£4

31/6

The Romantic Journey
The story of Thomas Cook and Victorian travel

The Romantic Journey

The story of Thomas Cook and Victorian travel

Edmund Swinglehurst

Pica Editions
London

Pica Editions
is the publishing imprint of
Pica Editorial Ltd
26 Parkway, London NW1

Design: Michael F. Hill

First published 1974

ISBN 0 904226 00 X

Text set hot metal in 12 on 14pt Monotype Gloucester
old style series 99. Captions filmset in Alphatype Souvenir.
Printed on 120 gsm WF coated cartridge by
Page Bros (Norwich) Ltd.

To Julian, Mark and Elissa

Acknowledgements

The author wishes to acknowledge his indebtedness to the following people and organizations who have made it possible for this book to be written.

Mr John Pudney whose excellent book *The Thomas Cook story* was published by Michael Joseph in 1963. Thomas Cook & Son Ltd whose archives have been an invaluable source of material. Mr William Cormack, Publicity Manager of Cooks, who made some useful suggestions about certain aspects of the history of the company. Mr Thomas Cook of Norfolk, great-great grandson of Thomas Cook who has allowed me to use some family photographs and to read Thomas Cook's correspondence. Mr R Searight, Mr Richard Carline and Mr John Price who have kindly permitted me to reproduce some illustrated material. The British Museum whose library is a pearl beyond price for all researchers. The British Museum Newspaper Library whose valuable volumes of the *Illustrated London News, Punch* and other publications gave much help. The Victoria & Albert Museum who have a fine collection of travel publications. Cie. Internationale des Wagons Lits et du Tourisme whose historical archives provided much interesting material. The Swiss National Tourist Office and the Musée des PTT Suisses, Berne for providing photographs. Mr A Moore for some interesting reminiscences of Cooks under the Cook family and Miss Janice Anderson for her editorial help. Many other people have suggested ideas which have put me on the track of useful information. I thank them all.   **ES**

THE WONDER OF 1851!

FROM YORK
TO LONDON AND BACK FOR A CROWN.

THE MIDLAND RAILWAY COMPANY
Will continue to run

TWO TRAINS DAILY
(Excepted Sunday, when only one Train is available)

FOR THE GREAT EXHIBITION,
UNTIL SATURDAY, OCTOBER 11.

Without any Advance of F

RETURN SPECIAL TRAINS leave the Euston Station on MONDAYS, TUESDAYS, THURSDAYS, & ATURDAYS at 11 a m., on WEDNESDAYS and FRIDAYS at 1 p.m., and EVERY NIGHT (Sundays excepted) at 9 p.m.

First and Second Class Tickets are available for returning any day (except Sunday) up to and including Monday, Oct. 20. Third Class Tickets issued before the 6th instant are available for 14 days, and all issued after the 6th are returnable any day up to Monday the 20th.

The Trains leave York at 9-40 a.m. every day except Sunday, and also every day, including Sunday, at 7-20 p.m.

Fares to London and Back :--

1st Class 15s. 2nd, 10s, 3rd, 5s.

The Midland is the only Company that runs Trains Daily at these Fares.
Ask for Midland Tickets !

Children above 3 and under 12 years of age, Half-price. Luggage allowed—112 lbs. to First Class, 100 lbs. to Second, and 56 lbs. to Third Class Passengers.

APPROVED LODGINGS, of all classes, are provided in London for Passengers by Midland Trains. The Agents will give Tickets of reference on application, without charge, and an Office is opened in London, at DONALD's WATERLOO DINING ROOMS, 14, Seymour-street, near Euston Station, where an agent is in regular attendance to conduct parties who go up unprepared with Lodgings.

The Managers have much pleasure in stating that the immense numbers who have travelled under their arrangements have been conducted in perfect safety—indeed in the history of the Midland Lines, *no accident, attended with personal injury, has ever happened to an Excursion Train.* In conducting the extraordinary traffic of this Great Occasion the first object is to ensure *safety*, and that object has hitherto been most happily achieved.

With the fullest confidence, inspired by past success, the Conductors have pleasure in urging those who have not yet visited the Exhibition, to avail themselves of the present facilities, and to improve the opportunity which will close on the 11th of October.

All communications respecting the Trains to be addressed to the Managers, for the Company,

October 2nd, 1851.

**John Cuttle & John Calverley, Wakefield;
Thomas Cook, Leicester.**

T. COOK, PRINTER, 28, GRANBY-STREET, LEICESTER.

Contents

Thomas Cook's first railway excursions were on trains very much like this one. Open 'tubs' without seats were the only accommodation available to passengers whose discomfort was aggravated by showers of soot and hot ash from the engine.

1 The shilling excursion

Eighteen hundred and eight was the year that Thomas Cook was born. It was also the year that Richard Trevithick exhibited an invention that made the railways, on which Cook later launched his excursion business, a practical proposition. Trevithick, an impatient Cornishman with an inventive mind, arrived in London with a load of iron rails, a steam locomotive and an open carriage. He assembled these in an open space where Euston Square now stands and surrounded his circular track with a wooden palisade. Not unnaturally, passers-by stopped to watch the activity.

However, to the majority of people, Trevithick's train was nothing more than a novelty. Like balloon ascents and paddle boats, it was a form of entertainment and aroused feelings of amazement at the ingenuity of Englishmen, and of trepidation at the uncertainty of the contraptions which their scientific genius was producing. Certainly none of the spectators, or those daring spirits who paid one shilling to ride on the railway, would have dreamt for one moment that his mechanical toy, puffing, hissing and clanking its way round the track on its flanged wheels, would revolutionise the life of England and do away for ever with the predominantly rural life of the countryside which was visible on the hills of Hampstead and Highgate.

In a world of horse-drawn vehicles, of a leisurely life in small communities dependent on agriculture, an industrial society as we know it was unimaginable; and people like Trevithick, and their inventions, were a little out of place in the prevailing atmosphere or, if not out of place, at least not given the recognition later accorded to engineers and inventors when the nation realised that its power and authority throughout the world was due to their ingenuity.

In 1808 at Euston Square the crowds came to be amused. Trevithick's locomotive, whose very name *Catch Me Who Can* suggested a fair-ground attraction, was a novelty, eliciting little shrieks of feminine alarm from the ladies in their high waisted dresses, as it belched its smoke and sparks in its giddy circling. For Trevithick the show was a disappointment. He had worked for years to perfect his locomotive and his system of flanged wheels which would keep it steadily on its track; before that he had built steam engines which ran on roads and which on one occasion had caused a good deal of panic by setting fire to the hotel at which he was staying. But he had never had any real recognition or support, even though one of his locomotives had shown itself able to carry out the job of transporting heavy loads at the Pen-Y-Darran iron works in Wales. In bringing the locomotive to London he had hoped to attract the attention of those who would help him, but he had failed. No one was yet ready to take locomotives seriously as a substitute for horses and carts and stage coaches: so Trevithick packed up his locomotive and dedicated himself to more profitable ventures such as the building of pumping machinery.

Inventors are never alone, however. For every new discovery that has ever been made, there have been scores of people working along similar lines to achieve the invention that finally becomes the milestone of progress. So while Trevithick gave up, others kept on and among these were Robert and George Stephenson.

George Stephenson studied Trevithick's engine and also the *Puffing Billy*, an engine built by William Hedley who had been Trevithick's agent, and he built his own locomotive, the *Blucher*. In 1823 Stephenson became manager of the Stockton and Darlington Railway and in 1825 formally opened it for public use. The railway was twenty five miles long and haulage was by means of horses, stationary engines and by locomotive. It aroused enormous public interest and on its first run carried over three hundred passengers as well as wagons with coal, horses, carriages and other vehicles. Crowds followed the train on foot, on horseback and on carts all the way.

The purpose of the railway was not, however, to carry passengers, for at that time the idea that large numbers of people might need or want to move away from their immediate environment was not universally accepted, and those who did travel about were the few whose journeys were prompted by duty or business rather than pleasure.

Before the first passenger-carrying railway was to open, five more years were to elapse. During this period Robert Stephenson, George Stephenson's son, built his famous *Rocket*, which won the prize for the most improved locomotive in a competition held on the new Liverpool-Manchester Railway.

The opening of the railway took place in Liverpool on September 15th, 1830 and was attended by the Duke of Wellington who, not many years earlier, had said that he could not see any general use for railways. Perhaps by now he had changed his mind, but the events of the day were hardly designed to win him over to the new method of transport.

It started off well enough with bands playing and flags flying and the presence of various people of distinction, including William Huskisson, Member for Liverpool, for whom the inauguration was to have fatal consequences. Also present was Fanny Kemble, niece of the great Sarah Siddons and a lively letter writer. Her description of the day in a letter to a friend paints a vivid and breathless picture of the scene. 'Though the weather was uncertain, enormous crowds of densely packed people lined the road, shouting and waving hats and handkerchiefs as we flew by them. What with the sound of these cheering multitudes and the tremendous velocity with which we were borne past them, my spirits rose to the true champagne height, and I never enjoyed anything so much as the first hour of our progress'.

But there was a sombre note to the day's celebrations, for the engine which could fill not only Fanny but all those present with such euphoria was also capable of inflicting pain and death. Here is how Fanny describes the tragedy: 'The engine had stopped to take in a supply of water, and several of the gentlemen in the directors' carriage had jumped out to look about them. Lord Wilton, Count Batthyany, Count Matuscewitz and Mr Huskisson, among the rest, were standing talking on the middle of the road, when an engine on the other line, which was parading up and down merely to show its speed, was seen coming down upon them like lightning. The most active of those in peril sprang back into their seat. Lord Wilton saved his life only by rushing behind the Duke's carriage, and Count Matuscewitz had but just leaped into it, with the engine all but touching his heels as he did so. Poor Mr Huskisson, less active from the effect of age and ill health, bewildered too, by the frantic cries of "Stop the engine! Clear the track!" that resounded on all sides, completely lost his head, looked helplessly to the right and left, and was instantaneously prostrated by the fatal machine, which dashed down like a thunderbolt upon him, and passed over his left leg smashing and mangling it in the most horrible way. (Lady Wilton said she distinctly heard the crushing of the bone.) So terrible was the effect of the appalling incident that, except for that ghastly "crushing" and poor Mr Huskisson's piercing shriek, not a sound was heard or a word uttered among the immediate spectators of the catastrophe'.

Although the tragedy provided ammunition for those who viewed the advance of industrial England with horror, it did not slow down for one moment the approaching avalanche of speculation in railways: in the next seven years no less than ninety-three railway acts were passed. Anyone with sufficient capital, it seemed, could open a railway, and most of them did during the course of the century, leaving a heritage to posterity which made widespread re-organisation of the system necessary later on. Although many people regarded the railways of the 1830s as the highways to a great new world, not everyone thought so: those who approved least of the new method of transport were the stage-coach proprietors, the canal barge companies and the landlords of large country estates. For the first two, railways were a threat to their business, and to the last an inconvenience which as Sir Isaac Coffin put it in the House of Commons, would, 'destroy the beauty of the countryside and the comfort of a gentleman's estate, and fox hunting'.

In many instances antipathy to the railways provided a common ground for landlord and transport owner and their employees, and the more obdurate of them were not averse to supporting strong-arm methods to prevent railways, surveyors and builders from doing their job. These encounters never reached the proportions of the railway feuds in the United States; most of the arguments were verbal.

Opinions were divergent. At one extreme there were those, who, ostrich-like, refused to believe that railways heralded any change in existing conditions: the very thought of trains superseding the stagecoach was laughable. 'What could be more palpably absurd and ridiculous,' says a contemporary, 'than the prospect held out of locomotives travelling twice as fast as stage-coaches?'. 'What persons would ever think of paying anything to be conveyed from Hexham to Newcastle in something like a coal wagon, and to be dragged for the greater part of the distance by a roaring steam engine,' says another. Stage-coach proprietors added fuel to the fire, giving maximum publicity to derailments, which were not uncommon, and spreading stories that passengers often fell off the open carriages.

Doctors were pressed to announce that travelling by train was injurious to the health, not because one could tumble out of them, but because of the rush of air, and the smoke which was damaging to the lungs. Others took the view that railways were detrimental to industrial life since they encouraged the working classes to travel and distracted them from their main duty, which was to work.

John Ruskin, who was not without his blind spots, joined the attackers, maintaining that he saw little advantage in the mobility which the railway brought the population. 'No change of pace at a hundred miles an hour' he thundered, stepping on his poetic accelerator, 'will make us one whit stronger, happier or wiser. The railways are nothing more than a device for making the world smaller'. Having launched this enduring cliché, Ruskin added acidly that someone with nothing to say in the first place was unlikely to find anything more to say by travelling faster.

The arguments and discussions, the reactionary prejudice and the wide-eyed optimism about the significance of railway travel were all expressions of fears and hopes that had been aroused in society by the changes in its circumstances, as well as an expression of a natural anxiety at the revolutionary new form of transport. The changes had already been in progress before the Napoleonic Wars, which had helped to accelerate the processes of production and the demand for better conditions for those on whose work the war production depended. After 1815 the problems attendant on the changes became intensified.

For many years after the introduction of the main railways most people travelled by stage coach much in the manner described by Charles Dickens in *The Pickwick papers.* This scene shows the staging post at the Elephant and Castle.

The decay of country life brought about by the intensification of the enclosure system was driving more and more people into the towns which were unable to cope with this sudden increase in population. Moreover, the social fabric once held together by the personal relationships between tenants and landlords, peasants and squirearchy, was disappearing in the country, and in the towns an impersonal relationship with foremen and managers separating the workers from their true masters developed. Recreation, which was a part of daily life in the country, almost vanished in the sordid slums where horizons were limited to dirty bricks and mortar or slag heaps and factories.

In such a situation everyone felt uneasy, the landed gentry feared the new, grimy, and often truculent city workers, the mill owners drove themselves and their labourers with ruthless energy, the working classes toiled and got drunk. Morale and morals decayed as everyone struggled to survive the industrial flood.

In the midst of this moral gloom there were, however, rays of light which shone more brightly and fiercely by contrast. There were the reformers, the Owens, the Mills, and the Places of the changing society, who concerned themselves with improving existing conditions. These people believed that the new industries would bring universal good, and agreed with Dr Arnold who, 'rejoiced to see it (the railways) and to think that feudality had gone forever'. Within a few years the growing mobility of the population had helped to bring about the changes that he foresaw; the system of rotten boroughs by which members of Parliament were enabled to represent non-existent voters was extinct, and the sad conditions of the majority of the population came home to the country as a whole, creating an awareness of injustice which led to changes in the laws relating to the people's welfare. The railways provided entertainment and encouraged leisure among people who had never strayed far from their native village because they could not afford the high fares demanded by the stagecoach companies. Above all the railways provided a means of escape from the dullness and drudgery of industrial life and travelling became a medium through which people could express the human need for change, for adventure and freedom.

Earlier in the century this need had been met by the steamboat, but this means of getting about was restricted to people who lived by rivers, by canals or by the sea. Railways made travel available to everyone and encouraged the formation of the concept of holidays: a social advance which took a hundred years to become universal.

The crowds that piled on to the trains, boisterous, gregarious and sharing the common excitement of the new experience, discovered increasingly that life, even in industrial regions, could have its bright moments. Often outings were organised with some purpose in view and there was a common affinity between the members of such excursions: on the outing for a Mechanics Institute from Nottingham, and the more macabre excursions to see a hanging which took place at Stourbridge.

For Thomas Cook, who ran his first excursion in 1841, the railways were a medium for bringing about reform in the social condition of the working class. At this time Thomas Cook was a publisher and the general overseer of the South Midland Temperance Association headquarters at Market Harborough. This was not a well-paid job, but it satisfied Cook's zeal for reform. Through temperance, Cook believed, working people could improve their lives and devote themselves more to their families and to self-improvement. The conditions of life in the cities did not, however, encourage temperate ways; there was little but boredom between work and the cheap gin shop.

Always a resourceful man, Thomas Cook hit on an idea which would give people an alternative way of spending their leisure. In later years he liked to refer to this idea as a revelation. 'About midway between Harborough and Leicester – my mind's eye has often reverted to the spot – a thought flashed through my brain – what a glorious thing it would be if the newly developed powers of the railways and locomotives could be made subservient to the cause of Temperance!'

Having had his inspiration, Cook instantly set about making it a practical reality by putting forward his idea at the next meeting of the Temperance Association. Calling on the support of the Chairman, Cook obtained approval for the organising of a special train trip from Leicester to Loughborough and back, and the following day he approached John Fox Bell, resident secretary of the Midland Counties Railway. Bell, like many railway people at this time, was keenly aware of the need to convert doubters to the merits of railway travel, and agreed to hire Cook a train, saying 'I know nothing of you or your society but you shall have the train'.

The Midland Railways had nothing to lose, for they were sure of getting their fee whatever the outcome of the exercise but, for Cook, the ensuing two weeks were an anxious time. He had to find enough passengers otherwise the South Midland Temperance Society would be out of pocket and he would be held responsible. He called on his Temperance friends in Nottingham and Derby for support, and obtained sufficient promises to enable him to set aside special carriages for them. He printed handbills and distributed them in Leicester and the surrounding villages; he printed a shilling ticket and set about selling it. To make the outing even more attractive, he arranged with Mr Paget of Loughborough, a man sympathetic to the cause of Temperance, to open his park for the benefit of the excursionists and he announced that there would be an added attraction in 'the shape of a gala'.

On Monday 5th, July 1841, an engine which seemed all funnel, boiler and wheels, drew nine carriages into Leicester station to the cheers of the five hundred and seventy passengers who held shilling tickets for the day's outing, and of the hundreds of others who had come to see them off. At first it must have seemed impossible that such a large crowd could squeeze into nine carriages, but as these were of the open variety with no seats, which were generally used for the common traveller at this time, their capacity was limited only by the passengers' ability to fit themselves in.

The ten miles to Loughborough were accomplished with cheers and good humour as

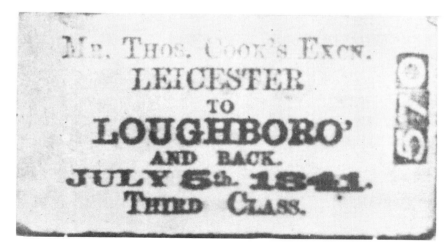

The ticket issued by Thomas Cook for his first excursion cost one shilling and included: return fare from Leicester to Loughborough, tea and buns at Mr Paget's Park and brass band music all the way.

well as showers of soot and hot sparks which flew out of the tall funnel as the train sped through the green Leicestershire countryside. At Loughborough, Cook's preparation had borne good results. A band met the train at the station and mingled its stirring airs with those of the band which, by some extraordinary magic, had been carried in the overcrowded tub carriages from Leicester. Banners waved, there were shouts of encouragement and welcome, and the excursionists and friends set off round the town to Mr Paget's park.

The Leicester Chronicle, reporting the event, reckoned that there were two or three thousand spectators to the great occasion. In the park each Temperance Group had set up its own tent, over which fluttered the flags of their towns: Leicester, Derby, Nottingham. Many groups had biblical appellations, such as Rock of Horeb, Ebenezer, Mount Sorrell, Sampson, and even the Junior Rechabites of Loughborough. The afternoon was taken up with games, cricket, tag, dancing and kiss in the ring, but the serious purpose of the excursion was not forgotten. As the leader writer of the Leicester Chronicle put it: 'The reason for the meeting was to show the Antis that some good can come out of teetotalism.' And he added, 'though not teetotallers ourselves, we could not but acknowledge that the steam generated by tea takes quite as long to condense as that generated by the "Fiend Alcohol" (as our friends the teetotallers somewhat unpoetically designate the whole class of fermented liquors.)'

There is no doubt that such excursions as the Loughborough one were planned as much to gain new adherents to a cause as to encourage those who were already committed to it. Thus many of the speakers at the Loughborough meeting harangued their listeners with tales of horror reminiscent of those moral set pieces with which Dickens peppered his work. The Rev Babington, Chairman of the meeting, described the work of his brother in a London hospital and concluded that a drunk was in a more pitiable condition than the blind, the halt, deaf and dumb because he was a madman. A speaker with a sense of humour put forward the idea that teetotalism was good for the body, the pocket and the mind, and good too for the drunken man's wife, while another, foreseeing the Imperial expansion of the latter part of the century, appealed to his listeners to help hoist the flag of teetotalism in the burning sands of Africa and the frozen regions of the North.

In an age when conversation was a form of entertainment, and speeches were judged much as today we judge an actor's performance, speakers were very aware of the importance of holding their audiences. At Loughborough, the speeches had not only a high moral purpose but seemed to be part of the entertainment provided for the crowd, which was made up not only of Temperance supporters but also of many people who had just gone along for the ride.

Certainly, the Chairman's final speech revealed the same kind of realistic approach as that of Thomas Cook when in later years he provided his tourists with facilities for obtaining liquor when on tours into uncivilised lands. In asking the gathering to support Temperance, Mr Babington requested that this should be done by a show of hands for he could not distinguish teetotallers by their faces as so many of those present had 'suspiciously rosy cheeks'.

The success of the Leicester to Loughborough trip fired Cook with an enthusiasm for excursions and gave full rein to his talent for organisation. He had at last, at the age of 33, found the medium in which the flair for leadership which he had demonstrated as a Baptist preacher, and his combative nature, could be allied with the cause of a social class of which he was a member.

2 The making of an excursion agent

Thomas Cook is a difficult person to know. His surviving photographs, taken when he had already achieved success, are deceptive, showing an impassive facade built up over many years of struggle, both public and personal, preserving carefully guarded secrets of the self. What was this man, who looks like a butler or perhaps a lawyer, really like? What was he like when he walked two thousand miles in one year on religious missions, or when he dealt with sheiks whose bands threatened the safety of the tourist caravans that he conducted over the Holy Land? His support of the Temperance Movement is legendary but the face seems at odds with the conventional picture of a moral crusader: there is something too generous about the mouth, even a touch of sensuality, and those large, well-formed eyes have a wide and passionate gaze that seem to hide as much as they reveal. People who develop strong moral convictions often do so as the result of an intense personal struggle. Was this the case with Thomas Cook?

Look again at this figure in the baggy suit who sits with one arm resting on a not very distinguished example of Victorian furniture. Remove him from the comfortable assurance of his Victorian background and set him down in Rome, where, arriving with a party and finding no hotel rooms, he hires a palace, or in Greece where he refuses to move without an armed escort for his tourists. It is in these settings and circumstances that Thomas Cook changes from a narrow fusty prig into the pioneer and visionary who opened up foreign travel for millions of his contemporaries.

Thomas Cook was born in 1808 at a time when Napoleon was master of Europe and Britain was undergoing agricultural and industrial revolutions which would make her mistress of the world. But world events seemed far away in the small village of Melbourne in Derby, where Elizabeth Cook gave birth to Thomas, and the villagers went about their daily tasks hardly aware of, or even interested in, what was going on in the next town. It is difficult to comprehend, in our age of instant and prolific communication, the isolation of the communities of a Britain of thirteen million people separated by poor roads, and without those links afforded today by rail, telephone and telegraph. Such was the world in which Thomas Cook grew up.

It appears that his family were in poor circumstances and when his father, John Cook, died and his mother married again Thomas had to go out to work. He was ten years old and was apprenticed to a market gardener. His wages were only sixpence a week but they helped the family finances, now badly strained by the birth of two step-brothers, Simeon and James Smithard.

Although poor, Thomas did not lack love, and the confidence with which he sallied out into the world suggests not only a natural determination of spirit but the assurance of affection at his back. Even at this early age his resolute character showed itself. John Roby, his master, was given to bouts of drunkenness. When these happened he neglected his market garden, leaving Thomas to worry about selling its products. Thomas was not one to waste time in inactive anxiety, and this young boy was often to be seen in the streets and market places of Melbourne hawking his master's products.

In his next employment, as an apprentice to his uncle, John Pegg, a wood turner,

Thomas once more came up against the problem of a drunken employer. It is hardly surprising, therefore, that he began to meditate on the evils of strong drink at an early age. Nevertheless, he stayed with his uncle for five years, during which time he learned a trade which was to provide him with enough money to live on.

These years between the age of fourteen and nineteen were vital in Thomas Cook's development, but we know little about them. An important influence on him was J F Winks, the Evangelical minister of Melbourne, who was also a printer and publisher of religious tracts. Winks introduced him to the craft of printing, and throughout his life, Cook produced a vast number of publications, on topics ranging from the evils of smoking to the glories of ancient Egypt. His enthusiasm for and belief in the power of the printed word were certainly inspired by Winks.

One wonders to what extent Thomas was aware of the course of world events when he was in his teens. Whether in his solitary fishing excursions on the Trent, to make time for which he would start work at four in the morning, he reflected on the significance of the currents of thought that were flowing through Britain at the time. There is evidence in the style of the company which he founded of a paternalism of the type associated with Robert Owen, and his lifelong interest in the condition of the working class may have sprung from a wider foundation than that of his own humble background.

In Cook's youth the decay of the old agricultural order, which William Cobbett had described in his 'Rural Rides', affected Melbourne, a small village set in agricultural country near growing industrial areas. According to Cobbett, this decay was due to a new and irresponsible gentry who did not reside on their lands and who, 'having no relish for country delights, foreign in their manners, distant and haughty in their behaviour, looking only to the soil for its rents, viewing it as a mere object of speculation,

unacquainted with its cultivators, despising them and their pursuits, relied for influence not upon the goodwill of the vicinage but upon the dread of their power'.

What Cobbett was regretting was the passing of the old rural communities where landlord and tenant were united by a common purpose and a common love. His views were exaggerated but they reflected the intranquillity of the time, the sense of changing ways of life caused by Corn Laws which impoverished the countryside, and by the humiliating Speenhamland system of poor relief which gave scope to greedy landowners who were prepared to allow the government to make up the meagre pay which they gave out to their workers. The problems of the countryside were no greater than those of the new industrial cities which were absorbing more and more of Britain's rapidly rising population, which was to double to 26 million by 1870.

The conditions which a large part of this population was condemned to, were appalling. Slum housing, disease, exploitation, drunkenness and moral decay were common. But this was also a time of public-spirited people who cared passionately about the condition of their less fortunate fellows and whose models were reformers like John Stuart Mill, Lord Shaftesbury, self-help enthusiasts from the working class like Francis Place, and the founders of innumerable societies whose interests ranged from Trade Unionism to Temperance.

Much of Cook's mature thought reflected the beliefs of those who were on the side of self-improvement and reform. His decision in 1828 to take up mission work for the Baptist Church suggests an inner compulsion to devote his life to the service of others. The influence of Winks, and perhaps a genetic inheritance from his evangelical grandfather, Thomas Perkins, made the church a natural medium for the idealism of the growing boy. Thomas, with his friend John Earp, was accepted '. . . as a suitable person

Thomas Cook's birthplace was at Melbourne in Derbyshire. It was here that Cook spent his childhood, working for a market gardener addicted to drink and fishing on the River Trent. He also used to practise public speaking in the church when no one was about. After he became successful he built some almshouses in memory of his daughter, Annie.

for the important work of an evangelist, so far as we judge him fit . . . '. The work consisted of preaching, distributing tracts and setting up Sunday schools and was not without its hardships, not least of which was the meagre salary of £36 a year.

Not everyone was prepared to listen to Evangelists and those who were not were often actively aggressive; Cook and Earp had to put up with heckling, jeering and rough handling as hazards of their chosen vocation. In their work they covered most of the distances between towns on foot since their pay did not allow for stage coach journeys. In his diary for 1829 Thomas recorded that he travelled 2,692 miles, 2,106 of them on foot: a precise annotation which reveals another aspect of Cook's character which was later to prove an asset to a rising young excursion agent.

Thomas Cook was evidently well liked, for he received numerous invitations to the houses of the people he met. But this popularity proved costly for it provided the Baptist Church with an excuse for reducing his salary. Eventually the Baptist funds dried up altogether and Thomas had to return to wood turning, setting himself up in a workshop at Barrowden. The years as a preacher had given him valuable experience which would enable him later to handle crowds with confidence, and overcome the stubborn resistance of short-sighted railway directors and hoteliers with persistence and determination.

Thomas moved to Market Harborough in 1832. Having settled himself in this larger community, he felt sure enough of his future to marry Marianne Mason, a young woman of twenty-three whom he had met three years before and who shared his religious convictions. Eighteen thirty two was the year of the first of the Reform Acts which were to change the system of parliamentary representation, a significant year for Britain as well as Thomas Cook. The repressive attitudes towards liberal ideas demonstrated by the landed gentry, industrialists and Parliament after the Peterloo massacre were softening, and the wealth of the nation was beginning to trickle into the lower strata of society.

For Thomas Cook, although he did not know it in 1832, the most significant development at this time was the improvement of steam locomotive engines, which, as Stephenson had shown in 1829, were now capable of speeds of up to twenty miles an hour, four times faster than the stage-coach. In 1830 the Liverpool and Manchester Railway opened the first regular passenger service. After his marriage, in 1832, Thomas worked at cabinet-making and wood-turning and found a suitable outlet for his crusading zeal in Temperance.

The need to curb drunkenness had occupied people's minds since the eighteenth century, but it was only in the nineteenth that the problem, aggravated by the growing population crowded into the town slums, became such that it aroused a national fervour of effort to deal with it. Gin could be bought for a penny a glass, and with nothing to do with their leisure hours people took to drink out of boredom or to forget the squalor of town life.

The well-meaning Beerhouse Act of 1830, which led to the opening of 50,000 more ale houses, in the hope that this would woo people away from spirits, only worsened the situation. Throughout the nation, consciences began to awaken and a national crusade for Temperance got under way.

Thomas Cook, with his personal experiences of drunken employers to arouse him, threw himself passionately into this new mission. But it was not only the repression of a vice that appealed to Cook, for the aims of the Temperance Society were closely concerned with general ideals of social improvement and self-help which were close to Cook's heart. Without too much resistance, Thomas allowed the Rev Francis Beardsall, the Market Harborough agent of the British and Foreign Temperance Society, to persuade him to sign the pledge to preclude the use of spirits, and to take other liquors in moderation, on New Year's Day, 1833. Marianne followed Thomas in taking the pledge and a year later was the first of them to dedicate herself to the cause of total abstinence.

Thomas himself was reluctant to give up his beer, and when he did decide to follow Marianne's example, after listening to the advocate of Teetotalism known as the Birmingham Blacksmith, he was still not sufficiently persuaded to pour away the beer he had in his cellar. There were ninety-six gallons of it and Thomas showed his common sense and ability to compromise by sending the best beer to his brother.

Later, in recounting the story, he could not resist the temptation to sermonise, claiming that the passage of the barrel through the countryside had been an advocacy of teetotalism throughout its journey. At the same time, there was a glimmer of awareness of the ways of the world when he added that he could not say that the barrel was not tapped on the way to its destination. After pouring away the inferior beer, Cook found that there now remained in the house two or three bottles of his wife's grape wine. Much to his surprise, the level in these bottles continued to go down. Eventually he discovered that one of his apprentices was taking a quiet nip at night. There is a mixture of common sense and dry humour in this account which gives an extra depth to the portrait of Thomas Cook.

The moral question of drunkenness apart, there is no doubt that it was the challenge of Teetotalism that appealed to Cook. Like so many of his contemporaries, he enjoyed a good fight, whether in the religious arena, or in lands far from home. By taking up the cause of Teetotalism Cook was stating his position in an unequivocal way and presenting a clear target to those whose commercial interests lay in the encouragement of drinking. Brewers, publicans and others in the business were not prepared to see it ruined by cranks and do-gooders and they hit back actively, even going so far as to employ bands of thugs to break up Teetotal meetings, damage the houses of leading abstainers, and cause them bodily harm. On one occasion Cook was felled by the leg bone of a horse, but being a man of spirit he ran after his assailant and hauled him before a judge.

None of this deterred Cook, rather it spurred him on, and very soon after becoming a Total Abstainer he took over the publication side of the South Midland Temperance Association, editing the *Monthly Temperance Messenger* in 1839 and in 1840 publishing the *Children's Temperance Magazine, A Cabinet of Instruction and Amusement of Little Teetotallers, edited by a father*.

The father was Cook himself and his son John Mason, born in 1834 was proudly proclaimed a teetotaller from birth. At the time, this was something of a curiosity as children were brought up to take alcohol from an early age. While Thomas was busy with his fatherhood, wood-turning and Teetotalism, destiny was already reaching out for him on the railway lines which were laid in 1840 for the first train from Derby to Rugby via Leicester.

3 Discovering Britain

The excursion fever which seized the working and lower middle classes in the 1850s was the result of a variety of forces; not the least of which was the desire of the railway companies to fill their trains, and the desire of the public itself to take to the rails. Having multiplied excessively during the years from 1845, the private railway companies fought to gain passengers, much as the package holiday companies do today, lowering prices to perilously low levels in order to increase traffic, and to deprive rivals of passengers.

The result of this acute competition was improved conditions of travel for the third-class traveller who had ridden in open trucks in the forties, but by the 1860s was riding in upholstered seats in enclosed carriages. Another result was a certain amount of negligence in the maintenance of rolling stock, which led to enough accidents to oblige the government to take steps to regulate the conditions under which railways were operated.

On the whole, the public benefited and showed itself more than willing to support the new system of locomotion: and the railway companies did everything in their power to encourage their enthusiasm. Special train services were put on to the famous spas which, although now decaying and deserted by the real gentry, still retained for those lower down on the social ladder the glamour of the days of Nash and Brummell. Most of these new visitors, however, were mere trippers; people who came and went overnight and who, if questioned about their previous visit, would have replied like Mr Pickwick, 'It's a very long time since I drank the waters certainly, for to the best of my knowledge I was never here before'.

There were hundreds of resorts and towns where the new excursionists had never been before and which they now began to visit as soon as a cheap fare was provided. The spectacle of hundreds of excursionists, more in quantity than a whole season of visitors, arriving suddenly by train was enough to cause a shock to those persons of 'distinction and fashion' who had hitherto made up the visiting populations, and who now complained about the vulgarity of those crowds. There were attacks from other quarters, too, in particular from factory and mill owners who disapproved of the time-wasting and distracting nature of excursions. Some of these received the support of the churches who frowned on the use of the Sabbath day for amusement and frivolity.

MIDLAND RAILWAY.

LEICESTER RACES.

On **THURSDAY**, September 10th, a Special Train will leave **NOTTINGHAM, DERBY,** and the under-mentioned Stations for **LEICESTER.**

Fares there and back and Times of Starting:—

STATIONS.						1st Class. s. d.	Cov. Car. s. d.
					A.M.		
Nottingham	...	...	...	...	9 30		
Beeston	...	...	...	...	9 40		
Trent	...	...	...	...	9 50	4 0	2 6
Derby	...	...	...	...	9 25		
Kegworth	...	...	...	...	9 55	3 0	1 9
Loughborough	...	...	...	...	10 10	2 6	1 0

Leicester, arrive about 10·45 a.m.

Children under Three years of age, Free; above Three and under Twelve, Half-fares. *The Tickets are not Transferable.*

The Special Train will leave Leicester in returning at 7·0 p.m. the same day, and the Tickets will be available for returning by this Train only. No Luggage allowed.

Derby, August, 1863.   JAMES ALLPORT, General Manager.

COOK'S EXCURSIONIST & INTERNATIONAL

EXHIBITION & BAZAAR ADVERTISER.

Price TWOPENCE; By Post, THREEPENCE.

CONDUCTED BY THOMAS COOK, Excursion and Tourist Manager, Leicester.

Registered for Transmission Abroad.

TOURS IN SCOTLAND, 1862.

SUMMARY OF TOURS & FARES.

TROSSACHS and LOCHCATRINE TOURS.

Special arrangements of the Edinburgh and Glasgow and Scottish Central Railway Companies. Tickets issued at Mr. Cook's Offices.

TICKETS GOOD FOR FOUR DAYS.	1st class.	2nd or 3rd class.
From Edinburgh to Stirling, Callander, Trossachs, Lochcatrine, Lochlomond, and Glasgow	19s. 0d	14s. 6d.
Same Route continued back by Edinburgh and Glasgow Railway to Edinburgh	23 0	16 6
From Glasgow to Lochlomond, Lochcatrine, Trossachs, Callander, Stirling, and Edinburgh	19 6	14 6
Same Route to Stirling and back, by Railway to Glasgow	17 6	13 6
From Stirling or Bridge of Allan to Callander, Trossachs, Lochcatrine, Lochlomond, Glasgow, and back by Railway to Stirling or Bridge of Allan	18 0	14 6
From Stirling to Callander, Trossachs, Lochcatrine, Lochlomond, and back, from Balloch to Stirling by Forth and Clyde Railway	17 0	12 6
From Perth to Callander, Trossachs, Lochcatrine, Lochlomond, Glasgow, Stirling, and back to Perth	23 0	18 0
From Perth to Callander, Trossachs, Lochcatrine, Lochlomond, Balloch, Stirling, and back to Perth	21 0	14 0

The above Fares cover the Coaches between Callander and Trossachs and Lochcatrine and Lochlomond, and all Pier dues; but Coachmen's Fees, 6d. each Coach, are not included.

EXTENDED TOURS, COMMENCING AT EDINBURGH AND GLASGOW.

First, Second, or Third Class, include Cabin of Steamer and Outside of Coach.

No. of Case.	TICKETS GOOD FOR 14 DAYS.	1st Class.	2nd or 3rd class.
1	To Stirling, Bridge of Allan, Perth, Dunkeld, Aberfeldy, Kenmore, Killin, Lochearnhead, Callander, Trossachs, Lochcatrine, Lochlomond and Glasgow	37s. 0d.	33s. 0d.
2	Same Route as No. 1, to Callander, thence by Railway to Edinburgh or Glasgow	31 8	26 6
3	Glasgow to Balloch, Lochlomond, Killin, Kenmore, Aberfeldy, Dunkeld, Perth, Stirling and Edinburgh or Glasgow	30 6	26 6
4	Stirling, Perth, Aberdeen, Aboyne, Ballater, Balmoral, Braemar, Spittal of Glenshee, Blairgowrie, Dunkeld, Perth and Stirling to Edinburgh, or Glasgow	50 0	40 0
5	Stirling, Perth, Aberdeen, Inverness, Blair Atholl, Pass of Killiecrankie, Dunkeld and Perth to Edinburgh or Glasgow	62 0	49 6
6	Edinburgh to Stirling, Callander, Trossachs, Lochcatrine, Lochlomond, Fortwilliam	32 0	......
7	Glasgow to Lochlomond, Inverarnan, and Fortwilliam	22 0	......
7A	Edinburgh to Stirling, Trossachs, Lochcatrine, Lochlomond, Tarbet, Inverary and Oban	32 2	......
8	Glasgow to Lochlomond, Tarbet, Tyndrum and Dalmally to Oban	20 0	......

Tickets to be had at Railway Stations, and at the Golden Lion Coach Office Stirling.

No. of Case.	TICKETS GOOD FOR 14 DAYS.	1st Class.	2nd or 3rd Class.
10	To Perth, Dunkeld, Aberfeldy, Kenmore, Killin, Callander and back to Bridge of Allan or Stirling	24s. 0d.	21s. 2d.
11	Balloch, Lochlomond, Killin, Kenmore, Aberfeldy, Dunkeld, Perth and back to Bridge of Allan or Stirling	28 6	24 6
12	Perth, Aberdeen, Aboyne, Ballater, Balmoral, Braemar, Blairgowrie, Dunkeld and back to Bridge of Allan or Stirling	40 0	32 0
13	Callander, Lochcatrine, Lochlomond, Tarbet, Inverary and Oban	28 0	
14	Callander, Lochcatrine, Lochlomond, Inverarnan, Glencoe and Fortwilliam	28 0	
14A	Perth, Aberdeen, Inverness	28 9	19 0
14B	Perth, Aberdeen, Inverness, Blair Atholl, Dunkeld, Perth and back to Bridge of Allan or Stirling	56 8	45 8

TOURS COMMENCING AT PERTH.

Tickets to be had at Scottish Central and Scottish North Eastern Booking Office, and at the British Hotel.

No. of Case.	TICKETS GOOD FOR 14 DAYS.	1st class.	2nd or 3rd class.
15	To Dunkeld, Aberfeldy, Kenmore, Killin, Lochearnhead, Callander, Trossachs, Lochcatrine, Lochlomond, Glasgow, and back by Rails to Perth	36s. 6d.	33s. 0d.
16	Aberdeen, Aboyne, Ballater, Braemar, Spittal of Glenshee, Blairgowrie, and back to Perth	33 0	27 0
17	Same as No. 16, to Braemar and Blairgowrie, thence to Dunkeld and back to Perth	34 6	28 6
18	Aberdeen Keith, Inverness, Blair Atholl, Dunkeld, and back to Perth	50 6	42 0
19	Dunkeld, Aberfeldy, Kenmore, Killin, Inverarnan, Lochlomond, Glasgow, Stirling, and back to Perth	30 0	26 6

See also Trossachs and Lochcatrine Tours from Perth, &c.

TOURS COMMENCING AT DUNDEE.

Tickets to be had at the Perth and Dundee Railway Booking Office, and of Mr. John Muir, Bookseller, 75, High-street.

No. of Case.	TICKETS GOOD FOR 14 DAYS.	1st class.	2nd or 3rd class.
20	To Perth, Callander, Trossachs, Lochcatrine, Lochlomond, Balloch, Stirling, Bridge of Allan, Perth and back to Dundee	27s. 0d.	19s. 0d
21	Same to Lochlomond and Balloch as No. 26, thence to Glasgow, Stirling, Perth and back to Dundee	27 0	21 0
22	Perth, Dunkeld, Aberfeldy, Kenmore, Killin, Callander, Trossachs, Lochcatrine, Lochlomond, Glasgow, Stirling, Perth and back to Dundee	41 0	36 0
23	Perth, Dunkeld, Blairgowrie, Braemar, Balmoral, Ballater, Aboyne, Aberdeen, Forfar and back to Dundee	37 0	30 0

By the 1850s there were all sorts of wonders offered in order to entice people on to the railways. Excursion trains grew in popularity because they offered a cheap fare and station platforms were crowded with excursionists, much to the disgust of the regular train passengers.

Thomas Cook was quick to reply to any suggestions that excursions might be against the will of the Almighty or in any way undesirable. 'Surely,' he asked 'there can be nothing inimical to religion in going abroad to behold the handywork of the Great Supreme?'

With critics who spoke for the owners of mills and factories he was more outspoken. 'A few years ago', he said, 'a visit to a watering place was a luxury beyond the toiling artisan or mechanic: his lot was to waste the midnight oil and his own vital energy in pandering to the vitiated tastes of the sons of fashion, who, after their debaucheries or voluptuousness, had to avail themselves of a change of air and scenery to recruit their exhausted powers'.

An insight to Cook's character and his flair for making every incident serve his purpose is revealed by a more specific criticism made of one of his trips on which, it was alleged, at least one of the passengers had been drunk. Yes, Cook admitted there was some drunkenness on this particular party, but he believed that the example of the drunks had been enough to persuade others to embrace the cause of teetotalism.

On the whole, the parties of excursionists were welcomed wherever they went: their fellow countrymen opened their arms to them with that warmth of hospitality usually offered by people to whom the arrival of a stranger is an event, as indeed it had been in the days when only stage-coach travellers journeyed about the country. The welcomes received by Cook's own excursions were reported: at Ashby de la Zouche a flag was raised over the castle on the arrival of the excursion and the church bells were rung, while a large concourse of well-dressed people turned out to cheer the visitors. In Glasgow bands played and there was a gun salute; in Edinburgh there was a special banquet.

Although spas and cities were popular destinations for the early excursions, then, as today, the greatest attraction was the seaside. To the characteristic romanticism of the Victorian mind the sea represented something mysterious, boundless, reaching out wider and wider into eternal truths and eternal progress. Charlotte Brontë, seeing the sea for the first time, was 'quite overpowered so that she could not speak', and Hazlitt's reaction was no less awe-struck at the 'strange ponderous riddle, that we can neither penetrate nor grasp in our comprehension'.

The grandiloquence of these expressions may seem exaggerated now, but at that time most people had never seen the sea; its immensity and its moods, specially its more unpleasant ones, were seen as examples of the power of the Almighty; the same power which was driving Britain forward in the accomplishment of her destiny.

On a more prosaic level, the seaside's popularity can be traced to the 'discovery' that sea-water was as beneficial to the health as was that of the spas. Belief in the efficacy of sea-water had existed in the seventeenth century, if not before, but no one had publicised the idea as effectively as did Richard Russell MD whose book 'A dissertation on the use of Sea-Water in the diseases of the glands, particularly the scurvy, jaundice, King's Evil, leprosy and the glandular consumption' ran into several editions.

The Royal patronage of Brighton by the Prince Regent gave the rise of the seaside resorts an additional impulse, but, even so, popularity was a relative term. Margate and Ramsgate which were easily reached by steamship, received a mere 17,000 visitors in 1812, and even thirty years later when Cook made his first excursion, places like Blackpool did not exceed a thousand visitors in the busiest month of the season, and the West Country resorts were lucky if they saw more then sixty or seventy.

The great change for the seaside resorts, as for the spas and the towns, came after the

seaside had two actions for the ursionists of the teenth century: water was uted to be lthy even when ed with alcohol seaside resorts e less class scious than the s. This picture ws the beach at logne, one of French resorts ch followed the mple of those he English side e Channel.

1850s when the railway excursion mania got into top gear. The seaside had particular appeal for the railway excursionist because it was classless. Unlike the spas, where the daily assembly was part of the ritual of life and where the social standing, financial status and breeding of all visitors were soon discovered, at the seaside everyone was anonymous and could therefore act with complete freedom.

The reason most people gave themselves for a visit to the seaside was much the same as that put forward today: it did them good. More specifically, they could explain in detail with the help of doctors who, no doubt, had a financial interest in the success of sea-water therapy, what good it was that they expected to derive from it.

Dr A B Granville, a doctor regarded as an expert in the matter of mineral waters, produced a handbook giving full instructions. The usual dose of sea-water that could be taken internally was half a pint and it could be mixed with port wine if desired. The variety of conditions which this universal remedy would cure grew in inventiveness. At Margate it was claimed that the sea would cure debility, St Vitus Dance, Hysterical affections, Epilepsy and Convulsions, while the waters of Hastings would banish Rheumatism, Gout, Consumption, Asthma, Indigestion, Hypochondria, Disease of the Liver, Rickets, Measles and Whooping Cough.

The enthusiasm for the sea grew throughout the century and the resorts grew with it but never, it seems, to a sufficient extent; for the promenades were always crowded with people on the move and the beach itself was a mass of men and women sitting on the sand and children running, shouting, quarreling or riding on the vast numbers of donkeys which trotted up and down by the water's edge. A familiar sight on the beaches was the bathing machine in which ladies were able to disrobe as they were pulled out to sea. The privacy offered by the machine was, however, shortlived for once in deeper water the ladies were helped into the water, kicking and giggling, by the stalwart bathing-machine attendants while, from the shore, gentlemen studied the scene through spy-glasses. Bathing for men was on a different part of the beach, where, it is surprising to discover, men bathed naked.

Overcrowding was not only a problem on the beaches. There were not enough boarding houses to accommodate all the visitors; at times more than a dozen people would share the same bed, and mattresses and cushions would be set up in every corner of the house to provide other places to sleep. Catering facilities for such vast masses of people, who sometimes outnumbered the local inhabitants, were also a problem and caused innumerable complaints. Jane Carlyle, holidaying on the Isle of Wight, complained that 'the butter tasted of straw and the "cold fowl" was a luke warm one and as tough as leather'. A visitor to Brighton described the fish as 'soles that perished from an original inability to flounder into the ark' and the beef as 'the fossil remains of a dead sirloin'. After several years as the unpaid organiser of Temperance excursions Cook, who had moved to Leicester in 1841, made his first venture into the excursion business for profit by arranging a trip to the sea at Liverpool in 1845. To make the arrangements, he had to negotiate with four railway companies, the Midland, the Lancashire and Yorkshire, the Manchester, and Manchester and Liverpool. Having established a fare of 15s first class and 10s second class, he went to Liverpool to investigate the restaurants where his excursionists could eat and the hotels in which it would be suitable for them to pass the night. Leaving nothing to chance, and having ensured that every service would be provided, Cook then wrote a guide book, *A Hand-book of the Trip to Liverpool*, which was possibly the first of its kind. In it, he detailed every step of the journey right down to the precise hour of departure and arrival at

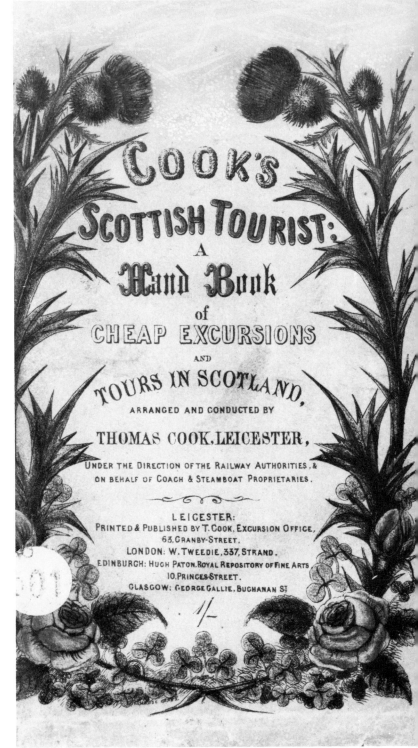

COOK'S
SCOTTISH TOURIST:
A
Hand Book
of
CHEAP EXCURSIONS
AND
TOURS IN SCOTLAND,
ARRANGED AND CONDUCTED BY
THOMAS COOK, LEICESTER,
UNDER THE DIRECTION OF THE RAILWAY AUTHORITIES, &
ON BEHALF OF COACH & STEAMBOAT PROPRIETARIES.

LEICESTER:
PRINTED & PUBLISHED BY T. COOK, EXCURSION OFFICE,
63, CRANBY-STREET.
LONDON: W. TWEEDIE, 337, STRAND.
EDINBURGH: HUGH PATON, ROYAL REPOSITORY OF FINE ARTS
10, PRINCES-STREET.
GLASGOW: GEORGE GALLIE, BUCHANAN ST.

1/-

stations en route.

Three hundred and fifty excursionists took part in Cook's first seaside trip. When they arrived in Liverpool they found that they could also take excursions to Caernarvon or Snowdon. Later, Cook, who was given to dramatising the decisions which led him on to new ventures, wrote that it was on Mount Snowdon that he had his next revelation. 'From the heights of Snowdon', he said, 'my thoughts took flight to Ben Lomond, and I determined to get to Scotland'.

Sound business sense, as much as a romantic desire to take his working class excursionists to the colourful and adventurous land depicted in the novels of Walter Scott, dictated Scotland as the next field for Cook's activities. Scotland possessed all the settings; wild highlands, misty lakes, ruined castles – essential to the romantic temperament of the early Victorians. It was a country full of magic and as profound as that offered by the sea; what was more it had become the holiday favourite of Victoria and Albert. There was only one drawback as far as Cook's plans were concerned: there was no railway over the border. Undeterred, Cook set about finding ways and means of setting up an excursion system to Scotland. He first explored the eastern route by train from Leicester to Newcastle, and there tried to negotiate with a shipping company to take his passengers to Leith where they could link up with the Scottish Railway system. But the steamship company was not interested, although Cook offered a guarantee of the fares. He had more success with another route up the west coast via Fleetwood. He arranged to charter a steamer which would take his excursionists from Fleetwood to Ardrossan where they could take the train to Glasgow, but despite all his efforts, he was unable to provide enough passengers to make a chartered steamer worthwhile and had to book berths on the normal service.

Three hundred and fifty excursionists set off from Leicester on Cook's first trip to Scotland in 1846. As far as Fleetwood everything went well. It was a rough night for the sea journey and there was a heavier demand for first class berths than Cook could fulfil. Like many a tour operator since, Cook had to put up with the complaints of his customers at his inability to satisfy their requirements and to live up to his promises.

Daylight and the arrival in Glasgow soon helped everyone to forget the discomforts of the night. A fine Scottish welcome more than made up for any feeling of disappointment. A band met the train as it drew up to the platform and cannons were fired in honour of the visitors: the excitement was intense and the excursionists felt like true pioneers. Later there was a soirée at the City Hall and hours of speech-making, which the excursionists took in their stride. In Edinburgh, there was another soirée at which William Chambers, the publisher, was present. He later wrote a description of the event in an article entitled *The Strangers Visit to Edinburgh*. Having completed the tour with visits to places made famous by Scott and Robbie Burns, Cook's intrepid excursionists returned to Leicester, and Cook began thinking of his future plans.

In the succeeding years, from 1846 until 1865 when he opened his first office in London, Cook had to strive hard to make his excursion business a success. The railways were not eager to give him concessions as either they believed that they could operate the excursions themselves, or they were not convinced that enough passengers could be found to make special services worthwhile. Cook's task was to persuade them that he could find the passengers and that he could find more of them than the railways themselves.

To do this, Cook launched himself into a variety of operations which would induce people to travel by the new railways and he enlisted the help of his son John Mason, still only a teenager, who would soon become as well known as his father for his remarkable strength and vitality.

The way to get people to travel, Cook decided, was to arrange journeys to places which the public had a special reason for wishing to visit. The seaside therefore became a feature of his handbills: Scarborough, Morecambe, Blackpool were among the most popular places. He also made arrangements for trips from the Midlands to the seaside resorts of the South coast: there was a 35s first class ticket, and a 5s second class ticket, which included 'almost every coast town including Hastings, St Leonards, Brighton, Portsmouth and the Isle of Wight'. Although he did not book hotels, he took advertisements for them and inspected them so that he could recommend them to customers.

At Ryde, there was the Yelphs family hotel, at Torquay, Mogridge's Union Family and Commercial Hotel, at Portsmouth the York Pier Hotel. Nor did Cook miss the possibility of advertising shops: Lewis's at Portsmouth sold photographic albums, cartes-de-visite with pictures of men of the time, the great masters, or humorous scenes, and elegant inkstands, china vases and 'beautiful toys for the amusement of juveniles'.

Famous towns and cities also featured in his excursions at this time, especially if they were the scene of an exhibition or special celebration. For a trip to York, for example, Cook's handbills advertised the Great Yorkshire Gala and Floral Fête which included a Great Bird Show, Military bands, Coxwell's balloon ascent, Miss Rose Fox, the marvellous skipping danseuse, Wainratta on the invisible high wire, and Mr and Mrs Paddy Miles, Irish duettists.

When the S S *Great Britain* ran aground in Dundrum Bay Cook ran trips to visit her, and Gretna Green was a regular attraction on his trips north. In his advertisements Cook pointed out that 'If any demand is made by ladies and gentlemen of the party for the special services of Mr Linton or Mr Murray (the famous marrying blacksmiths) the special shall be detained to enable them to terminate "single blessedness"'.

It was not enough, however, to arrange excursions to interesting destinations. Cook always had to consider the activities of his competitors and ensure that his own arrangements were more attractive than those of others. One attraction was to include in his excursion parties his own brass band and the Shapcott family whose playing on a completely new instrument, the saxaphone, was featured.

Despite his growing success as an excursion agent, the indefatigable Cook found time to carry on with many other interests. He produced a pamphlet, *The Cheap Bread Herald*, to protest at the high cost of bread and used a window in his house in Leicester as a platform from which to address the public on the subject. Through the correspondence column of the local newspaper, he attacked the police for the manner in which they dealt with the 'cheap bread' demonstrators and was himself attacked through the same column for exaggerating the police brutality.

After several visits to Iona, Cook felt impelled to start a fund for the local fishermen. He asked his tourists to contribute to the cost of new fishing boats, nets and tackle for the impoverished islanders who, inspired by his encouragement, formed a society for self-improvement and invited Cook to be an honorary member. Their letter of invitation began 'There has been for some time a growing desire among the young men of this island to adopt some measure for their own mental improvement and thus enable them, to a certain extent, to overcome the disadvantage which their isolated condition entailed upon them' and was signed by D H McVean, Alex McGregor and Donald Black.

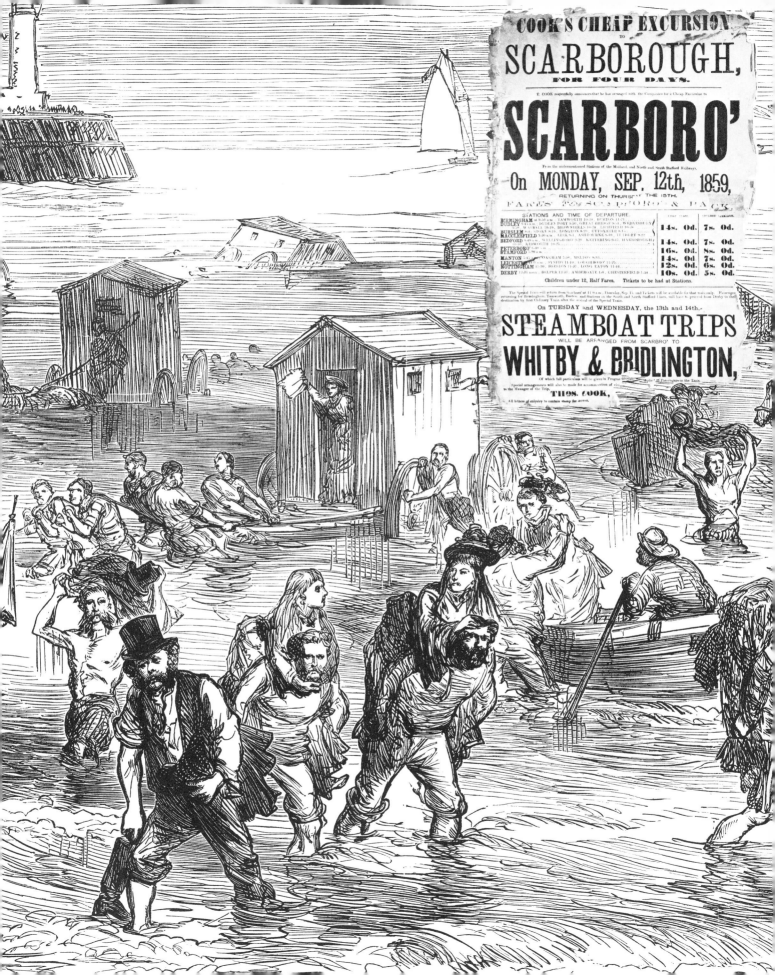

Cook had not stopped his public speaking on the subject of Teetotalism, and was able to deal with any hecklers he might encounter. The Leicester Mercury's correspondence column records one such encounter. Cook had accused a Mr Brewin Grant of hissing at one of his meetings: 'Gooseism and Snakeism' he had called it. Mr Brewin Grant's spirited reply in the Leicester Mercury referred to, ' . . . the grave accusation you levelled against me. What could it be? For you were eager and excited to a high pitch of moral indignation. Was it a case of felony, seduction or murder? No, worse. I hissed John Sturge about teetotalism. Well. What then? Is there a law against hissing'? He ended by accusing Cook of being 'an impertinent meddler' to which Cook riposted: 'Mr Brewin Grant had better return to Jericho until his beard is grown. Let us have no more of this puppyism and cowardly sidewinds'.

Ever one to involve himself in arguments, Cook also challenged such national institutions as the Anniversary of the Battle of Waterloo, calling on the Iron Duke with passionate intensity to cancel all preparations for the celebration of the victory over Napoleon and set an example so that, 'Wars shall cease to the ends of the earth'. Throughout his life, Cook's idealism and business sense were often in conflict; not long after his outburst against war he was running trips to the very battlefields which he so abhorred.

Cook was much involved in purely philanthropic activities at this period of his life. He provided 15,000 gallons of a 'strong superior' soup during one of those local famines which were not uncommon in nineteenth century England, and brought in barge-loads of potatoes during another. In 1846 he opened a Temperance Hotel in Leicester and gave it over to the management of his wife Marianne, who proved to be an excellent administrator in this and other later enterprises.

It was a time of tremendous activity for Cook and in his efforts to establish himself and survive he was not averse to knocking his competitors' conduct which in our times of mutual protection would be regarded as in bad taste. 'We are often amused', Cook said in one broadside 'at the pretensions of some bustling upstarts who seem as though they would kick the world like a ball . . . and it is especially laughable to see their puffery. Some make a feat about taking visitors to Paris, keeping them and bringing them back to London for £5. These presentations are all bosh to those who know anything about Continental travel'.

In fact, at the time Cook was an absolute beginner at the business of Continental travel, but he did not lack experience of how to promote and organise travel for large groups of people. He had learnt a great deal in the most important venture of his early years as an excursion agent: his excursions to the Great Exhibition of 1851.

In 1850, Cook's thoughts had turned to America and during the winter of that year, when the excursion business was dormant, he set off for Liverpool to talk to the shipping companies about his plans for an American trip. Stopping at Derby on the way, Cook met John Ellis MP, Chairman of the Midland Railways, and his friend and associate Joseph Paxton.

Ellis knew of Cook's work in promoting excursions and, although Paxton did not know Cook personally, it is likely that he felt a certain kinship with him since he himself had started life as a gardener's boy at Chatsworth. The Duke of Devonshire, his employer, had taken him to London, and now Paxton was the designer of the Crystal Palace which was to house the Great Exhibition. With Ellis, he was concerned about getting the crowds from all over Britain into London; it was almost inevitable that the three men should come together over this project. The deal was made, and Cook was given exclusive rights in moving Exhibition traffic over the southern part of the Midland Line, but he had to work together with Cuttle and Calverly who controlled the Northern section. In return for his efforts, Cook was to receive several shillings for every excursion passenger he found.

At one swoop, Cook had been given the opportunity to further some of his most heart-felt ambitions: to bring travel to the people, to stimulate their desire for learning, and to make them aware of the glorious future which the Great Exhibition presaged.

Cook immediately set about planning his campaign with the help of his son John Mason, who had been working for a printer as the excursion business had not been profitable enough to provide him with a living. John Mason now left the printer, and father and son began to tour the Midlands and the North, setting up Exhibition Clubs into which working men could pay a weekly quota, making arrangements for accommodation in London, and founding a travel magazine which was called *The Excursionist*. Cook contributed numerous articles to it, one of which was entitled 'How are working men, their wives and children to get to the Exhibition?' 'The Great Exhibition', he claimed, 'is mainly indebted for its astonishing interest to the skill and industry of mechanics, artisans and other operative classes. And in many instances the honour of invention and execution which properly belongs to those classes is monopolised by the principles of manufacturers (who may be mere noodles) or the wealthy millionaire, whose gold had made him representative of the products of better men's brains and hands'.

When the great day came for the first train to leave for London, Cook and John Mason felt that they had done their work well. Then Cook suddenly discovered to his horror that the Great Northern Line were cutting their prices to 5s, which left his own price of 15s uncompetitive. In a price war, the only possible strategy is to meet the competition, and this was what Cook now proposed to the Midland Railway directors. They reminded Cook that his earnings within the terms of their agreement made this impossible. Cook's answer to that was to tear up his contract and the price came down to 5s.

In London Cook had arranged accommodation at the Ranelagh Club where bed and breakfast was to cost 2s and included a bed, hair mattress, sheets, blankets, coverlid, soap, towels. Boot cleaning was a penny extra, there was a barber in attendance, and Thomas Abrahams, a surgeon, would attend each morning. The breakfast menu included soups, cold roast beef, mutton, pork, sausages, and bacon. Tea and coffee were the beverages. Whatever dreams Cook might have had of making money on this enterprise must have almost vanished when he tore up his contract, but he was not dismayed. With furious energy, he set about increasing the number of passengers to compensate for his diminishing margin of profit.

With John Mason, still only a boy of seventeen, he set about an incredible exercise in direct selling. First he arranged that every train on the Midland line except the Express should be available to the excursionists. Then he and John Mason travelled with the trains to and from London and to any city on the Midland System where he thought he could persuade people to visit the Exhibition. In Leeds, Bradford, Sheffield and Derby, the Cooks paraded round the town in a van advertising the Exhibition trips. Often they had a band with them; they made many speeches and they even extended credit to those who were unable to raise the fare.

The year of the Exhibition was a significant one for Cook. His great achievement in persuading 165,000 people to travel to London made his name known farther afield and confirmed the faith of Paxton and Ellis in his talent for organisation. However, it had not been financially successful, and Cook had to return with renewed energy to his Scottish tours in the following season. These, though perhaps the most lucrative, were not the only venture in which he was engaged in the years following the Exhibition. Soon there came other exhibitions in Dublin, Manchester and one in Paris in 1855 which drew Cook abroad for the first time.

The first tourists abroad were encouraged by Thomas Cook through the pages of his magazine *The Excursionist.* The rigours of a customs examination did not deter the ever growing number who went abroad for cultural reasons or to attend events such as the Paris Exhibition.

PARIS EXHIBITION, 1867.
COOK'S ANGLO-AMERICAN AND EUROPEAN TOURS.
RETURN TICKETS TO PARIS AND BACK,

For the Double Journey, from THE UNITED STATES AND CANADA, giving a choice of SIX LINES OF STEAMERS.

As per following Programme

Line of Service across the Atlantic	Fare to LIVERPOOL and back	Fare to GLASGOW and back	Fare to Paris and back, via Liverpool First Cabin, & First Class Railway	Fare to Paris and back, via Liverpool First Cabin, & Second Class Railway	Fare to Paris and back, via Liverpool First Cabin, & First Class Railway	Fare to Paris and back, via Liverpool First Cabin, & Second Class Railway	Fare to Paris and back, via Glasgow, First Class Railway	Fare to Paris and back, via Glasgow First Class Railway
			Tickets between Liverpool and Paris good for One Month	Tick'ts between Liverpool and Paris good for One Month	Tickets between Liverp'l and Paris good till used	Tickets between Liverpool and Paris good till used	Tickets between Glasgow and Paris good till used	Tickets between Glasgow and Paris good till used
	Dollars.	Dollars.	Dollars.	Dollars.	Dollars.	Dollars.	Dollars.	Dollars.
Montreal Ocean Mail Line from Portland or Quebec	150	...	176	170	181	173	...	...
Do. 2nd Cabin	120	...	146	140	151	143	...	...
National Steam Navigation Co's. Line from New York	150	...	176	170	181	173	...	...
Cunard Extra Line, from New York	150	...	176	170	181	173	...	...
Anchor Line, from New York to Liverpool or Glasgow	120	120	146	140	151	143	170	156
Montreal S. S. Co's. Glasgow Line from Portland or Quebec	...	120	...	...	...	...	170	156

SAILINGS OF STEAMERS AND REGULATIONS FOR RETURNING.

The Montreal Ocean Company's Canadian Mail Steamers—Line of Hugh and Andrew Allan, Montreal.

The Steamers of this Line, by which the Tickets are available, leave Portland every Saturday to May 4, and after that date to October, leave Quebec for Liverpool.

The Tickets issued for this Line will be available for returning by the Lines of the same Company, from Liverpool or Glasgow, or by the "Anchor Line" of Handyside and Hendersons, from Glasgow, at any time within Six months from date of departure. Steamers leave Liverpool every Thursday for New York; Glasgow for Canada, every alternate Thursday; and Glasgow for New York (Anchor Line) every Friday. The Steamers of this Line are

AUSTRIAN	MORAVIAN	BELGIAN
NESTORIAN	HIBERNIAN	NORTH AMERICAN
PERUVIAN	NOVA SCOTIAN	DAMASCUS

The Montreal Ocean Steamship Company's Glasgow Line of Hugh and Andrew Allan, Montreal.

Until May 4, the Steamers of this Line leave PORTLAND for Glasgow every alternate Saturday, returning from Glasgow every Thursday. After May 4, from QUEBEC, returning from Glasgow every alternate Thursday, from May 11 to October.

The Tickets are available for returning by any Steamer of the service for 6 months after date of departure; or they will be available for returning by the same Company's Ships from Liverpool to Portland or Quebec, on payment of 20 dollars extra at Liverpool; or by the "Anchor Line" of Handyside and Hendersons, from Glasgow to New York, without extra charge, at any time within 6 months. The Steamers of this Line are
ST DAVID—ST. ANDREW—ST. GEORGE—ST. PATRICK.

The Anchor Line of Transatlantic Steam Packet Ships, of Handyside and Hendersons

Tickets may be had for leaving by this Line from New York to GLASGOW every Saturday; returning from Glasgow every Friday, for New York, within 12 months from date of departure.

These Tickets will also be available for returning by the Montreal Lines of Messrs. Allan & Companies, from Glasgow free; or Liverpool to Portland

or Quebec, by Canadian Mail Line, on payment of 20 dollars extra to the Canadian Companies before leaving Liverpool. The Steamers of this Line are

| EUROPA | HIBERNIA | BRITANNIA | UNITED KINGDOM |
| COLUMBIA | CALEDONIA | IOWA | ACADIA |

The Line of the National Steam Navigation Company.
(LIMITED.)

These Steamers leave New York every Saturday, taking passengers to Queenstown or Liverpool. The tickets are available for any day of departure, and for returning from Liverpool by the same Line only, on any Wednesday, for 6 months after date of departure. The Steamers of this Line are

FRANCE	ERIN	PENNSYLVANIA
ENGLAND	DENMARK	VIRGINIA
QUEEN	HELVETIA	LOUISIANA

Cunard Extra Line.

The Steamers of this Line leave New York every Wednesday for Liverpool, calling at Queenstown. The Tickets are available by any Steamer in which there may be room, for any day of departure; and for returning from Liverpool or Queenstown, any time within 12 months. The Steamers of this Line are

ALEPPO	HECLA	MARATHON	PALESTINE	SUMATRA
ATLAS	KEDAR	MOROCCO	PALMYRA	TARIFA
CORSICA	MALTA	OLYMPUS	SIDON	TRIPOLI

Liverpool and Great Western Steamship Company's New Line of Guion and Co.

These Steamers leave New York every other Saturday for Liverpool, calling at Queenstown. The Tickets are available for any day of departure; and for returning from Liverpool or Queenstown by same Line, on any day of sailing within 12 months. The steamers of this Line are
MANHATTAN—MINNESOTA—CHICAGO—NEBRASKA—
With other first-class Steamers building.

Although these vessels are fitted with First Cabin berths for 60 passengers, the Acts of Parliament will only allow of 20 First Cabin passengers travelling by them from Liverpool to New York; consequently it is only advisable to issue a limited number of Return Tickets, particulars of which may be had of the Agent.

IMPORTANT NOTICE—APPLICABLE TO ALL LINES OF STEAMERS;—Holders of Cook's Tickets by the above Lines of Steamers will be treated precisely the same as ordinary passengers, and will have equal accommodation in the Saloon; but to ensure comfort it is necessary to give as long notice as possible to the Agent, to enable him to secure good State Rooms—they being all attained according to priority of application. This Notice applies equally to leaving both sides of the Atlantic; and all passengers will be subject to the usual regulations of the various Companies. The holders of these Tickets will be entitled to all the privileges and facilities afforded by

Mr. COOK'S TOURIST and EXCURSION TICKETS, for Travelling in
GREAT BRITAIN, FRANCE, BRITTANY, NORMANDY, GERMANY, SWITZERLAND, ITALY, &c.;
being the only system in operation by which passengers can book through from Great Britain to Switzerland, Italy, &c., and back again, on one payment; thus obviating the loss and inconvenience arising through passengers travelling in a Foreign Country having to re-book at various points en route; they will also be entitled to avail themselves of Mr. Cook's Hotel arrangements, by which accommodation is secured in PARIS DURING THE EXHIBITION for 2000 VISITORS PER NIGHT, at fixed charges, varying from 8 to 20 Francs per day;—a similar arrangement is also made for Mr. Cook's passengers in every City and Town of interest combined in his Continental Tours.

RETURN TICKETS FOR THE AMERICAN RAILWAYS will be issued by the regular Agents of the principal Companies for travelling in various parts of the STATES AND CANADA to the Port of embarkation in connection with Mr. COOK'S TICKETS

For further particulars, and to secure passage, apply to the Agents of the Grand Trunk and Great Western Railways of Canada, the Michigan Central, Erie, Pennsylvania Central, Atlantic and Great Western, Little Miami, Baltimore and Ohio, Philadelphia, Wilmington and Baltimore, and Vermont Central Railways; also to the Agents of E. P. Beach, in various parts of the States, and to

E. P. BEACH, 176, Broadway, New York; | CAIN & WALKER, Gibson House, Cincinnati;
J. WARBACK, Dearborn Street, Chicago; | Mr. TUGBY, Bazaar, near Goat Island, Niagara;
Mr. FOGG, Planters' House, St. Louis; | FOWLER & WELLS, 389, Broadway, New York
J. L. BUTLER, 3, Union Merchants' Exchange, St. Louis.

All American communications for Mr. COOK, to be addressed to 339, BROADWAY, NEW YORK.

GREAT WESTERN RAILWAY.
THROUGH ROUTE
BETWEEN
ENGLAND & THE CONTINENT
VIA WEYMOUTH AND CHERBOURG.
FIXED SPECIAL SERVICE
(DAILY, EXCEPT SUNDAYS)
BY FAST TRAINS AND STEAMERS.

The service has been organised by arrangement between the Great Western Railway and the Western of France Railway, and affords a convenient, attractive, and economical route to Normandy, the West and South of France, Paris, and Spain.

The passage between Weymouth and Cherbourg occupies about six hours.

The Steamers from Weymouth to Cherbourg start daily at 11.30 p.m., in connection with fast Trains from London, Bristol, Plymouth, Exeter, Liverpool, Manchester, Swansea, Cardiff, Birmingham, Worcester, and all important towns on the Great Western Railway, reaching Cherbourg in time for a fast Train to Paris which arrives there in time for the evening Trains to the interior of France, Switzerland, Germany, and Italy; and also having a connection via Mezidon, Le Mans, and Tours, with the Paris and Orleans Railway.

The Steamers from Cherbourg to Weymouth start daily at 7 p.m., after the arrival of fast Trains from Paris and other parts of the Continent, reaching Weymouth in time for fast Trains to the above-mentioned towns on the Great Western system.

Single Tickets are available for Seven Days, and Return Tickets for One Month.

Through Passengers to and from *the interior* of France are each allowed to pass 66 lbs. weight of baggage, free of charge. All extra weight will be charged. Children, who travel at half fares, are allowed 44 lbs. weight of baggage, free of charge. To and from Cherbourg, every 1st Class Passenger is allowed, without extra payment, 120 lbs., every 2nd Class Passenger, 100 lbs., and every 3rd Class Passenger, 66 lbs. of luggage, such as is authorised by the different Acts of Parliament relating to the Railway. All other Luggage must be paid for according to weight.

Luggage can be registered between Stations in England and France at a fee of 1s. per passenger.

Passengers may break their journey at Weymouth and Cherbourg, or at any Station on the Western of France Railway.

The Steamers are provided with commodious State Cabins, which can be retained by application at the Station at which Through Tickets are taken. Three First Class Tickets is the minimum number for which a State Cabin can be retained. Berths can be reserved by application to the Company's Agents at Weymouth and Cherbourg.

PADDINGTON TERMINUS. | J. GRIERSON,
 | *General Manager.*

For the service via Weymouth and Cherbourg see page 8.

4. Elders and betters

The Paris Exhibition of 1855 took place while the Crimean War was in progress but this did not dim the brilliance of the occasion. Opened by the Emperor Napoleon III and his Empress, it aroused considerable interest in France's ally, Britain. To Cook, the Exhibition was one more portent of the millenium of peace and plenty which was to come and he was enthusiastic to take people to see it, realising too, from his past exhibition experience, that an event of this kind predisposed the public to travel.

When he approached the railway and channel steamship companies he realised that achieving his aims would not be an easy matter. The railway company controlling the ports would not give him any help and the only facility he was able to obtain was for a trip from Leicester to Calais. Cook did, however, have an arrangement with the Great Eastern Railway which permitted him to take passengers via Harwich to Antwerp at a reduced price. Other arrangements with the Belgian, German and French railways enabled him to plan a tour which would take in the Rhine and Paris.

As so often happened in later years, Cook had a faithful Boswell among his customers. On this first overseas tour, this was a lady called Matilda. She made the trip with her three sisters and enthusiastically recorded everything they did. She wrote:

'Mr Cook has mapped out for us a most delightful route. We visited Antwerp, Brussels, Cologne, Mayence, Manheim, Heidelberg, Strasbourg and Paris . . . Many of our friends thought us too independent and adventurous to leave the shores of old England, and thus plunge into foreign countries not beneath Victoria's sway, with no protecting relatives, but we can only say that we hope this will not be our last excursion of this kind. We could venture anywhere with such a guide and guardian as Mr Cook for there was not one of his party but felt perfectly safe when under his care. We calculate an estimate of our expenses for travelling, guides, hotels etc. for ladies, to be about £10 0s 0d for a fortnight's trip'.

It says a great deal for Cook's ability that he was praised for the first trip he had undertaken abroad, and, although there is no record of his doing so, he almost certainly went over the route in detail as was his custom, making a note of times, arrangements for baggage transfers, hotels, restaurants and all the other items which the journey involved. It is interesting to reflect on the effect of Cook's tours on the emancipation of the women of England, for Matilda was only the first of many ladies who felt themselves safe in his care and were thus able to launch themselves with tremendous daring into a world beyond the confines of their daily life. It was often remarked later that the travellers on Cook's parties were predominantly female. Of course, long before Cook had arrived on the scene with his Continental excursions, a few women were travelling throughout the world. Names like Hester Stanhope, Emmeline Stuart Wortley, Ida Pfeiffer and others may have meant nothing to the ordinary, middle-class women who travelled with Cook, but these pioneers were the spearheads of a female army of travellers who found a romantic escape from a dull and restricted existence in foreign countries to which such

Victorian romanticism found its expression in travel as well as the arts. Young ladies swooned at the visions of the Jungfrau, Lake Como and the Grand Canal and daring thoughts dwelt secretly in their minds as they went on bathing parties with members of the opposite sex.

figures as Byron had pointed the way.

What is so amazing in the journals of such women, was the matter-of-fact way in which they faced the hazards of travel. Lady Emmeline, for example, whose travels began after the death of her husband, and who justified her long journeys with a delicate daughter on the grounds of health, fearlessly travelled across the bandit-infested roads of Mexico and by canoe across the Isthmus of Panama before she finally succumbed to dysentery in the Middle East. Or think of Ida Pfeiffer fighting off a maddened negro in Brazil with the aid of a parasol, or persuading cannibals in Sumatra not to eat her on the grounds of her age and the toughness of her skin. It was not only the skins of these ladies that were tough but their spirits also and this applied in a lesser degree to the less wealthy, more socially constrained sisters of the middle class.

Cook's parties gave the latter the opportunity to travel in safety and with economy, providing enough of the challenges of life in a foreign environment to be exciting, but keeping away from any real risks other than those of contamination by ideas and social conventions different from those they were accustomed to at home. On a Cook's tour, men and women could emulate those travellers of a higher level of society who since the end of the Napoleonic Wars had been flooding into Europe from Britain at the rate of 150,000 a year. While the Cook customers followed in the footsteps of squires and sons of the squires, they did so with guide book in hand and were as determined to acquire the charisma of those for whom they felt a certain awe, as were American tourists to Europe between the wars, or the Russian tourist of today.

Like these, the Victorian tourist took care to prepare himself for the travel experience by assiduous reading. A popular guide book had been written by Dr Abraham Eldon in 1828. It was a book which reflected the attitudes of travellers throughout the century and was entitled The Continental Oracle or Maxims of Foreign Locomotion'. The Doctor begins at once with ironic humour: 'To the untravelled portion of the British nation if such there be, the following work (in which the art of travelling is made easy, and the most ignorant and indolent rendered, in the space of a few months, illustrious tourists, tour writers and diners out) is presented with all due tenderness and humility by their fellow countrymen and devout well wishers. The author'.

After some sharp comments on travel in general, Dr Eldon gives instructions on how the traveller should get the best out of each country. 'In France, praise the French, in Italy, contempt is a fine quality: it grows nowhere so well as in England, and this is the secret of our power and influence over all nations. It's outward signals are a high cravat, a well-made coat, and English stride and silence'.

Throughout the century the English were to be admonished for their superior attitude to foreigners, without, it would seem from reading similar twentieth century comments, much effect. 'Let every man who leaves England,' Dr Eldon wrote, 'convince himself of one thing – that he will see nothing like it until his return. England was, is, and always shall be the envy of surrounding nations . . . .'.

Considering the pleasure to be won from recounting the experience of a foreign holiday to those who had had to stay at home, Dr Eldon advised a tantalising silence in the first instance. 'By saying little, smiling less and listening not at all you will soon obtain what you claim', he wrote, 'a *toto vertice* superiority over the multitude who have had the misfortune of having a home and of never leaving it'. Having had his say about the English abroad, Dr Eldon then warned his reader against certain foreign hazards. 'Never drink the soup or the wine, but take brandy and water instead. Every traveller should carry his own sheets and look at his bills carefully, for Frenchmen will present

More prosaic than rowing boats but providing a quicker and more comfortable way of seeing lakeside sights, the paddle steamer vied with the railways as a popular means of transport.

a "long bill with an even longer compliment" '. Most important of all, Dr Eldon recommended his travellers to carry a pair of pistols and to have a table and chair placed across the bedroom door on retiring.

Advertisements in Cook's *The Excursionist* reveal other conveniences not mentioned by the good doctor. Among these were Keatings Powders, 'the remedy for bugs, and beetles', Seymours' Patent Magnetic Amnyterion Appliances that provided protection against sea sickness, and Dr Collis Browne's chlorodyne that cured the diarrhoea which the tourist was almost certain to get. For the safety of the person there are a number of other items which are essential to the traveller, among these is a portable door fastener and a Gladstone bag which included a rope and pulley which could be fixed to the window frame and served as a fire escape.

These items solved the practical problems which the Continental traveller was likely to run up against, but there were others which caused even greater anxiety to the prospective newcomers to foreign travel. These were largely of a moral nature, and were founded on the unvoiced but long-standing belief, still surviving today, that all foreigners were heathens, or papists, and given to all sorts of immoral habits which would not be tolerated in England.

Typical of the reaction of ladies who found themselves in a milieu where the difference between the sexes was regarded as natural and not requiring obsessive segregation, was that of the wife of a Mr Roget who took a trip to Paris with her husband in the 1820s.

"OUR FRIENDS THOUGHT US TOO INDEPENDENT!"

Mr Cook had mapped out for us a most delightful route. We visited Antwerp, Brussels, Cologne, Mayence, Manhcim, and Heidelburg – a return route by Strasbourg and Paris......
Many of our friends thought us too independent and adventurous to leave the shores of old England, and thus plunge into foreign lands not beneath Victoria's sway, with no protecting relative, but we can only say that we hope this will not be our last Excursion of the kind. We would venture anywhere with such a guide and guardian as Mr Cook, for there was not one of his party but felt perfectly safe when under his care..... Matilda and Three Sisters

Young ladies were often impelled to keep journals of their travels. Many of those who travelled with Thomas Cook were gushing in their praise of his careful arrangements. One of these was Miss Matilda and her three sisters who went on Cook's first (1855) tour of the Continent.

'The dismay of an English lady', she wrote, 'was considerable to find this room (her bedroom) was but a step above the courtyard, a tiled floor without a carpet and two very high windows with thin muslin curtains half way up, opening into the court or public entrance, so that it was exactly like sleeping in the street. I did not like the idea of undressing in so exposed a situation'. Things had not changed much forty years later when Cook's tourists were visiting Europe, as Viator Verax pointed out in his book of 'Cautions for the First Tour.' 'We expected fifty years ago that familiarity with our tastes, notions, and habits would speedily work a marvellous change in those of our intelligent neighbours. Such anticipations were far from sanguine'.

Alas! the French had remained incorrigibly lacking in modesty and Viator reported, 'a gentleman of my acquaintance *saw* a French lady, *stripped to the waist* washing her neck and arms in the presence of her husband and one of the hotel waiters who was speaking to them about dinner . . . ' Foreigners, it seemed, would go to any lengths to intrude on the privacy of others, even going to the extent of boring holes in doors in order to provide themselves with a peepshow of life in adjoining rooms.

Even more appalling were the habits of foreigners concerned with the natural needs of the body. It was possible for a respectable Englishman to open a chest of drawers and find that the previous occupant of the room had used it for a purpose other than that for which it was intended. The toilet facilities were repugnant, as indeed they continued to be until recent years, and ladies were recommended to invest in an artefact which for less than 25s would avert the 'wretchedness, contamination and defilement of the public toilet'. This object was a metal pail, disguised as a bonnet box, with a removeable polished mahogany rim and metal lid, the possession of which would save ladies from 'having to encounter, to meet and glide by the moustached foreigner (be he noble or pedlar) with his waistcoat unbuttoned, cigar in mouth, and his hands fumbling at his braces, in the corridor. They will not be subject to the insult of coming upon such a personage seated with the door open'.

But it was not only in these personal matters that foreigners displayed their lack of breeding. The restaurant was another place where an English lady or gentleman's sensibilities were liable to be disturbed, for foreigners had the habit of splashing their food around their plates with their knife and fork, spitting on the floor three or four times during a meal and indulging in the barbaric habit of extracting filaments of food from their teeth with the point of a dagger-shaped knife or one of the tines of a fork. Despite all these dire warnings of the conditions travellers were likely to find abroad, their numbers continued to increase and when Cook finally managed to come to an arrangement with the Brighton and South Coast Railway for the regular passage of his customers to Paris, thanks once again to Joseph Paxton, he had no difficulty in finding customers.

This new contract arrived at an opportune moment. Cook had had a very successful season with his Scottish tours in 1861, but these were soon to end because the Scottish railway companies were preparing to take them over and deprive Cook of his concessions. Moreover, Cook had been unable to repeat his 1851 Exhibition success with the 1862 Exhibition, as once again the railways had decided to provide the excursions themselves. Thus, although he did well in providing accommodation in London for the Exhibition excursionists at hotels supervised by Mrs Cook and his daughter, he must have felt disappointed that his services as an excursion agent had not been required. Even to a man of resilient character like Cook, this was a blow and in *The Excursionist* of that year he wrote, 'Our desire is to follow the leadings of Providence; to live while we

Paris and Switzerland satisfied two different dreams. The former, via such public places as the Champs Elysees, awoke desires for a more colourful and easy-going life than at home. The latter stimulated heroic ideas about man and nature.

live to some useful purpose, cultivating and strengthening those influences which ripened and matured on earth, bear fruit beyond the grave'. As he wrote those words Cook could hardly have been aware that he was on the verge of a development which would transform him from a Leicester excursion agent to a world-renowned figure and would make his business into the greatest travel organisation in the world.

While Cook had been busy with his excursion business in England, the railway system of the Continent had been growing and extending across the Alps. In 1846 a line was established between Vienna and Trieste, .the Turin-Genoa line driven through the Italian maritime Alps, the Mont Cenis tunnel excavated and the French railways system completed to the Côte d'Azur, and to Geneva. It was the latter city that set Cook's imagination alight, for from here he could arrange an excursion to the lower slopes of Mont Blanc, a mountain, like Snowdon and Ben Lomond, which symbolised man's eternal and 'successful' struggle to climb ever upwards.

Although for Cook the appeal of the mountains was in their symbolic meaning, the actual climbing of them had also become an activity which aroused much enthusiasm, especially among the English, who had founded the Alpine Club in 1857. Cook, therefore, had a powerful ally to help him in encouraging customers to join his Swiss trips. Moreover, the Alps could provide the health ingredient which justified the taking of holidays. Cook's first trip to Geneva and Mont Blanc took place in 1863 and once again he was lucky in having a passenger who kept a careful record of events. This was Miss Jemima Morrell, whose description of the trip is recorded in the following chapter.

From Switzerland, Cook took his travellers to Italy where they visited Turin, Milan, Rome, Florence and Pompeii. Switzerland well served those who felt their romanticism in terms of Rousseau and nature. But Italy had a more direct appeal. It was the cradle of that Roman civilisation and Pax Romana of which the English people were beginning to consider themselves the true heirs.

As the British seaside was invaded more and more by the common people those who considered themselves a cut above them escaped to the Continent where they could meet others of their own class.

5 Miss Jemima's journey

In 1863 Miss Jemima Morrell, her brother William and six friends joined a Cook's party of 130 people bound for Paris, Geneva and Mont Blanc. This group was typical of those that Cook was to attract on his foreign tours in the next fifty years; William was a young banker, another man was a teacher, and the three young women in the party were presumably of no occupation except that of waiting for marriage. Miss Jemima, as hundreds of later Cook's tourists were to do, kept a journal of the tour, describing the scenery and making comments on the manners and modes of Switzerland at a time which Leslie Stephen, the father of Virginia Woolf, writing thirty years later, was to regard as its golden age.

Whether 1863 was a golden age is a matter of opinion but it was certainly a watershed in the history of Switzerland as a tourist country. Visitors had been coming to Switzerland since the eighteenth century, and by 1840 it was regarded in the same way as the Lake District in England – a holiday region which satisfied those romantic yearnings which were not only fashionable but represented the spirit of the times. The numbers who went to Switzerland at this time were few however, and restricted to those more fortunately placed in the society of the period. Nevertheless, there were enough of them to stimulate the Swiss to invest in amenities for tourists, to foster the establishment and good maintenance of small hotels and inns, and to keep a supply of horses, carriages and guides for the visitor. 'And then', Stephen wrote, 'in the fullness of time arose the Alpine Club. There is, I am told a fruit which can only be eaten in perfection at a particular moment; ten minutes too early it is still sour and ten minutes too late the flavour has already begun to decline perceptibly. So the Alps culminated for a few years'.

It was in these few years that Cook arrived with his first tour. Miss Jemima, paying hommage to the Alpine Club and all it symbolised named her own party 'The Junior United Alpine Club'. To Stephen, however, Cook's first tour was not the development of a desirable trend but the end of the Switzerland he cared for. He wrote:

> 'The fortunate generation is passing away, and the charm is perishing. Huge caravanserais replace the old hospitable inn; railways creep to the foot of Monte Rosa and the summit of the Wengern Alp and threaten even the summit of the Jungfrau. The tourist despatches Switzerland as rapidly and thoughtlessly as he does Olympia; and the very name of the Alps, so musical in the ears of those who enjoyed their mysterious charm, suggests little more than the hurry and jostling of an average sight-seeing trip'.

Stephen, looking back in 1894 was not the first to regret the popularisation of travel and one wonders what he would have said today on learning that the Himalayas, which he contemplated as a possible substitute for the Alps, are undergoing the same tourist pioneering as the Switzerland of 1863.

Neither Cook nor Miss Jemima thought about their visit to Switzerland in these terms; their feelings could be summed up in a truism about travel, which is that all

49

D

places are new and unspoilt to those who have never seen them before. To Miss Jemima and her party, every step of the way was a new experience: as if they had been the first ever to set foot in Switzerland. The opening words of her journal express the excitement: 'Friday 26th June 1863. Waking at four o'clock there was a rustle in the household; at four thirty the Travellers break-fasted, and at six some 130 tourists who were travelling under Mr Cook's guidance, and his Tickets, started from London Bridge Station for Newhaven . . .'.

Miss Jemima was not the only one to feel excited about this tour; at Dieppe a large and curious crowd turned out to see the arrival of such a large number of English people. In fact, throughout the journey, the tourists were regarded with special interest and attention, which was not unjustified, for it must have been the first time that a tour of this magnitude had been abroad. According to the official records of Swiss tourism, Cook's 1863 tour shared with the Alpine Club the credit for founding the Swiss Tourist Industry.

At Geneva Miss Jemima made the first of many remarks about the food and service at meal times. This was a subject of enthralling interest to her, as it was, if we are to judge by Mrs Beeton's success, to all English people; for food in Victorian times was more generally regarded as a matter for serious thought than it is in the average household today. The Geneva lunch described by Miss Jemima consisted of ten courses, including soup, salmon, roast beef, boiled fowl, sweetbreads, roast fowl, artichokes and several kinds of dessert. It seems to have met with everyone's approval but the same

could not be said for the service which Miss Jemima criticised several times throughout the journey for being too quick. 'On a silver stand', she wrote, 'is placed for one moment the dish which we are to regale, which being, it is supposed, duly eyed by the company, is removed to be carved by an official aside, whose dexterity in dissection is only surpassed by the agility of the waiter who, if for a second you lay down your knife and fork, makes a dart at your plate like a cobra's and carries off your bonne bouche as his prey'.

For the drive to Mont Blanc the Cook's party consisted only of Miss Jemima's group, another one of similar size, and one or two other people including a Mrs H whom Miss Jemima named The Solitary Companion. On the way to Chamonix the party came across some early tourist attractions. At one point there was a cannon which, when the visitor paid one franc, was fired to produce echoes in the mountain valley; at another there was a sale of cherries; and then finally there was the view they had all come to see: Mont Blanc.

The highlight of the expedition was the climb to Montanvert and the walk on the Mer de Glace. Everyone bought alpenstocks at $2\frac{1}{2}$ frs. each, only to discover that they had been overcharged. On Montanvert they met some German tourists, a German gentleman of comfortable dimensions and his wife and daughter. The latter was surprised that the young English ladies should be allowed to travel on their own. At Martigny Miss Jemima's party left Cook and struck out on their own for a tour into central Switzerland. Since this was the prototype of many subsequent Cook's tours, Miss Jemima and her friends representing the kind of people who would tour Switzer-

The Berner Oberland became a British preserve and especially resorts such as Interlaken and Grindelwald. British tourists had a delight in scrambling over glaciers in clothes which were quite inappropriate especially when caught in an avalanche.

land in ever increasing numbers, it is worthwhile following in their footsteps, reconstructing the feelings and attitudes of early tourists to the country that was to become the playground of Europe.

The party went on to Sion where they stayed at the Hotel du Lion d'Or, which still stands in a leafy avenue of the town and then continued up the Rhône valley. They turned off to Leukerbad, climbing to this thermal spa in a carriage. Leukerbad today is still much as it was in Miss Jemima's time, a small village overlooked by 3000 ft cliffs which lead up to the Gemmi pass. On the cliffs can be seen the narrow zig-zag path up which Miss Jemima and her friends toiled in their crinolines; today everyone takes the cable car to the top. Food was the most important topic in Miss Jemima's journal at Leukerbad: there were seven courses at lunch this time, and each of them received the kind of critical attention meted out by food writers in our contemporary press.

'The soup' [Miss Jemima opines] 'was decidedly watery – the slices of beef with its border of fried potatoes – starved – the mountain trout had exchanged its natural element for one of oil. The fowl and the rice were passé. Slices of chamois, alias chèvre, were served in a vinegared gravy and were evidently an important and popular course. But we never loved the dish, and here we rejected it to the contemptuous astonishment of the waiter who with a pity for ignorance of its superior merits, entreatingly asked, "N'aimez vous pas le chamois?"'

Ladies often rode up the mountain passes or were carried up in sedan chairs. Mountain tops were ideal spots on which to rhapsodize over sunrises and as platforms for poetry readings.

Next day Miss Jemima and her party visited the thermal baths, as observers, and were torn between a slight guilt at their curiosity and a desire to giggle at what they saw.

'In one bath we recognised a lady who was our vis-a-vis at a table d'hôte the day before. She was taking her next meal up to her shoulders in water; on a wooden tray was placed a tiny coffee pot, a pat of butter and slices of bread. We could discern the seat or benches running round the bath on which were seated persons in dark blue or dark red gowns. A moustached gentleman, who would consider himself in the prime of life, was cutting leather work on his floating table, other bathers were preparing for a game of draughts, whilst one portly round-shouldered party of some sixty summers was executing a roving commission across the water to salute some ladies in the opposite corner'.

The walk up the narrow track cut out of the face of the Gemmi began on muleback, but as the ledge narrowed the party decided it would be safer to walk. In this way they scrambled to the top and, after a walk across the pass, descended to Kandersteg. In the Lauterbrunnen valley where they visited the Staubbach falls, in much the same way as tourists do today, they found plenty of evidence of tourist development. There were shops selling carved wood souvenirs, and young beggars offering flowers and pebbles for sale. This was to be a recurrent image of Victorian travel: the English parties, ladies with crinolines and parasols, gentlemen in side whiskers and narrow-trousered suits

53

moving at a dignified pace, aloof yet interested, through crowds of beggars, hawkers and others who hoped to profit by their presence.

After crossing the Wengeralp, where they were entertained by a man sounding an alpenhorn, and gazing in awe at the Jungfrau, which obligingly staged an avalanche for them, Miss Jemima's party went on to Grindelwald where they stayed at the same Hotel Adler which stands there today. From Lucerne, the party carried on dutifully to the next obligatory stop on a tourist's itinerary: the Rigi, which not only provided a view over Switzerland but also, at three o'clock in the morning, the ritual of the sunrise worship. Miss Jemima's description of the scene expressed those mixed feelings of censure of her fellow travellers and romantic awe at nature's wonders which were characteristic of Victorian tourists.

'There was as motley a group as the guide-book and descriptive articles ever assemble there. Some three or four care-for-nobody characters appeared as New Zealand chiefs, wrapped in those scarlet blankets that are vetoed in black and white behind every bedroom door, a charge that seems only to remind the inmates of the peculiar adaptability of the said blankets for outdoors as well as indoor service. Most of the gentlemen were in buttoned mackintoshes, a costume not extraordinary, though their neckties of varied qualities and dyes might be inadmissible in full-dress assemblies. But although the ladies of all nations were really unexceptionable in the matter of plaits and hats, some (here I speak personally and honestly as becomes a delineator of facts) were so very exceptionable indeed, it is a question whether the parents of our party would have recognised their off-spring in their Gibeonitish condition. If the good-natured beau in grey, who was supposed to see no wrong in ladies, had his organ of order daily vexed by the toil-honoured and soiled robe of "la plus jolie dame", then to what extent of odium would they have been subjected in their native towns, and what amount of censure levelled against them by their maternal orderlies!

We counted about a hundred and fifty early risers, most of whom wore that miserable expression that would find words in Dr Watts moral song "You have waked me too soon, I must slumber again". The peripatetic vendors of carved needle cases, etc., seemed to awake to their interests as they offered their itinerating stores. Vain men! to think that they could break the monopoly of the rising sun on the Rigi, as in stately process he rises from the dusky mist and with one glance of his ruby eye suffuses the ashy visages of that snowy congress with the waxen hues of the celestial rose called "The Maiden's Blush" '.

There is little more to recount of Miss Jemima's journey. The highspot had been reached, and it is worth meditating on it, for, to borrow Miss Jemima's own style of rhetoric, the year 1863 also marked the dawn of another age of tourism, the hues of which were considerably less boisterous and spontaneous than the early working class outings to Scarborough and Morecambe.

The new attitudes among Cook's tourists were merely a reflection of the changes within society itself. In his foreign tours, Cook was dealing with the rising middle classes, people who were becoming increasingly comfortably off and who, as a result of the wider franchise established by the Reform Acts, were able to exert a powerful influence on government and, by their numbers, on the social manners and attitudes of the country as a whole. This middle class had arisen largely from the manufacturers and merchants of the Midlands and North and it carried with it, like flotsam on a tide,

55

Tägliche Fahrten der Dampfboote

ZWISCHEN

LUZERN UND FLUELEN

mit Berührung der Stationen

Weggis, Buochs, Beggenried, Gersau, Seelisberg und Brunnen.

LUZERN und KÜSSNACHT.

LUZERN, STANSSTAD und ALPNACHT.

Im Anschluß an die Bahnzüge der Centralbahn und in Verbindung mit den Posten von und nach

Mailand, Turin, Genua (über den St. Gotthard) Schwyz, Einsiedeln, St. Gallen, Nid- und Obwalden; mit dem Brünig-Pass und Berner-Oberland; sowie mit den Dampfschiffen des Zuger- und Zürchersees.

Vom 1. Juli 1863 bis auf weitere Anzeige.

The Lac des quatre Cantons, renamed Lake Lucerne by British tourists who regarded every resort they invaded as an extension of England, admirably combined all the attributes desired by the nineteenth century tourist.

all the trends of thought which had characterised the earlier generations of industrial society. Because it was made up of people who had come up in the world it was unsure of itself and clung obstinately to principles, the roots of which lay among the Evangelical and reforming movements of the first half of the century. It also subscribed to the idea of a divided society in which ladies and gentlemen were a totally different breed from working men and women, and wives were a different kind of female to the tens of thousands of fallen women of whose services the gentlemen availed themselves.

Aware of their power but also aware that they were not the ruling class gentry, and fearing too close a connection with the working class from which so many of them had sprung, the middle class cultivated a form of gentility which lasted until 1939 and is still fighting its rearguard action. It is this gentility which is apparent in the tourist of the late nineteenth century and which Cook went to such extraordinary lengths to serve.

In 1863, while Miss Jemima and her party were toiling over the Alps, Cook was having some thoughts that he later expressed in an article entitled *Alpine dreams and realities*. Most of this was taken up with a description of the tour, but there were one or two hints of a change of attitude. The response to his advertisement for the tour was far greater than he had anticipated. There were 140 customers, the majority of them ladies, and he sold more first class than second class tickets. Of the 140 travellers, 62 accompanied him to Switzerland, and the rest remained in Paris. Cook referred to the former as 'my select party'.

Here was a turning point in tourism, and being the capable businessman that he was, Cook sensed it, in the same way that others in more recent times have foreseen the change in the travel market and have created the modern mass package holiday. When, therefore, Cook wrote that 'France and Switzerland now present to me new and almost unlimited fields of human endeavour', he was not only thinking of territorial expansion but of the new potential market of thousands of Miss Jemimas and friends who seemed ready to avail themselves of his services. In the year following Miss Jemima's tour, Cook began his Continental excursions in earnest. He sold 1,200 tourist tickets, of which 140 were over the Alps into Italy. This was a tour to Rome and Naples for which Cook engaged his first courier, although more by chance than intention. The story has a truly Dickensian flavour.

When Cook advertised his Rome tour he received a letter 'from an anxious mother asking for our assistance, if possible, in the restoration of her child left in Rome under trying circumstances'. The circumstances were considerably more than trying, for it appeared that the child had been born in Rome while the father was working there as a courier. The mother, having fallen ill of 'Rome fever', had been ordered back to England instantly by her doctor. The father had to continue on his journey and left the child in the care of a nurse. Returning to England in straitened economic circumstances, the father had then set himself up as a tobacconist and newsvendor and the mother had become pregnant once more. Under these circumstances, and in view of the difficulties and expenses of the journey to Rome, neither of the parents had been able to retrieve their child and the amount they had to pay for her keep made it impossible for them to save money for its return.

Cook, whose philanthropic tendencies were later to cause some disagreements with his son, John Mason, could not resist becoming involved. 'With a case so clear and interesting', he said, in recounting the story to his customers 'it was impossible to give a cold negation, and the question arose how we might best promote the attainment of

The advent of Cooks tours led to a rapid increase of hotel building in Switzerland. The hotel at Schwarbach on the Gemmi pass, the Hotel de la tour at Martigny and the Bains Froids on the Rigi were much patronised.

After Switzerland, Italy became a popular holiday
country and tours often combined the two.
Winter sports did not arrive until the end of the
century, however.

the desired end. Our profits on Tourist Tickets do not afford a margin sufficient to enable us to pay the expenses of a courier: but relying on the generosity of our Tourist friends we have ventured to promise the father the means of visiting Rome in connection with our next excursion'. The 'generosity' of the tourists whom Cook was not slow to appeal to when there was a good cause to be supported, brought the child safely back to England and thus the story ended happily.

Having broken the ice of an Alpine crossing in 1864 Cook set off in the winter of 1865 with his son John Mason to make preparations for the following year, a critical one for Cook as he had decided to open an office in Fleet Street and engage his son in the business. The description of the reconnaissance trip was written by John Mason, who was accompanying his father to Switzerland and Italy for the first time. This account gives a glimpse into the condition of Cook's business at this time, and hints at the growing recognition of the value of his service to foreign railway companies and hoteliers.

'On arriving in Paris' [John Mason wrote] 'we met with the usual hearty reception, and received the usual kindnesses from everyone with whom we had to transact in business, and it was exceedingly gratifying to find the Directors and Managers of Railways and Diligences were also perfectly satisfied with the result of last season's labours, that several opportunities were offered of extending our tourist arrangements. We were also glad to find that our ideas of *giving* to the public of Great Britain all the information possible respecting general arrangements for transit of either passengers or parcels, through the medium of our new offices was considered by the various companies as one likely to facilitate travelling arrangements generally, and the Directors and Managers willingly offered to keep us supplied with all OFFICIAL time tables, maps etc'.

The tourists swarming over the mountains aroused the indignation of real mountaineers but didn't prevent the Miss Jemimas of Cooks parties from enjoying their mountain excursions.

Surrounded as we are today by easily obtainable information, this may not seem a very remarkable innovation, but in 1865 it must have been a very useful service to tourists. It established the tradition of supplying information to the public which was later extended by the national tourist offices.

Crossing the St Gotthard pass in mid-winter was hardly a joy ride but neither of the Cooks seem to have been put out by the cold and the hazards. They set off in sleighs during a snow storm, as John Mason wrote afterwards:

'The snow continued falling, and as we neared the summit the wind arose, and in addition to the falling snow drifted considerable quantities off the mountain, but through the whole ascent the writer never felt any painful sensation of cold . . . and going into the Hospice at the summit, he suffered from hot-ache which soon passed off, and after having a *café noir* (without the cognac) was quite ready for the descent to Airolo'.

After completing their business in Italy, the Cooks returned via the Mont Cenis pass, inspecting the tunnel which would soon provide a way for the railways to cross the Alps to Turin. They had bad weather again crossing the pass. The diligence (stage-coach) of the Messageries Imperials company on which they were travelling over-turned in the snow. 'The instant this occurred' John Mason wrote, 'we heard a loud barking and howling of a dog and on looking out ascertained for the first time that we were followed by a magnificent animal, somewhat of the celebrated St Bernard species.'

Back in London, the Cooks set about advertising their tours for 1865, offering every service which their tourists might require. Passports were not necessary in France, Italy or Switzerland at the time, but Cook offered to get them for travellers to Austria

and the Papal States at the cost of two shillings plus one shilling service charge. Specially mounted passports embossed with the customer's name were worth 2s 6d. Guide books were another sideline. Murrays, Baedekers and Knapsack guides were the most recommended and Cook grudgingly adds Gaze's as the best of the low priced guides (perhaps because he had less commission on them) '. . . they call for much hard labour for the ordinary Continental Traveller', he said 'and may possibly mislead some as to the cost of a trip to Switzerland. Had he based his calculations on our system of Cheap Tours he might have got through with the same amount of money and with much more ease than he prescribes for doing Switzerland for Ten Guineas, to which he adds the wise precaution of putting another £5 in the pocket to meet contingencies'.

In the summer after his winter trip to Italy, Cook opened his season with a 3000-mile tour including Switzerland and Italy. The party consisted of a family of five New Zealanders called Clark, a brother and two sisters from Australia, a family from London, a friend from Yorkshire who had travelled with Cook eighteen years earlier and now was accompanied by his wife, an elderly gentleman and his lady from Lancashire, some ladies on their own from Cheshire and Lancashire and a brave lady from Hertfordshire who had been on previous Cook trips. This party visited Milan, Florence, Rome (19 hours) Naples, Pompeii, Pisa, (25 hours), Genoa and Turin. The high spot of the tour was Pompeii and there we find the party sitting in the Amphitheatre having a picnic at which, 'we have a sumptuous spread of chickens, tongues, sandwiches, cakes, fruits of various kinds and drinks for all palates consisting of cognac, Lachrymi Christi (the tears of Christ!) made from grapes grown at the foot of Vesuvius, and simple essence of lemon for that portion of the party who "neither drink wine nor strong drink" of whom there were not less than a third of the party'.

On his 1866 excursion to Italy, Cook was obliged to hire a palace in Rome for there was no room in the hotels. He paid £500 for this and later published the exact cost of the arrangements, revealing that he had lost £6 14s 8d on the deal. The difficulties of finding accommodation and the trials and tribulations of travel by rail, diligence, and steamer caused weariness which sometimes led to frayed tempers and irritation, and although Cook's descriptions of the journey were generally painted in glowing tones, he now and again spoke out sharply. 'We have but one parting request to make', he says after describing his plans for an autumn trip to Italy, 'and that is, that any who cannot accompany us in a genial, sociable and confiding spirit, will be kind enough not to trouble us with their communications or attempt to join our parties. It has been our lot through many years, to enjoy the greatest social pleasures in these great and responsible undertakings; we have had the confidence and esteem of thousands; our travelling companions have become, in many instances, attached friends; the social feeling has risen above the commercial; and as we began, we desire to continue, and to close the peculiar work, free from petty jarrings and paltry ebullitions of temper and distrust. We have been accustomed to look upon our work in the character of a mission of goodwill and universal brotherhood, and we cannot succumb to unworthy feelings, or bend to an inferior position. Those who wish next to accompany us to Italy or elsewhere will please note these observations, and act in accordance with their spirit and bearing'.

A year after opening his office in Ludgate Circus, Cook was evidently becoming confident of his success, but it is difficult at this point to separate the voice of Thomas from that of his son, John Mason. From now on the two became indistinct as the business expanded in the hands of the indefatigable and relentless John Mason.

The success of the Cooks' business lay in the fact that their offices, such as the London Office in Fleet Street, were able to supply through tickets on the tangled private lines which ran through Europe and that their representatives provided a link with home at foreign ports and stations.

6 The Cooks' barbarians

That travel broadens the mind is indisputable; that it does so in a mood of harmony and tolerance is more open to doubt. Written records and the voice of the modern tourist suggest that where travel is concerned discord is never far off. Firstly, the traveller himself is the subject of criticism by the person who stays at home, in particular the foreign traveller who does so to show off, to keep up with the Joneses; then the foreigner becomes a butt of criticism for the traveller himself. Nothing the foreigner says or does is right, or rarely so, except to the would-be connoisseur of travel who can find nothing but good abroad and nothing but bad at home. Equally a subject for criticism is the fellow traveller who is in different circumstances to one's own. The coach tour party people, or the ones who arrive in that pretentious car, or the ones who think they know about wine, or the ones who drink nothing but orangeade and as for the fish and chip brigade . . . *Plus ça change* . . . as Sterne might say were he alive today, for it was he who made the remark about ' . . . idle people that leave their native country and go abroad for some reason or reasons which may be derived from one of these general causes – Infirmity of body, Imbecility of mind or inevitable necessity'.

He was not the only one of his day to hold this opinion. Adam Smith, too, had a low opinion of the traveller who, 'commonly returns home, more conceited, more un-principled, more dissipated, and more incapable of any serious application, either to

The physical energy of the British tourist, when not exhausted by mountain climbing, was often relieved in boisterous horseplay.

he facade of respectability of the British middle
lasses sometimes cracked in a continental
limate and tourists sometimes behaved in ways
hich would have been inconceivable at home.

The first Cook party to Pompeii arrived in 1864 and aroused the wrath of the British resident bourgeoisie who resented the intrusion of strangers.

study or to business, than he could well have become in so short a time had he lived at home'. And it is not only the English who take part in the game of denigrating travel and travellers; it was a Frenchman who remarked about the English tourist that, 'In a hundred there are not two who seek to instruct themselves. To cover leagues of land or water; to take punch and tea at the inns; to speak ill of all nations, and to boast without ceasing of their own; that is what the crowd of the English call travelling'. These criticisms were voiced nearly two hundred years ago and referred in particular to the young sons of the gentry whose education was completed by the Grand Tour. Today, perhaps, those of us with more idealism than objectivity might claim that the modern tourist is more enlightened in his outlook. Perhaps.

Whether he is or not he will continue to be criticised and to criticise and will find his detractors and his champions giving voice to their opinions. It has always been so and will always be so. No story of the growth of tourism would be complete without an account of the great era of controversy sparked off by Cook and his tourists. When Thomas Cook began his tours abroad critics of foreign travellers were provided with an increase in the variety and quantity of the targets on which they could vent their humour or their spleen. There were the workers from the industrial towns who travelled with Cook to British cities and resorts, there were the artisans and tradesmen who went across the Channel to Paris and Amsterdam, Brussels and the Rhine and there were the school-teachers and professional classes who went to Italy, Germany, Switzerland and the Middle East.

The most resented of all the parties that travelled abroad were those which arrived in Italy, trooping in and out of museums and churches and disturbing the tranquillity enjoyed by those British residents of long standing who considered Florence, Siena, Rome and Venice their private property. The feelings of these people were voiced by a man called Charles Lever who, writing under the pseudonym of Cornelius O'Dowd, began a malicious tongue-in-cheek campaign against the tourists and in particular against the tourists who were arriving in Italy under the care of Thomas Cook. 'It seems', he wrote 'that some enterprising and unscrupulous man has devised the project of conducting some 40 or 50 persons, irrespective of age and sex, from London to Naples and back for a fixed sum'.

O'Dowd then announced that, these people did not represent the nation, but that the tourists were part of a government scheme for disposing of convicts by sending them on tours and dropping them off here and there on the Continent.

'I have already met three flocks' [he said] 'and anything so uncouth I never saw before – the men mostly elderly, dreary, sad-looking, evidently bored and tired, the women somewhat younger, travel tossed, and crumpled, but intensely lively, wide awake and facetious. The cities of Italy are deluged with droves of these creatures, for they never separate, and you see them, 40 in number, pouring along a street with their director – now in the front – now in the rear – circling around them like a sheep dog and really the process is as like herding as may be'.

In a later piece O'Dowd returned to the attack, himself not unlike a dog that has discovered the pleasure of chasing sheep, or of a journalist who has found a fruitful vein to dig at for the amusement of his readers.

'Foreigners may say, we desire to be able to pray in our churches, to hear in our theatres, to dine in our restaurants, but your people will not permit us. They come not in two's and three's but in scores and hundreds to stare and laugh at us. They deride our church ceremonies, they ridicule our cooking, they criticise our dress, and they barbarise our language. Take my word for it, if these Excursionists go on, nothing short of another war or another Wellington will ever place us where we once were in the estimation of Europe'.

When Cook read this article he exploded with the same energy that he had previously demonstrated in his encounters with Leicester hecklers and would-be competitors.

'Let me ask' [he wrote] 'why Mr Lever's susceptibilities should be outraged, and his refinement trampled on, because thirty or forty Englishmen and Englishwomen find it convenient to travel in the same train, to coalesce for mutual benefit, and to sojourn for a time in the same cities? Reference to a modern compilation shows that this hyper-critical gentleman started upon a career as student of medicine in Dublin, that he subsequently took a German degree, and that after practising for a short time he foresook his profession for novel-writing as being more profitable and less laborious. Apart, then, from his talent for producing fiction – of which I would speak with all possible respect – Mr Lever is an Irish gentleman of the precise class to which the English clergymen, physicians, bankers, civil engineers and merchants, who honoured me by accepting my escort to Italy last year, indisputably belong. By what right, then, does he constitute himself their censor?'

O'Dowd, no doubt enjoying a good fight like a true Irishman, had other things to say about the Cookites.

'These people, from the hour they set out, regard all foreign countries and their inhabitants as something in which they have a vested right. They have paid for the Continent as they paid for Cremorne and they *will* have the worth of their money. They mean to eat it, drink it, and junket it to the uttermost farthing. When the cutlet is overdone, or the cathedral disappoints them, it is not merely unsatisfactory – it is a do – a sell just as if the rockets should refuse to go up at Vauxhall or the Catherine wheels to play. Europe, in their eyes, is a great spectacle, like a show-piece at Covent Garden; and it is theirs to criticise the performance and laugh at the performers at will'.

It would be incredible if Cook was not aware that O'Dowd's criticisms were justified, though exaggerated, for he himself had experienced the complaints which are the lot of all who make travel their business. However, Cook would never admit to his clients' defects; like a good public relations man he had to look continually on the bright side and defend even that which he knew to be indefensible in order to maintain his customers' loyalty. But there was more to it than that. O'Dowd had his public too and in Cook's eyes these were people who, because of their status in society, considered themselves better than those who did the work; they were the gentry and aspiring gentry of the upper middle class, the snobs who were alarmed by the rising lower middle class and who attacked those who were climbing up through society by sneering at their social deficiencies. In this way O'Dowd was in line with the later humourists in *Punch* to whom the lower orders were a constant source of inspiration. From what we know of Cook's earlier attitudes there is no doubt that O'Dowd's heavy irony was like an ermine

CANNIBAL CHIEF (releasing victim)

"Why didn't you say before that you were from Cooks—I'm their Local Agent"

cloak to a socialist bull; so he tore into O'Dowd with gusto.

At the same time it is worth noting that he had no quarrel with Arthur Sketchley, a humorous writer. Sketchley expressed his opinions and made comments on the contemporary scene through a character called Mrs Brown, an outspoken Cockney lady whose indiscreet comments and criticisms were made palatable to readers by the fact that she could be dismissed as an uneducated woman whose opinions did not have to be taken seriously because the social gulf between her and her readers was unbridgeable.

Cook invited Sketchley to join one of his tours and the result was a book describing the tour to Switzerland and France in a straightforward manner and another with Mrs Brown's version of it. This satire was more kindly than that of O'Dowd and no doubt Cook felt that in view of the public acceptance of Mrs Brown and her comments on everything from the law to the Commons he had no need to worry about his clients' susceptibilities. Like Molière's audiences, no one would recognise themselves in the Cockney woman. Besides, as Mrs Brown said, 'I'm sure as Mr Cook did ought to 'ave 'is statutes by law stuck about all over the world, as is a wonderful man: and as to Brown, I never see a man take more to another in this world, never'.

But although there was no doubt about where Mrs Brown's loyalties lay, this did not prevent her from giving a telling description of the tourists who were brothers under the skin to O'Dowd's barbarians.

> 'I've 'eard parties talk a deal about French cleverness,' [she says while on a visit to Paris] 'and it is wonderful how Frenchmen can make out what you mean when you don't speak no French and will bring you anythink as you want at a 'otel by guest work, but of all the stupids over their own languidge they beat anyone as ever I knowed or 'eard tell on, for I'm sure there was one waiter as only took and stared at me a 'askin' 'im for the butter, as said I to 'im quite plain "gasson" as means waiter, "Dele bour, sival play", as is "butter if you please", all the world over and then for the other one to pretend not to know as I wanted two heggs, and kep me awaiting ever so long tho' I said to 'im, "Doo-oos" twenty times as means two heggs, tho' when you want one, you must call it "Huff aller cock", or you won't get a 'ens egg as is their contrairy ways of callin' thinks, just like forriners'.

Apart from her low opinion of the intelligence of foreigners, Mrs B did not trust them an inch. In Rome she found the carriage drivers urging her to mount their cabs. One day, pressed against a wall by an importuning cab, she stepped into it to save herself from being run over . . . 'Afore I could get right, that boy 'ad drove on ever so fast, so I takes my umbrella and pitches into 'is back as 'ard as I could, a-'ollerin' stop and the more I 'it and 'ollered the faster he went on till, as luck would 'ave it, the wheel went ag'in a cart and pitched me out'. Mrs Brown was not without her faults and these are such as would have infuriated the O'Dowds of Naples, Florence and Rome. At Pompeii she was told about the eruption of Vesuvius and destruction of Pompeii. 'Yes, says that gent, and was kep' covered up for 'undred of years, thro' hashes never bein' took away. "Ah", says I, "the dustman's the dustman all the world over . . ." '.

Cook's tolerance of Sketchley seems to have escaped O'Dowd's notice, who, while confessing surprise at Cook's indignation to his editor John Blackwood, does not realise that in Cook's attitude too, there is more than meets the eye at first glance. 'He pitches into me most furiously for my O'Dowd on the "Convict tourists" and seeing the tone of his paper I only wonder he did not make the case actionable.' O'Dowd's final words to

Blackwood revealed his true feelings, for he said 'Heaven grant that I may fall in with his tourists. I'll certainly go and dine at any table d'hôte I find them at in Florence'.

Cook's preoccupation with the effects of press criticism of his tourists was much more evident in the case of William Howard Russell's articles in *The Times* describing the Prince and Princess of Wales' tour to Egypt. This tour, as it happened, coincided with Cook's own first Egyptian tour of 1869. Not unnaturally, and probably correctly, W H Russell surmised that the object of Cook's tour was not only the study of Egyptian antiquities but also the opportunity to follow in the footsteps of a royal party.

To Russell, the royal trip, after his experiences as war correspondent in the American Civil War and in the Crimea, must have been a very routine assignment and the arrival of the Cook party gave him that peg which every journalist stuck with a dull story looks for. At any rate he used it as the leaven with which to make his bread digestible. In Russell's reports, the Royal party, attempting to pursue its dignified way up the Nile,

Empress Frederick of Prussia, Queen Victoria's eldest daughter (Vicky), who shared the Royal family's passion for travel. Her own daughter, Sophie, married Constantine, Crown Prince of Greece, and Vicky suggested that Mr Cook should be invited to Athens to see how the tourist trade could be extended to that coun so that 'poor little Greece would become rich at once'.

seems to be constantly in danger of being caught up by the Cookites who provide a kind of comic relief throughout the expedition.

' . . . a cloud of smoke rises from a steamer astern', [writes Russell]. 'The Tourists are coming!' [Or, in another passage,] 'We went so slowly that the fear grew upon us lest Cook's tourists should overhaul the flotilla'. [And again] 'Cook's tourists have arrived! Their steamers are just below us in the stream. The tourists are all over the place. Some are bathing off the beaches: others with eccentric head-dresses are toiling through the deep sand after an abortive attempt to reach Philae. They are just beaten by a head in the race. Another day and the Prince and Princess would have been at their mercy!'

William Howard Russell was having a bit of fun and entertaining his readers, but Cook could not see it that way. This was his first Egyptian tour and he feared that the ridiculing of his clients would affect the susceptibilities of his future customers and kill his business. He had a lot at stake in the Middle East. So he wrote to the Prince of Wales himself, and published the letter in *The Excursionist*, sending a copy of the letter to Lord Clarendon, the Foreign Secretary. After apologising for his inability to 'wield a pen in literary tilt with the pen-proud hero of the Crimea and other battlefields', and for any rudeness or indecorum in addressing a letter to His Royal Highness, Cook launched into a description of his tourist trip, and managed to suggest that far from wishing to escape from his tourists he believed that the Prince was in fact hoping to meet them, an encounter that had been made impossible by an accident to a paddle-wheel of Cook's steamer, and the refusal of the Governor of Kenneh to let him proceed on another ship. With ingenuous guile Cook wrote 'I will not say that Mustapha Aga (the Consul who had told Cook that the Prince wished to meet the party) really meant what he said for the Egyptians have such a peculiar way of expressing themselves, that he might have intended the reverse: and it is not impossible that the unaccountable conduct of the Governor of Kenneh, in not authorising a steamer to proceed, while the other was being repaired was owing to some secret communication of the wire . . . '. Officially, Cook received nothing more than a routine acknowledgement of his letter, but from his customers there came an avalanche of support. Whether or not he had planned his strategy with this in mind, the results were very satisfactory and encouraged Cook on the road to one of his most important ventures; the tourist conquest of Egypt.

Perhaps the last and best word on the subject is that offered by the ubiquitous Mrs Brown who had been a member of the Cook's party and who subsequently commented, 'As to anyone a'saying as I went to Egyp' a follerin' the Prince of Wales about, I'd scorn the action, as never was one for to intrude myself on no-one, and 'ave a 'usban of my own to foller, and foller 'im I will. Some parties we was a – stoppin' and was talkin' at breakfast one day a 'ole party as ad come out from England for to foller the Prince of Wales about and one gentleman said as it was a impertinent intrusion. I says "Fiddle-de-dee. Impertinent indeed, 'A cat may look at a king' as the sayin' is and I'm sure 'is Real 'Ighness would be glad for to fall in with some good honest Hinglish faces arter seein' nothink but there 'ere Turkey Blackamoors about." "Oh", says the gentleman, "Wulgar people thinks alike"'.

7 The lure of the Middle East

To British people the Middle East has a particular significance, and has given rise to more legends, aroused more emotions, demanded more attention, and caused more expense than probably any other part of the Empire. In the late 19th century the Middle East was, if not the heart, at least the main artery of the Empire. It was through here that the material and the spiritual blood flowed. It was a strategic lifeline and more than that, it was the Land of the Bible, the birthplace of the representative of that Divine Providence which had arranged that the British should lead the world to enlightenment and truth. For these reasons the Middle East aroused more interest than the more mysterious and more distant lands east of Suez. It was an arena in which the conflicting characteristics of the British temperament could struggle, like Jacob and the angel, for self-revelation and for the expression of that innate romanticism of the Victorian soul. Also the Middle East was accessible, within reasonable reach for someone with four weeks and a couple of hundred pounds to spare. The opening of the Middle East to the tourist could not be more clearly marked. The year was 1869, the year of the opening of the Suez Canal and of the royal visit to Egypt by the Prince of Wales.

Thomas Cook had already explored the possibility of a trip to the Middle East in 1868 and had received an invitation to the opening of the Suez Canal from his friend de Lesseps. As usual his preparations were impeccable. He planned for a party of sixty people and, since there were no hotels or other amenities available in the Holy Land, he set up his own travelling camp. This consisted of 21 sleeping tents, with beds, carpets, tapestries and other amenities to make them as comfortable and home-like as possible. For meals, he supplied three dining tents with field kitchens. Transport was supplied by 65 saddle horses and the whole caravanserai was moved by 87 pack horses and as many mules as were necessary, led by 56 muleteers. All this was a far cry from the trains and diligences with which he transported his Continental tourists, but Cook was not at all put out by his new field of operations.

The prospect of travelling through wild territories occupied only by Arab tribes, who were not only often at war with each other but who frequently threatened and stole from passing travellers, was one which concerned but did not deter Cook. Whether this danger was as real as he assumed is perhaps open to doubt; there are conflicting opinions. According to Isabel Burton, the wife of the explorer Sir Richard Burton and an intrepid traveller herself, the numbers of the tourists were themselves a safeguard and in her opinion the Arabs regarded Cook's tourists as 'Hum Kukiyejeh' not 'travellers but Cookii'. Perhaps Isabel Burton's opinions were coloured by the fact that tourists wandering in large groups through the lands which had been the preserve of pioneers and explorers tended to detract from the glamour of their exploits. John Murray, whose guide book to travellers in Syria and Palestine began with a humble admission that the best handbook was the Bible, did not underestimate the dangers and warned all travellers to choose a good guide from the tribe through whose territory the tour was to go, otherwise unpleasant encounters might occur.

For the tourists themselves the expedition through the Holy Land must have pro-

people who led austere and righteous lives the Middle East
posed a problem. It offered self indulgence and exoticism. Most
people managed not to succumb by reacting indignantly at
everything they saw.

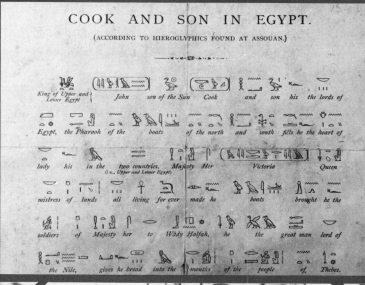

COOK AND SON IN EGYPT.

(ACCORDING TO HIEROGLYPHICS FOUND AT ASSOUAN.)

King of Upper and Lower Egypt | John son of the Sun Cook and son his the lords of

Egypt, the Pharaoh of the boats of the north and south fills he the heart of

lady his in the two countries, (i.e. Upper and Lower Egypt) Majesty Her Victoria Queen

mistress of lands all living for ever made he boats brought he the

soldiers of Majesty her to Wâdy Halfah, he the great man lord of

the Nile, gives he bread into the mouths of the people of Thebes.

duced tremors of excitement and fears as they listened to stories of ferocious horsemen who stopped caravans and made off with the women, and of travellers whose bleached bones were found months later in the shifting sands of the desert. Murray was on the whole, reassuring. He advised that in the event of trouble a 'calm and conciliatory bearing' was the best way of dealing with the natives, and that on the happy outcome of an encounter, but not before, a small gift was advisable. 'Be firm, but kind', he directed. 'Browbeating may compel submission but will never secure respect and wholesome deference which is so essential to the peace and pleasure of a Syrian Tour'. In an age of Palmerstonian gunboat diplomacy this was very sensible advice. No doubt those who followed it were the ones who left behind the legend of the imperturbable Englishman which still receives homage from people all over the world, even today.

Whether the dangers were real or imagined, Cook was taking no chances. Among his entourage he included guards, guard dogs and those genies of the tourist parties, the dragomen, who acted as guide, mentors and friends to the tourists. Cook himself once described a typical desert trip in the Holy Land:

'Let us begin the day. It is still dark . . . five, and sometimes four o'clock when the dragoman's whistle is heard to summon the camp; and two men go round all the tents, one ringing a large bell and the other beating some kitchen-pan by way of a gong. There was no sleeping after this. Now there are a variety of cries. "Light, No. 2", "Water, No. 8". With clapping of hands in the dark to direct the attention of the servants. We must needs be on the alert, for before we can possibly dress and repack our luggage we hear the men removing the tent pegs. Suddenly down comes the canvas and we are left to finish our toilet in the open air'.

Whether this was intentional or not is not clear, but possibly the servants were not above having a bit of fun at the tourists' expense, in the same spirit as that of Italian waiters who knock and enter simultaneously as they deliver breakfast to some attractive signorina. Once they were dressed the party had breakfast: 'Tea, coffee, and milk, with boiled eggs or omelette are at once handed around. Then follows a course of hot chicken, and then another of cutlets'. The servants are also not above letting the tent down on the heads of the breakfasting tourists, so they hurry through the meal and saddle up for the day's ride. At lunch time there is a break. The servants have laid out carpets under the palms of an oasis and every traveller is provided with a tin plate, tin mug and cutlery. They then set to with a will on hard-boiled eggs, cold chicken, cold lamb, sardines, cheese, bread and oranges. Not surprisingly, this snack makes some of the party feel sleepy and so they have a siesta before setting off again.

Later that afternoon they spot the camp which the servants have gone ahead to set up, and are delighted to see the Union Jacks flying over every tent. They are even more delighted to note that the cook is preparing the evening meal which, when it arrives, consists of 'hot soup of the best quality', mutton or lamb, goose or wild boar, chicken or turkey, then some capital pudding. There are, of course, vegetables and fruit in abundance and it is impossible not to agree with the writer when he says, 'the wonder is how these comforts can all be packed and carried with us day by day'.

By 8 o'clock the party is 'fit for little else than sleep'. But one wonders how much sleep the intrepid tourists, used to the silence of some English town, actually did get.

'Now and then the soundest sleeper is aroused by the piercing cries of the jackals prowling very near, responded to by the vehement and angry barking of our dogs. The tinkling of the bells of our mules and the occasional bray of a donkey, a song from the muleteers squatting around their fire, the croaking of frogs in the neighbouring stream, or the hooting of an owl, with an occasional snore from some sleeper in the tents, are other sounds which sometimes break the silence'.

Cook controlled an army of workmen who regarded him as the most powerful man in Egypt. Among his employees were the dragomen, guides and guardians of the parties in the Middle East. The one in this picture was called 'Charlie' by his customers.

There were moments of high excitement during these desert trips and moments which even Cook's careful arrangements could not prevent. One of these was caused by bad weather which, on the occasion described by Cook, brought torrents of rain and wind which blew down one of the tents. 'Looking in that direction (of tent No 8) we saw the pole prostrate, the canvas collapsed, and the unfortunate ladies, in their camp beds, exposed to the elements'. With speed and resourcefulness other members of the party rushed to the rescue and carried the ladies' beds into another tent. But no sooner had they done so than another tent blew down, and then another. Finally, the party had to squelch their way through the mud to a nearby hut where the men crowded into one badly ventilated room and the ladies into another. An ever-present danger was that of the wild Bedouins. Whenever the party passed through Bedouin territory the dragomen and muleteers fired their rifles as a warning, while the travelling trumpeter, or tumbreler, blew on his instrument and went into a wild song.

The first tour was full of unexpected events, one of which was recounted by Miss Riggs of Hampstead in her journal. One of the ladies of the party had become ill and had gone to a convent at Ramlah where she had died. The problem of what to do with her body was solved in an original manner, as Miss Riggs described.

'Arabs have a great supersitition with regard to the dead – and as she (Mrs Samuels, the dead woman) was to be taken to Jerusalem to be buried, the natives were told that she was ill and she was packed up and carried on a palanquin. A dead person could not be taken from the convent without government permission. So altogether it was thought advisable to act this deception – she died at 3 (night) and was conveyed thither at 6 in the morning and buried that night – eastern burials are so awfully rapid – we all felt the solemnity of the event and I felt, and I am sure others also, how God in his merciful goodness had conducted us safely and well through so much of this wonderful land of Promise, so interesting to the infirmities and weaknesses of the flesh'.

Despite this sad incident the tour continued on its way with Miss Riggs keeping a scrupulous tally of the number of times that each tourist fell off his or her horse.

Cook did not mention Mrs Samuels' death, but reported at length on a robbery at his encampment. The story appeared in *The Times*, *The Daily News*, *The Evening Standard* and *The Pall Mall Gazette* and aroused considerable interest despite John Mason's attempts to tone down the exaggerated reports which merely reflected the growing self-importance of a nation that easily became indignant at the impertinence of foreigners who dared to upset its citizens.

The English tourist who visited the Middle East was a very different person from the one who had joined Cook's working parties to Paris. He was a man or, in the majority, a lady, of some substance, aware of his position in society and of himself as a representative of the most powerful and most civilised nation in the world. He therefore expected proper respect, and a visible expression of gratitude for the benefits which his country had bestowed on mankind. It would be a mistake, however, to think that the Englishman abroad was a self-righteous prig, turning away from anything which might offend him or his wife. On the contrary, in the Middle East he was far enough away from home to be able to indulge openly in harmless entertainments which he would not like to be associated with publicly in England. Even the ladies seemed less liable to fainting fits from shocks to their susceptibilities. Miss Riggs quite unblushingly recorded the

80

In the last quarter of the century tourists became more demanding of their creature comforts and Co provided them with iron bedsteads to sleep on and porridge and boiled eggs for breakfast even in the desert

sight of naked Arabs along river banks and the dancing girls 'which the gentlemen patronised'.

Another amusement which did not turn tourists away, although it produced the same conventional indignation as stories in the more imaginative Sunday newspapers do today, was the visit to the slave market described by John Ripley, one of Cook's early couriers.

'We entered and found ourselves in the presence of a slave owner and his slaves. The man stealer was a stout, sensuous, lazy-looking Turk about sixty years of age, sitting wrapped up in costly eastern robes, with the everlasting pipe in his mouth. The slaves consisted of five women and two boys. Three of the women were comparatively young, ranging from nineteen to twenty-four years old, the other two about thirty, and the boys about thirteen or fourteen. We were asked to sit down and coffee was immediately brought to us. We asked through our guide what was the price of the best-looking of the girls. The old man told us £300 and ordered her to stand up, which she immediately did, showing a fine form and an erect position.'

On their departure the tourists handed out the usual baksheesh and 'left the dirty den with our hatred of Eastern abominations very much intensified'.

Cook's first tour arrived in Egypt before the opening ceremonies of the Suez Canal, but the tourists had another exciting prospect, that of following the Prince of Wales up the Nile. Miss Riggs made careful notes in her journal of the movements of the royal party, also mentioning that Cook was very nearly drowned while bathing in the Nile. There exists a good deal of written material on British tourism on the Nile in the last two decades of the century, and from the various journals and books it is not difficult to imagine the sights and scenes of a British party on tour. Cairo was the starting point

and Shepheard's Hotel the centre of tourist life. There, around its terraces, gathered all the local people who depended on the tourists for a living. There were donkey boys and their donkeys, conjurors and snake charmers, sellers of ancient jewellery, pimps and con men. On the terraces, separated from the Egyptian crowd by an iron railing, sat or walked the visitors, discussing their excursions or the results of their souvenir hunts.

It was the period of extravagent elegance in dress, with draped overskirts and tight bodices which gathered up behind in the 'Dolly Varden' style or draped gracefully from the hips à la 'Princess Polonaise'. The apparel contrasted strangely with that of the Arabs who stared with respect and perhaps some amazement at the visitors. The spectacle of a party of these ladies, in their voluminous dresses, and their men bowler-hatted and often dressed no differently from the way they did at home, setting off to visit the Pyramids astride donkeys named Lily Langtry, Sir Robert Tichbourne and Benjamin Disraeli, must have been awe inspiring. Off the party would go, up the avenue which had a familiar Continental look because of the French influence on the architecture, past the open-air cafés where British soldiers sat reassuringly, past such pictu-resque sights as a wedding party with the bride borne along in a covered palanquin, or a funeral procession with the deceased man's wives, prostrate, and veiled, on a low cart behind the bier.

Approaching the Pyramids the donkey boys could not resist the temptation to give the donkeys a prod that would send them off at a gallop with their riders hanging on desperately and often falling off. When this happened the donkey boys were all solici-tude and apologies and no-one thought that their mischievous behaviour had been intentional. The visit to the Pyramids was a 'must' but there were hazards other than the ascent: beggars, guides and pedlars swarmed round the tourists like the flies that buzzed about their heads and, although Cook's dragomen had strict orders to protect their charges, they were easily outnumbered and outmanoeuvred. The advice given by some

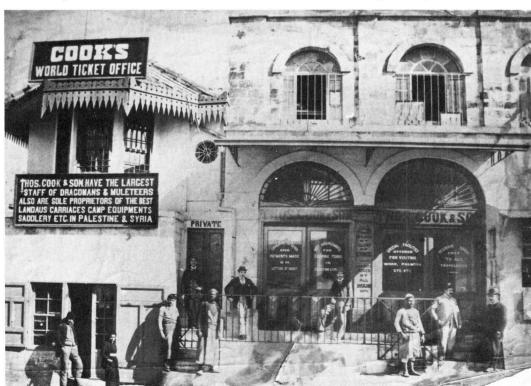

The first Cooks office in Egypt was opened in the grounds of Shepheards Hotel. Soon others followed at Luxor and Port Said.

There were no mountains in Egypt so tourists
climbed the Pyramids. This exercise was usually
aided by three men who pushed and pulled stout
ladies and gentlemen to the summit.

guide books, and often taken by the tourists, was to set about them with a stick and, if they did not possess their own to take one of those offered by bystanders in the hope of receiving the ever-present baksheesh.

The ascent of the Pyramids was usually accompanied by three Bedouin escorts, two to pull and one to push. The climb was worth it for, from the top, the British tourist could feel, like Napoleon, that thirty centuries were looking down upon the British in Cairo and that in all that time there was no worthier master of the Middle East. Another 'must' was the Cairo Museum where antiquities, including mummies which had been discovered by Englishmen, were on view and even for sale in an adjoining room. The daughter of one of Cook's dragomen of the turn of the century, a Mr Aquilina, remembers that the illicit sale of antiquities continued long after the Egyptian Government closed down the Museum sales and that any objects dug up were often sold to interested parties in secret. One such discovery and sale related to a sarcophagus dug up by her father in the grounds of a villa he intended to build. This object took the fancy of an American tourist who, convinced that it contained the remains of Queen Cleopatra, outbid the British Museum and arranged for its secret conveyance to the United States.

Truth, as the British knew it, was certainly difficult to pin down in Egypt if one is to believe the indignant comments of A N Montgomery, a former captain in the Royal Fusiliers, writing in 1882. 'In this country', he said 'all men are liars, you cannot be certain of anything being done. You'll get civility but not truth or gratitude – but sometimes you may be agreeably surprised'. Whatever Captain Montgomery may have thought of Egypt he was certain that Britain must fulfil her role there. 'It is to be hoped,' he says, 'that Great Britain, having commenced her beneficent work, will falter not until she has established in Egypt liberty and security for native and alien'. Not every tourist set the example that Captain Montgomery or Cook himself would have wished. The stuccoed interiors of tombs were often defaced or large chunks removed. Candlegrease and finger marks appeared on the wall paintings while the more sordid aspects of life in Alexandria and Cairo flourished with tourist support.

Cook quickly realised that the success of his Egyptian tours would depend on isolating his customers from the less acceptable realities of Egyptian life, a truth about certain types of tourism that still applies today. He therefore set about providing on the Nile steamers a home from home refuge from which his tourists could observe life at a safe distance. As the century progressed, he became master of his own fleet of ships but, throughout the period that he controlled the Nile steamers, the aim of the service remained the same: to provide all the comforts of home in palatial style.

Cook's steamers were Grand Hotels afloat. They had public rooms where the passengers could congregate, play cards or write their journals, a reading room in which the English papers and magazines provided a constant link with home, and a promenade deck which was covered with an awning and, completely closed at night, provided a place where the elegantly-clad ladies and the men in evening dress could discuss the day's excursions as they watched the starry Egyptian night through the smoke of their cigars. At hand there would be the servants, white robed, white gloved, wearing red fez and cummerbunds and ready to give instant and unobtrusive service at the wave of a hand. These same servants would be there at breakfast time, handing round the English papers that had arrived on the mail steamer, serving a reassuringly English breakfast of porridge, bacon and eggs, fish, ham, tongue and other hot dishes. Everything that Cook, and John Mason Cook in particular, could think of for the comfort of passengers was provided, even a bar. Such pests as the mosquitoes, fleas, flies, lice and bugs against which Keatings promised protection in advertisements in Cook's *The Excursionist* found it difficult to come aboard. 'Very little medicine is needed, for Egypt is delightfully healthy, and on each Cook's steamer there is a doctor with plenty of drugs'.

The cost of Cook's tours to the Holy Land and Egypt was 150 guineas for a 100 day tour and 100 guineas for one of seventy days. He offered a special fare of 50 guineas for the opening of the Suez Canal in November 1869. This fare provided a ticket but no accommodation, and there was a choice of routes via the Mont Cenis, St Gotthard or the Simplon Pass to Trieste for embarkation on the SS *America*. The opening of the Suez Canal was the biggest event of an eventful year for Egypt, and Cairo was *en fête* for the occasion. Shepheard's Hotel was crowded with eminent people. The Empress Eugenie, the wife of Napoleon III and considered the most beautiful woman in Europe, was there for the opening and so was Theophile Gautier. A new opera house had been built and an opera with an Egyptian theme commissioned from Guiseppe Verdi. (Unfortunately he did not finish *Aida* in time and *Rigoletto* was performed instead). There was a ball for 5000 guests, parties on the yachts and Nile steamers, processions, bands and endless merrymaking in the streets.

It was a great historical moment and everyone knew it, including Cook who early in the following year wrote:

'Thirty years have passed since the first thought of applying the powers and facilities of railways and locomotion to the purpose of social and benevolent organisation led to proposals and labours which have culminated in visits to Jerusalem, to the land of Pharaohs, to Asia and Greece: and now we are pressed to go wider still, to extend these Oriental efforts to India, to China, to Australia, to California and then, like our namesake of old "Circumnavigate the World".

The Cooks obtained the monopoly of Nile passenger traffic and set up a Nile fleet of steamers. These were built in Scotland, shipped out piecemeal and assembled at the Boulae Shipyards.

8 The carriage trade

'It is, or has been, the fashion among some empty-headed persons to sneer at "Cook's Tourists". Pretending to imagine that the pleasure of travel should be reserved for the upper classes, they protested against the beauties of Nature being examined by any but persons of the highest quality and seemed to think that the grey Highlands, the quaint Belgian cities, the castled Rhine crags, the glaciers, the mountains and waterfalls of Switzerland, the blue plains of Italy were exhibitions which should be open only to the holders of high priced stall tickets. What little mischief those notions occasioned was soon blown aside when, in the course of the last thirty years, a man has catered for the comfort of upward of three million persons – numbering among them Dukes, Archbishops and members of every class of respectable society – not merely to their satisfaction, but without the occurrence of a single accident throughout the whole period, he can well afford to disregard either spoken scoff or printed satire'.

In these words *The Daily Telegraph* of 1872 accepted the fact that its public were in favour of Cook's tours. The newspaper justified its opinion by pointing out that even the Quality patronised them, a fact often used by Cook himself to encourage new patrons from the middle and upper middle classes. It would be wrong to assume that Cook had turned his back on his earlier ideals of cheap travel for everyone, for workers' holidays continued insofar as there was a demand for them; but a greater demand was being made by the middle classes, many of them workers of a previous generation.

The fact was that the evolution of society was continuing. The enormous gulf between the rich and the poor, the literate and the ignorant, still existed; but was now filled with a solid mortar of the kind of people who voted governments in, set the pattern of social manners and morals and had money to spend on gracious living. The poor were still there, perhaps with their poverty made more apparent by the general affluence of the sections of society who employed them: Disraeli's concept of 'two nations' was a reality which worried the more thoughtful, but the consumer society that had been created had to be served, and those who were in business could not ignore it.

A hint of things to come, as far as Cook was concerned, had already been announced in his disagreement with the organiser of a party of working people for whom Cook had planned a tour to Paris for the Exhibition of 1868. The quarrel arose over the accommodation and its cost which the client thought too high. The business was taken away from Cook, who promptly changed the character of the rooms he had prepared to make them more suitable for a 'class above that of the workers'. The direction taken by the company, officially called Thomas Cook and Son in 1872, was, one suspects, very largely dictated by the business sense of John Mason Cook who knew exactly where the future lay. That was in what the majority of the travelling public wanted, and what, if the business was to survive, it had to be supplied with.

One of the first steps taken by the Cooks to serve their increasing clientele in the new era which had opened by the '70s was the extension of their premises by a move into a large office at Ludgate Circus. Here they dealt not only with tickets and tours, but also ran a goods receiving office, a branch post and telegraph office, provided a reading room

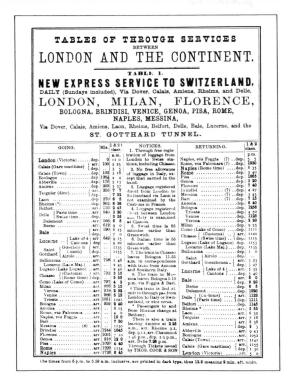

and a waiting room, and posted up a daily notice of weather conditions abroad. In 1873 they also began the publication of the Cooks Continental Timetable, a book which is still published today.

Addressing their clients through *The Excursionist*, the Cooks wrote, 'It has been a great annoyance to us to know that many of our patrons have had to exercise their patience for one or two hours at a time awaiting their turn, and we have no doubt we have lost a few good customers, simply because their time and patience have been exhausted'. They went on to describe the new facilities offered the public and also answered those who thought they should have more assistants by pointing out that it was difficult to find people qualified to reply to questions put by customers, some of whom often wasted the assistants' time.

'We have just had two ladies in the office', the editorial complained, 'one and a half hours, purchasing tickets to the amount of £40 only'. Without doubt, it was John Mason Cook speaking up in the interests of better service for the growing number of people who were flocking into the Cooks' headquarters, and in the interests of better profits for the firm. 'People overlook, the fact that business has grown so enormously in the last eight years that it has become almost impossible to keep pace with it', he pointed out.

If the manner in which the Cooks dealt with their clientele appears a little more peremptory than in the early days, this was due not only to their confidence in their situation but to the fact that the public had become more demanding and intolerant. No longer were people content to pile higgledy-piggledy into open carriages or find themselves on a steamer without reserved cabins. That spontaneous, devil-may-care enjoyment had begun to disappear except among those pioneering spirits who were following Cook into the Middle East and across America. The rest were demanding that the Cooks live up to their reputation as organisers. Travel was on the threshold of the age of the cossetted tourist who blames the travel agent if a cockroach happens to find its way into his room.

Evidence that quantity did not always go hand in hand with quality where tourists were concerned can be glimpsed in the newspapers of the day, which, while accepting the Cooks, continued to belabour some of their clients. 'It is desirable', says *The Illustrated London News*, 'that they should think somewhat less of themselves, and should endeavour to study, with more liberal sympathies, and more earnest desire of knowledge, the foreign lands and nations they visit'.

Although prepared to berate his clients for wasting the time of his staff, Cook was not inclined to question their motives for going abroad, and he continued to provide them with reasons for joining his foreign tours. 'The intense and passionate desire to escape from the drudgery of the shop or counting house, forms an all-powerful motive annually compelling thousands of our fellow countrymen to rush from the precincts of the crowded towns and cities for the purpose of inhaling the fresh, invigorating mountain air, or drinking in the rich beauties of nature . . . ' A half admission of his true feelings was revealed however in the concluding paragraphs, in which his future hopes seemed to admit to an imperfect dream. 'We are learning to correct our social deficiencies; much of our natural uncouthness and want of politeness arose from our insular position'. The early dream of continual and universal self-improvement which would lead to a perfect society of affluent cultured people, was beginning to fray at the edges, and so perhaps were those of the Cooks. Certainly, a letter such as that received from the Earl of Shrewsbury, who had given Cook permission to take excursionists to Alton Towers, was not encouraging.

'Dear Sir,

Willing as I am to allow every facility for excursionists to visit this place, I cannot but take notice of the disorderly conduct of the party from Wednesbury that came here today. I am sorry to say there were many of them half drunk when they came, and finished the day in a state of intoxication. My intention in opening this place to the public is to afford reasonable recreation. I must, therefore, as this is the second offence on the part of the Wednesbury people, instruct you not to arrange for any excursion train from that district for the remainder of the season.
Believe me, sincerely yours
Shrewsbury'.

The letter was addressed to John Mason Cook whose growing absorption with overseas tours did not mean that he neglected home business. An 1870 issue of *The Excursionist* advertised tours to the Nottingham Goose Fair, to the Workmen's International Exhibition in London, to the seaside resorts, and to the beauty spots of England, Wales, Scotland and Ireland. Foreign tours, however, were of longer duration and more expensive, and left a larger margin of profit. Moreover for the Cooks, who had travelled the length and breadth of England, they provided the stimulus of a new worlds to conquer.

Those who went abroad were a different class of society from those who travelled on the excursions at home, and they were more deeply imbued by the concept of Britain's supremacy in the world; or if they were not, they soon acquired it as they surveyed the teeming mobs of less privileged, poverty and disease-ridden people in the countries they visited.

Empire was beginning to have a real meaning for the British in the latter part of the century, and *The Illustrated London News* abounded with illustrated reports of the wars in Bechuanaland, Zululand, the Sudan, Ashanti, the North West frontier and other places where the natives were reluctant to appreciate the advantages of membership of the greatest Empire on earth. The Cook traveller overseas, journeying with his fellows, accompanied by a personal escort, met at ports and stations, waited on hand and foot on board ship and housed in the best hotels abroad, naturally regarded himself as a land-lord visiting his property and demanded respect and admiration from those who served him.

'It is mere truth to affirm', remarked one of them, 'that in some respects the foreigners are two centuries behind us'. This was not pure arrogance, for Britain was materially far in advance of other nations, particularly those nations where a great deal of overseas tourism took place, and where the British Army maintained the *Pax Britannica*. How-ever, it did produce a certain superiority of attitude, a benevolent despotism which characterised the British tourist of the period. But this was not universal; though some might shout and beat the importuning or disobedient natives with sticks, others kept their sense of humour and were as ready to be amused at their own mishaps as at the efforts of the natives to get the better of them.

A Mrs Bridges, whose journal described 'A lady's travels round the world' was a typical representative of the British tourist, firm when required to be so, and not without a dry humour. Apart from the flies, one of the most persistent pests in the Middle East tours were the boys and beggars forever offering help and demanding baksheesh, and Mrs Bridges once found herself and her male companion besieged by a mob of boatmen. As her companion's patience began to run out, he 'raised a stout walking stick, and I assumed an offensive attitude in the rear with a large umbrella', Mrs Bridges recorded. On the occasion when she was being badgered by guides offering to pull her up the pyramid, she deals with the difficulty with irony, 'Oh, Sheik,' she exclaimed, 'we have often climbed mountains six times as high as your Pyramid and will not be pushed up like the daughter of an ass'.

A writer who has left us a lively record of travels in Europe in the 1870s is Fanny Kemble, now no longer the young girl who was excited by her trip on the Liverpool and Manchester railway 47 years earlier, but a well-travelled actress who has returned from America for a holiday in Europe. She visits Switzerland, now alive with tourists, and is disappointed at what she finds. In the Engadine, 'every hotel in every village is crammed with people, sleeping two, three or four in a room. The hotel keepers are the direct descendants and representatives of those robber knights of old, fleecing the wretched wayfarer and adding insult to injury by telling you in the most pathetic way that their season only lasts two months'.

Reading this, it is easy to understand the success of Cook's hotel coupons with their fixed rates for food and accommodation. But the result of Cook's work in the new hotels, and amenities that were springing up all over Switzerland, did not please Fanny who wrote from Brunnen.

'The inns or hotels, begging their pardons, are all like palaces (gin palaces, I think I ought to say) magnificent, flaring, showy, luxurious, in all the public apartments, but noisy, disorderly, dirty and quite deficient in comfortable *private* accommodation . . . To the attractions of these huge houses of entertainments are added musical bands, fire works, fire-balloons, and spectacles of every kind, *besides* that of the sweet, solemn, sublime natural features of the beautiful scenery – all which seems to me very vulgar – bread and butter, and *paté de foie gras*, and marmalade and jam, and caviare, one on top of the other; but I am thankful for what I have enjoyed, and do still enjoy, though under such different conditions'.

Like O'Dowd and Leslie Stephen, Fanny Kemble was regretting the growing numbers of the new type of traveller on the Continental scene and their effect on the people who had once received visitors with simple hospitality but now did so with a sharp eye to business. St Moritz was to her the epitome of villages ruined by commercialisation. 'The place itself is less attractive than any other where we have stopped in Engadine, and its essentially watering place character, crowded with overdressed dandies and equivocal or unequivocal ladies, with a perfect fair of booths filled with rubbish, at extortionate prices, incessant *braying* of bands and ringing bells, the eternal inrushing and outrushing of arriving and departing travellers, made it altogether an unpleasant residence'.

Among Cook's tourists there may have been some who thought like Fanny Kemble, and no doubt there were many who were as horrified as she was to find bed-bugs in their beds; but they were not deterred from visiting foreign countries. Indeed with Cook

The dream of a British corridor from Cairo to the Cape was shared by Cook who organized trips on the Uganda Railway.

there to protect them from the hazards of the journey, and sheltering them in places where the servants understood English tastes, they increased in numbers. Cook was very much aware of the changing character of his clientele and, eager to spare them any unpleasantness which might offend their sensibilities, he worked indefatigably to protect them as much as possible from direct contact with the local populations and the more squalid sections of cities in which they stayed. He provided personal conductors to accompany them, often going himself or sending John Mason; he ensured that the hotels he sent them to were suitable; he stationed representatives in splendid semi-military uniforms at all main destinations and transfer points; and he gave them streams of reassuring advice through the columns of his magazine.

In particular, he was eager that his prospective clients should be made aware of the 'respectable' character of his parties.

'A glance through the lists of persons composing our excursion parties of former years shows that the various professions are largely represented. In nearly every one, the clergy have been represented by one or more persons and usually one or more

members of the medical fraternity are to be found. We have never found it necessary to require persons wishing to join our parties to furnish special references, because we do not think this at all necessary, and because it really amounts to nothing. If we should find an objectionable person in one of our parties, we should immediately refund the amount paid and quietly bid him depart in peace'.

The respectability which became such an essential quality among the late Victorian middle classes was the descendant of the earlier quality described by Jane Austen as breeding, refinement or distinction, and those who professed it were therefore concerned with doing the right thing. Cook's advice often took the form of instruction in dress, and comportment. 'It is the greatest mistake', says the introduction to a book of advice to ladies travelling abroad, 'to suppose that anything will do to wear on the Continent. Is the credit of our country nothing to us, that we should be content to rest under the assertion that Englishwomen, though renowned for their beauty, are the worst dressers in the world? A little care in choosing and in the manner of wearing articles of dress would soon put us on a level with our critics'. Suggestions for dress throughout the season are described: from January to March a serge costume is best and silk stockings with button boots. The latter point is stressed and, in anticipation of the endless walking through ruins and art galleries, churches and museums, it is pointed out that elastic-sided boots make the ankles swell. Soft felt hats are advised and veils are worn to protect the face from mosquitoes and flies. In June, an alpaca costume is recommended. Oil of almonds is essential to ward off mosquitoes, while Kalydor preserves that pale complexion which is fashionable and separates the ladies of the

middle classes from those whose labours expose them to the darkening effects of sun and wind.

On the subject of comfort while travelling, Cook advised the taking of a small lunch basket fitted with knives, large and small forks, glass, plates and napkins. This could always be replenished with cold viands, wine etc at a very small cost from any hotel and, as the distance was often great between the railway buffets, it would be found a pleasure and comfort to refresh the exhausted nature when required: nothing adds to the fatigue of travelling so much as hunger and thirst. This was before the age of dining cars, and Cook might have added that the station buffets, when existing, were the scene of a wild and uncouth scrimmaging as everyone on the train fought to buy food and drink in the ten minutes or so during which the train halted.

At about this time, more and more advertisements directed at Cook's travelling public began to appear in *The Excursionist*. Keatings proclaimed their power to kill bugs, fleas, and black beetles; Rowlands Kalydor promised to dispel clouds of langour and relaxation, restore elasticity to the skin, remove freckles; tan spots, pimples, and was also useful for sunburn and mosquitoes. Hunters Chloral was good not only as an aid to sleep but as a means of preventing sea sickness. Goffs of Covent Garden and James Carter of Oxford Street offered among other practical items such as trunks, travelling baths, and drinking flasks, items for the protection of the tourist – sword sticks, revolvers and, for ladies, that indispensable item, the door fastener.

Cook's success had led to competition and imitation from others and he kept a wary eye on his rivals. Having expanded his business and taken on new premises, he could not afford to lose customers. In 1873 he devoted a whole page in *The Excursionist* to the subject of 'Competition, Comparisons, Counterfeits and Collapses'. Even at the age of sixty-five, Thomas Cook had plenty of fight left in him. The competition came from imitators of his system of Circular Tickets and Hotel Coupons, and Cook had little time for his competitors. In particular, he attacked a 'Berlin Copyist' whom he had met on a Mediterranean boat when 'the Teutons clamorously took possession of all deck cabins, even to the exclusion of our ladies'. Cook's own ladies had had to go below into other cabins, 'as though they had been French citizens under the German hoof', Cook said bitingly.

One earlier attempt by Teutons to make inroads into his business had ended in bankruptcy, and another had 'skedaddled'. But it was not only foreigners who were trying to infiltrate into Cook's hard-won territory. The railway companies were constantly trying to keep for themselves the passengers whom Cook was booking on their railways. When Cook opened up in New York in partnership with a Mr Jenkins, who had been one of his own tourists, and who is referred to extensively in Chapter 9, the railways also opened up in competition, but Cook triumphed. 'Mr Jenkins proved more than a match for the English representative, and, as far as we could learn, the opposition collapsed without the booking of a solitary passenger'.

America was the new scene of Cook's activities, thanks to the development of a new type of ocean steamer, the *Oceanic*, built by Harland and Wolff of Belfast, and capable of providing a reliable and reasonably comfortable passage across the Atlantic. This would now become the greatest tourist route of all.

9 Britannia rules the waves

The Napoleonic Wars had established Britain's supremacy on the seas, but most of the people who travelled by sea were those who absolutely had to. The soldiers, sailors and administrators who were expanding and establishing control of British territories overseas sailed abroad in increasing numbers on the route to the East round the Cape of Good Hope and, after 1825, on the Suez overland route, and on voyages to America and the Caribbean. Their numbers were small and they could be accommodated on existing ships like the beautiful but ponderous East Indiamen which carried the cargoes of the East India Company.

The first big increase in shipping traffic arose out of the Industrial Revolution which

drove emigrants to seek abroad better living conditions than those which they had to suffer in the slums of industrial cities. In the 1830s emigration to distant colonies created a need for some system of dealing with bookings of passages. This had previously been done by direct arrangement with the ship's captain. On board ship there was a need for proper arrangements for accommodating passengers, maintaining discipline among them and looking after their health and hygiene. In the early days, such arrangements as were made for the emigrant passengers were primitive in the extreme. Wooden bunks were set up between decks, there was a pump at which to wash, and emigrant passengers often had to cook their own food on deck. In bad weather the seas washed the ships from stem to stern and water leaked through the decks and down the hatches, sloshing about in the confined space where the passengers huddled together without light or ventilation. Even with the advent of the clipper ship in mid-century, living conditions did not improve, although the speed of these elegant ships, almost twice that of existing ships, did mean that passengers suffered for a shorter time.

There were of course, good times aboard as well: periods of calm sailing in trades with the sails ballooning out against blue skies, and dolphins and flying fish leaping through the water. But on the whole conditions for emigrants were hardly better than those for the herds of sheep and cattle that were carried on board to provide fresh meat. Nevertheless, people were travelling in increasing numbers, going to the new promised lands that cost only £10 to reach, and which in California, Australia and New Zealand at least, promised the richest of all rewards: gold. Most immigrants never found gold but they stayed in the countries where they had gone to seek a new life and turned their hands to developing the communities which later grew into nations.

A big growth in sea traffic took place at the same time as the development of the railways, and steam played an essential part in its expansion. In 1819 a sailing ship called the *Savannah*, fitted with paddle wheels and an auxiliary steam engine, crossed from America to Europe in 29 days. Her engine was used for only 24 hours, but her voyage marked the beginning of a new age in sea travel. From now on steam would gradually replace sail though it wasn't till the 1890s that shipbuilders and owners had enough confidence in engines to dispense with sail altogether. One of the earliest uses of steam, in 1825, was on the route to the East from England to Egypt, when passengers went overland on the Isthmus of Suez and then by East Indiaman down the Red Sea to India and on to China.

The route to the East was vitally important to British interests and the ships of the East India Company, whose operations in India had established British influence on the sub-continent, ploughed their way to and from Europe laden with Indian spices and silks and took back the products of British factories. The new steamships offered a better and faster service, but there was some reluctance on the part of the East India Company to give up the ships which made up its own fleet. Nevertheless the new steamships soon took over running to Alexandria, from where passengers and goods were taken on the overland route to Suez. This route became famous and was still in use in 1888, almost twenty years after the Suez Canal was built. It involved a journey

97

by tug-drawn barge from Alexandria to the Nile, up the Nile by steamer to Cairo, and across the ninety miles of desert to Suez. The Orient Line book of information for passengers described this part of the journey as follows:

'A journey of some 18 hours under these circumstances (on a two wheel horse-drawn vehicle which took six passengers) could hardly be called enjoyable, even when the tedium was relieved by drinking innumerable cups of coffee at the various stations where horses were changed. Still the experience was one which impressed the imagination in no ordinary degree. A moonlight journey was most striking. The seemingly boundless expanse, the silence broken by the voice of the driver and the muffled sound of the horses feet, (which seemed somehow to accentuate the sense of stillness) the caravans loaded with mail and baggage passing with silent stealthy tread; the whitened bones of countless troops of camels, which had died in harness, glistening in the moonlight; then the sudden day break, the solitary Bedouin family mounted aloft on their desert ship, the mirage so wonderful when first seen – these and other impressions remain indelible in the minds of people who knew the Overland route as it was'.

The steamer service to Alexandria was run by the Peninsular and Orient line (always known as the P & O), which began life in 1837 as the Peninsular company after its

founder, Arthur Anderson, had obtained the mail contract to Portugal. Anderson and his partner Wilcox extended the service to Egypt in 1840, after some initial difficulty in getting bank credit for their venture. By 1852 the route had been extended to Australia, with ships calling at Alexandria and Suez and passengers, goods and coal being transported across the Isthmus. The opening of the Suez Canal was by no means a boon as the British Government, who subsidised P & O to the tune of £160,000, hesitated to give up using the Overland route. Moreover, the invention of the compound engine made the P & O fleet obsolete. Undeterred, Anderson set about rebuilding his fleet, and in a few years was running the latest steamships through the Canal and all the way to Australia, New Zealand and the Far East.

Despite the importance and the pioneer significance of the Eastern route, it was the Atlantic that became the scene of the great dramas and battles of passenger shipping. Shipping companies competed for passengers in a fierce, though polite, contest in which speed and luxury were the measures of success. The first transatlantic ships were neither speedy nor luxurious, however, and offered little more comfort than the sailing vessels. The *Sirius* was the first ship to cross the Atlantic driven only by steam. Less than 800 tons in size, she took eighteen and a half days to cross from Cork to New York. The *Great Western* which followed her a month later was hardly any bigger.

The *Sirius* pointed the way to the future of transatlantic travel and it was not long before businessmen became interested in this new field of enterprise. One such was

The Suez Canal, opened in 1869, provided steamships with an opportunity to show their advantages over sail. However, many steamships still carried some sail until the end of the century.

99

The nineteenth century saw a remarkable change in journeys by sea. As travel expanded, conditions improved accordingly. Bottom right: A dance on board the ship Randolph taking immigrants to New Zealand in 1850. Bottom left: An afternoon in the tropics in May 1857 aboard a P & O paddle steamer. Top right: Dinner aboard a liner in 1890 obviously during a storm, but well attended nevertheless. Top left: The Palladian lounge on the Aquitania built in 1914. The ideas were copied from existing buildings by Christopher Wren in a colour scheme of wine red and grey.

Samuel Cunard, the Nova Scotian who founded the Cunard Steamship Line. From the start, Cunard realised that there were three sources of revenue for shipping lines: mail carrying, cargo and passengers, and that services needed to be regular and frequent. He obtained a royal charter for carrying mails to the West Indies, and gathered a fleet of 17 ships, fourteen of which were paddle-wheel steamers. He named the company the American Royal Mail Steam Packet Co. and started operations in 1841, eventually linking up by an overland service across the Isthmus of Panama with the Pacific Steam Navigation Company which operated up and down the west coast of America.

Improvements in the comfort of sea voyages were slow in appearing, largely because the ships were small and had to carry large cargoes, livestock and mail. There was simply neither the room, nor the inducement at the emigrant fare, to improve matters.

Charles Dickens who sailed to America in 1842 on the steam-packet *Britannia* described the experience in his American notes. The shock on finding that his 'state-room' was hardly bigger than a cupboard is expressed in what he describes as 'one-fourth serious and three-fourths comical astonishment'.

' . . . that this utterly impracticable, thoroughly hopeless, and profoundly preposterous box had the remotest reference to, or connection with, those chaste and pretty, not to say gorgeous little bowers, sketched by a masterly hand, in the highly varnished lithographic plan hanging up in the agent's counting house in the city of London: that this room of state, in short could be anything but a pleasant fiction and cheerful jest of the captain's, invented and put in practice for the better relish and enjoyment of the real state-room presently to be disclosed: these were truths which I really could not for the moment, bring my mind at all to bear upon or comprehend'.

The first shock having worn off, Dickens, like most travellers, begins to make the most of what he has got and even persuades himself that the cabin is just the right size. 'By very nearly closing the door, and twining in and out like serpents, and by counting the little washing slab as standing room we could manage to insinuate four people into it, all at one time; and entreating each other to observe how very airy it was (in dock), and how there was a beautiful port-hole which could be kept open all day (weather permitting), and how there was quite a large bull's eye just over the looking-glass which would render shaving a perfectly easy and delightful process (when the ship didn't roll too much); we arrived, at last, at the unanimous conclusion that it was rather spacious than otherwise: though I do verily believe that, deducting the two berths, one above the other, than which nothing smaller for sleeping in was ever made except coffins, it was no bigger than one of those hackney cabriolets which have the door behind and shoot their fares out, like sacks of coal, upon the pavement'.

In the 1840s screw propulsion came in and the sailing ships were doomed. The first sea-going ship to use screw propulsion was the *Great Britain*, built in 1843. After three years on the Atlantic run, she ran aground in Dundrum Bay in Ireland. Until she was hauled off and repaired, she provided Thomas Cook with one of the destinations for his Irish excursions. The *Great Eastern* was an abortive attempt to use screw propulsion, but the monstrous size of Brunel's brainchild doomed her to failure. She was designed to carry 4,000 passengers, had six masts and five funnels and was hailed as the 'Crystal Palace of the Sea'. Thomas Cook, always eager to adopt anything new in travel, was soon advertising the new shipping lines; in *The Excursionist* for 1866 appeared the Inman Line, Montreal Ocean Mail Line, Guion and Co., Handyside and Henderson and the Montreal Ocean Line, all offering trips to America.

Mark Twain, the American writer, travelled to Europe in 1867 on a paddle steamer, and wrote a vivid description of life aboard.

'At seven bells the first gong rang: at eight there was breakfast, for such as were not too seasick to eat it. After that all the well people walked arm-in-arm up and down the long promenade deck, enjoying the fine summer mornings, and the seasick ones crawled out and propped themselves up in the lee of the paddle boxes and ate their dismal tea and toast, and looked wretched. From eleven o'clock until luncheon and from luncheon until dinner at six in the evening, the employments and amusements were various. Some reading was done: and much smoking and sewing, though not by

For most tourists sea travel meant going across the Channel, an introduction which did not encourage longer voyages.

the same parties; there were the monsters of the deep to be looked after and wondered at; strange ships had to be scrutinized through opera glasses, and sage decisions arrived at concerning them; and more than that, everybody took a personal interest in seeing that the flag was run up and politely dipped three times in response to the salutes of those strangers; in the smoking room there were always parties of gentlemen playing euchre, draughts and dominoes, especially dominoes, that delightful harmless game; and down on the main deck, the for' ard of the chicken coops and the cattle – we had what was called "horse billiards". Horse billiards is a fine game. It affords good active exercise, hilarity, and consuming excitement. It is a mixture of "hop scotch" and shuffle-board played with a crutch. In the evenings life continued its even tenor with dinner, a stroll round the deck and prayers, but after prayers came the most important acitivty of all. Behind the long dining tables on either side of the saloon, and scattered from one end to the other of the latter, some twenty or thirty gentlemen and ladies sat them down under the swaying lamps, and for two or three hours wrote diligently in their journals'.

No wonder so many travel books were written by travellers in the second half of the nineteenth century! Apart from all these activities, one of the main events of the day, then as now, was the next meal. Thomas Croal, writing in 1877, gave the menu on one transatlantic steamer: Breakfast: Beefsteak and onions. Omelettes and mutton chops. Findon haddies. Fresh fried fish. Grilled sausages. Rice cakes. Devilled bones. Corn Bread. Porridge. Digby Herrings. Irish Stew. Mashed, chopped and jacket potatoes. After a turn around the decks or a game of horse billiards the traveller then went on to dinner which consisted of: Ribs of beef and potatoes. Leg of mutton and onion sauce. Loin of pork and apple sauce. Duck and green vegetables. Spring chicken and bread sauce. Oxhead forced. Rabbits and bacon. Turkey and oyster sauce or Baked pork and beans. There were cold meats and vegetables as well, and to follow, Gooseberry and bread and butter pudding, Apple Hedgehog, *Vol au vent* Rhubarb, Compôte of pears, Chocolate creams, sweet sandwiches and, in case anyone was still hungry, some Nelson cake and marmalade as a reminder that England expected that everyone should do their duty. Croal was, of course, travelling first class and enjoying some of the benefits that passengers received as a result of the rivalry of transatlantic shipping lines. There was a general improvement in shipboard life after the launching of the *Oceanic*, a ship that marked the beginning of a new era in sea travel.

The *Oceanic* was built in 1870. She was a 2,200 tonner with public rooms for the cabin class placed amidships and with a large deckhouse which stretched right across the ship, preventing big seas from sweeping over the deck from bow to stern, as usually happened on other ships. The *Oceanic* was made of iron and had iron under the deck planking; eliminating the flooding and leaking below decks which was common on earlier ships. This great step forward in the comfort of ocean travel was soon followed by others. Ventilation systems were introduced, based on the trunk ventilating of the *Germanic* in 1874. Then gas lighting came in to eliminate the smells of the earlier lamps. Electricity was used in the *City of Bremen* in 1875.

Thomas Cook showed his faith in the future of ocean travel by organising a trip round the world. This began at Liverpool in 1872 on the *Oceanic*, went across the Pacific on the SS *Colorado*, sailed from Japan to Ceylon on the *Mirzapore* and ended with a voyage across the Mediterranean on the *Hyaspes*. As it happened, Cook's trip coincided with the publication of Jules Verne's 'Round the World in Eighty Days' and reflected the avid

Jules Verne's *Around the world in eighty days,* was serialised in a Paris newspaper in 1872, the year that Thomas Cook made his first world tour. The Cook party's adventures, however diverting, were not quite as thrilling as those depicted in these illustrations of the Jules Verne story.

public interest in the idea of 'encircling the globe' by steamship, a feat which excited the imagination of the public at large. Thomas Cook's letters to *The Times* described his experience. 'My pioneering party,' he explained in his initial letter, 'is not large, eight today and maybe eleven when we sail tomorrow; but we represent in pleasing harmony England, Scotland, Russia, Armenia and Greece'.

On the transatlantic crossing the *Oceanic* was carrying 778 steerage passengers, who may have given Cook the idea of advertising emigrant fares for £3.10, which he did on his return. The cost to emigrants of this particular trip was £6 and conditions, Cook noted, despite outcries in the Press, were reasonable. At least he did not hear any complaints other than that the beef was too salty and too hard. Because of the sleeping arrangements on board, the sexes were separated, as the emigrants slept in dormitories. The cabin class passengers, of whom there were 117, were comfortable and well cared for. After five days in New York, Cook's party crossed the United States and boarded the SS *Colorado* in San Francisco. From here, except for a southerly deviation because of storms, they sailed across the Pacific to Yokohama in Japan, a distance of 5,525 miles which took 24 days and four hours.

The days crossing the Pacific were tedious, travelling at nine miles an hour because of the need to save coal. 'Over that vast expanse of waters we never caught sight of a sail or craft of any description and for 580 hours the engines never stopped or lost a single revolution; and we made our best progress when the sea was most disturbed, although the wind could seldom be called fair.' The *Colorado* was a paddle steamer. She had evidently caused a sensation on her inaugural trip to Yokohama when British sailors had exclaimed, 'What a mountain!' on seeing her hull, which Cook compared to a New York ferry steamer and quite unlike the neat design of the P & O steamer which operated from Japan to India and then on to Suez. In Japan, Cook was delighted to find that 119 Englishmen were employed by the Imperial Japanese Government, more than double the number of the next most numerous foreigners, the French, and that Japanese Railways were manned by British engineers.

In India, where he arrived on the P & O steamer *Mirzapore* after a brief visit to Ceylon, Cook examined hotels and means of transport with an eye to future tours in the Empire. His party travelled about in a railway coach reserved specially for them, provided with sleeping compartments, baths and closets, and stayed at hotels like the Great Eastern in Calcutta where each of them had a personal servant. Some of the sights they visited caused Cook much distress, especially in Benares. ' . . . around the filthy purlieus of that centre of idolatry, hovered, from windows and balconies, shameless dancing girls, inviting the passers in the narrow streets to their dens'. Idol worship and prostitution were not the only evils that worried Cook. Even in India, there was more drunkenness than he cared to see. 'The free sale of drink is having its natural effect on the population. Young men released from restraints of home are dying of drink rot; morals are sapped and undermined, the Church loses its members, and the standing and withering question of the heathen, when pressed and beaten in argument, is, pointing to drunken sailors, soldiers and civilians. "Is it like them you wish to make us?"'

With an enthusiasm that belied his age Cook set about giving Temperance talks during his visit to India and organised a library for 'men who have ceased drinking and have a voracious appetite for mental food'. From Bombay, Cook and his party sailed on the P & O *Hydaspes* for Aden and the Red Sea. When they arrived in Egypt, they dispersed and chose their own homeward route. The tour had taken 220 days. Cook meanwhile had made his notes and placed his proposals for regular round-the-world-tours at the moderate price of 220 guineas before the steamship and railway companies. Improvements in ship design were becoming widespread and, with increasing demand for their services, cargo and passenger ships became bigger and better.

'The motto of the P & O Company,' Cook told his readers of *The Excursionist*, 'seems to be "Larger and Larger" for not only is the company continually making additions to its fleet, but each time it does so, the size and tonnage of the steamers are increased'. The *Himalaya*, advertised by Cook in 1892 was a 7,000 tonner, 466 feet in length and able to travel at 18 knots. She carried 269 first class saloon passengers and 144 second class. 'The cabins for the first saloon are fitted with every comfort it is possible to introduce in the space, viz. fold-up lavatories, chests of drawers, what-nots, writing tables etc. of dark mahogany . . . '. Every cabin was supplied with electric light and there were 24 baths of solid marble with spray, douche and waves.

Size, speed and luxury were to become the three essentials for any steamship company that hoped to attract customers. By the eighteen nineties the rivalry between shipping companies, which was to last until the 1930s, had begun. Steamship companies vied with each other to make their ships like the Grand Hotels which were attracting the tourist to the Continent, their decor became more and more fantastic; saloons emulated Renaissance palaces, Gothic cathedrals and Roman temples, trying to make the passenger feel that he was not on board at all, but in some vast holiday dreamland from which the humdrum facts of everyday life were carefully excluded. A vivid picture of one of these luxury liners, the *Majestic*, was included in a book by William Smith, a Yorkshireman who crossed on her to New York in 1892.

'The saloon,' he says, quoting an unknown writer whom he calls a journalist of repute, 'is a banqueting hall of superb brilliancy. The style is Renaissance and the tones of ivory and gold. Nearly all the sides of the great room and the vast canopy which covers it is a sea of ivory and gold crowned with a dome of mirrors. Bas relief golden figures of tritons, nymphs and other members of Neptune's court gambol in the ivory sea beside the ports, and classic ornaments and electric lamps flash and glow across the ceiling'. A passenger with a taste for the Middle Ages could if he chose spend his time in the smoking room where 'the woodwork is all of that particular rich, dark mahogany one sees sometimes in old mansions. The walls are covered with a richly embossed gilt leather of a dark tone. Fitted with panels are large, bright oil paintings, representing the picturesque Mediterranean shipping of the Middle Ages. Figures in high relief, carved in pear wood, fill many niches. The ceiling reproduces an extremely handsome Old English plaster pattern in quaint, variously shaped panels and is pierced with two lanthorn lights of stained glass'.

These Hollywood settings, like those of the Grand Hotels, provided the dream environment in which the fantasies of holiday life could take shape. They set the stage for tourism in the following century.

10 Cook's American dream

The Civil War which ended in 1865 with the surrender of the Confederate Army had postponed the opening of America to Cook's tourist parties. Thomas Cook made an exploratory tour in November of that year, and in 1866 John Mason took a party of thirty to New York, Niagara Falls, Michigan, Chicago and Ohio by rail, and then by river steamer to Kentucky where they visited the Mammoth Caves, and on to Baltimore, Washington and Richmond to visit the Civil War battlefields. This promising start to a system of tours did not develop as the Cooks had hoped. Thomas Cook blamed the discord among railway companies and the jealousy of the agents for his lack of success.

Eighteen seventy one brought a change to Cook's fortunes when he met a man called Jenkins, leader of a Knights Templars' party to Europe whose trip Cook had arranged. Jenkins was enthusiastic about Cook's ticket system and persuaded him to form a partnership to operate the American business. Cook agreed and in 1873 Cook, Son and Jenkins opened an office at 362 Broadway, New York.

Thomas Cook had already done some reconnoitring of the U.S. territory when he crossed from New York to San Francisco on his way round the world in 1872. What he found did not displease him. On his route he rode in a Pullman car along the Delaware, on the Great Western Line to Michigan and then on to Chicago on the Central Line. From Chicago he went to Omaha on the Burlington route. Across the prairies of Illinois the Indians kept everyone in a state of almost constant excitement, as the Sioux, 'armed to the teeth', kept pace with the train. At Omaha Cook joined the Union and Central Pacific Railway and travelled via St Louis, Kansas City and Denver to San Francisco. As he travelled he took notes of the facilities and standards of accommodation that were available. He was impressed by the open car plan of American trains, to which he compared unfavourably the British compartment system. He also liked the method whereby a Baggage Express Company took charge of the luggage leaving the passenger free to board the train unencumbered.

He was not so impressed by the speed of the train which averaged only 19 miles an hour, but he made allowances for the fact that the railway had to ascend the Rocky Mountains and the Sierra Nevada en route. Seven nights were spent in sleeping cars on this journey and he found the 'admixture of strangers and sexes very repulsive to English travellers'. Although this route was one which was used by the thousands of settlers who were streaming west with high hopes of becoming rich, he did not travel with the 'emigrants' who, instead of covered wagons now rode on special trains which ran twice as slowly as the regular service and consisted of freight as well as passenger cars. Always bearing his customers in mind, Cook made a careful study of the hotels and found a great deal to praise in them. He particularly liked the special public rooms: some provided for ladies and others for those who wanted to partake in intoxicating liquids. The existence of a saloon nurtured a habit of drinking before rather than with meals, and Cook praised the facts that on every table in the hotel dining rooms there was a jug of iced water, and tea and coffee could be had during every meal.

'The dinner table', he observed, 'is free from that slavery and exaction often seen and

American trains had a rough pioneer atmosphere about them that contrasted strongly with the growing luxury of the European railway system.

felt at English tables, where some old "heavy wet" manages to get in the chair, calls for wine and holds all responsible for payment of equal shares, and if anyone dares to object he is regarded as mean and exceptional'. The food he found copious and appetising with a choice of fifty to a hundred dishes from which it was usual to order twelve. This enormous menu was available three times daily, at breakfast, lunch and dinner. He voiced his enthusiasm for the American system in *The London Echo* in an article entitled 'Captain Cook II'. In this, Cook was quoted as saying that he preferred American hotels over those of other countries and quoted an average price of 3 to 4½ dollars a day.

Fanny Kemble preferred a world with less propinquity of classes and sexes. Describing her tour to America with her father she wrote that 'the very cheap rate of travelling which enables *everybody*, without exception, to travel, and the absence of distinctions of place or price in the public conveyances, which compels *everybody* to travel together, of course brings refined and fastidious pilgrims in most painful proximity with their coarse and unpolished brethren . . . '

In spite of these disadvantages of a classless way of life, Fanny Kemble also found much to praise in America, not least the courtesy towards women. ' . . . but (well I have said my say in my time upon the subject of American tobacco chewing, cigar smokers and question askers) a woman cannot possibly travel in any part of the world with equal security as in America; the law of the land – public opinion – secures to women the first choice of accommodation on every road and at every inn; a look, word, or gesture of intentional impertinence will not assail her, nor a single offensive expression reach her ear in passing from one corner to another of that vast and half savage continent'.

American tours in Europe were an important part of Cook's plans for the New York office. From here, he saw himself drawing into his fold the thousands of Americans who had made their money in the Eastern States and the Middle West; the farmers, the cattlemen, the dwellers in the dynamically evolving cities, the school teachers and preachers all were potential customers, and, which was even more pleasing, they were tourists who would travel with an eagerness to learn about and absorb the noble and mind-uplifting facets of European culture. Perhaps it was his high expectations that made his disappointment the greater at finding that things did not go as smoothly as he would have wished. 'There have been times when we have thought ourselves somewhat unfairly suspected and harshly treated by American travellers', he once commented.

Unlike Cook's middle-class British clients, the Americans were extroverted and outspoken, indulging in what Cook called 'high airs and tall talk'. A constant cause of friction was the Continental breakfast which seemed like an insult to people used to starting the day on steak. 'At home they can order a dozen varieties for breakfast, and one charge covers the whole: on the Continent each separate article is charged, and though but little, or even nothing of what was ordered is consumed, the bill for breakfast à la carte swells to enormous proportions, and for articles not covered by Coupons, the settlement is often attended by hot disputes'.

Another source of friction was the expectation of hoteliers that hotel guests would order wine with their meals, and the American determination to drink iced water, and coffee, and not pay extra for it. On this question Cook showed a sympathy with the hoteliers surprising in someone dedicated to the cause of abstinence. 'On this side of the Atlantic, the wine feature in a dinner bill is calculated upon by the Hotel-keeper as his chief source of profit, and many proprietors grumble when two score Americans sit down to dinner with perhaps a single half bottle of wine, and maybe, out of a little consideration for the landlord, a very few glasses of beer before them', he pointed out.

In the two-way traffic of Americans to Europe and of Europeans to America, which was to grow into a flood in the '80s and '90s, there was bound to be criticism for, like father and son, here were the old world and the new eyeing each other with a new-found rivalry. Whatever rivalry existed, it would make no difference to the eagerness with which Europeans emigrated to the United States in search of a new life or the enthusiasm with which Americans flocked to Europe to explore the birthplace of their forefathers. Mark Twain, visiting Europe in 1869 in one of the first transatlantic cruises on the *Quaker City*, has left a good-humoured account of an American's visit to Europe in 'The Innocents Abroad'. On the whole he finds things to his liking or at least acceptable. 'We are getting foreignized rapidly with facility', he wrote. What he had got used to were the tiled floors, the 'tidy noiseless waiters', and deliberately leisurely service at table, the wine and the siesta and cigar after the meal. He disliked his fellow Americans who 'talked very loudly and coarsely, and laughed boisterously where all others were quiet and well-behaved'.

With prospects appearing very bright, Cook decided at last to give way to the demand from customers that he should provide some system which would make money available abroad against money deposited at the point of departure. In New York in April 1894 Cook announced, rather tentatively, that he was prepared to give cheques, or circular notes as he called them, to the value of £5 and £10 against money deposited in the New York Office. In order to safeguard himself and his customers against fraudulent encashment of the cheques, Cook provided a letter of Indication to every cheque bearer and this served to vouch for the bearer's identity. Thanks to his wide connections in Europe Cook was able to arrange that his cheques could be cashed at hotels as well as banks and *bureaux de change* and the convenience of this arrangement soon brought him an increasing number of cheque customers. Among the tourists of his first year's operation in America, Cook had 150 school teachers who visited Europe and a number of smaller parties to the Middle East as well as several times the number of these as individual customers.

Although the traffic to and from America grew, the partnership of Cook, Son and Jenkins did not prosper as each of its members had hoped. Within a few years John Mason, who was taking more and more control of the management of the business, was writing to Jenkins telling him to take down a sign that had been painted on the New York office and not to put notices up without authority; this instruction was repeated three times for emphasis. In 1876 there was worse trouble, with John Mason accusing Jenkins of lack of financial integrity. In his blunt forthright manner, he wrote that 'Unless the

111

Cook's American Excursions and Tours.

OCEAN STEAMBOAT ARRANGEMENTS FROM ENGLAND, SCOTLAND, AND IRELAND, TO AMERICA.

RETURN TICKETS may now be had on application to the TOURIST OFFICE, 98, FLEET-STREET, LONDON, for the Passage from Liverpool, Glasgow or Queenstown to New York or Canada.

First Class Fares for the Double Voyage,
including Provisions, in accordance with the general regulations of the Companies,

TWENTY-FIVE GUINEAS,

By all the Lines except the Montreal Ocean Glasgow Line and the Anchor Line of Handyside and Henderson, Glasgow, the Return Tickets for which are

TWENTY-ONE GUINEAS.

Places are secured on payment of a Deposit of £5, £1 of which will be forfeited if the Contract is not completed within ten days prior to the time fixed for departure.
State Rooms and Berths will be registered in the order in which Deposits are paid.
The following is the list of Companies for which the Tickets are available :—

The Liverpool, New York and Philadelphia Steamship Company—Inman Line of Mail Steamers.

Special arrangements are made with this Company for the Tickets to be available for leaving Liverpool on the last Wednesdays in July, August, September, October, November, and December, or for departing from Queenstown on the following days.
Tickets available for returning from New York by this Line only, on any Saturday for 12 months from the date of the Tickets.

The Line of the National Steam Navigation Company, (LIMITED).

These Steamers leave Liverpool every Wednesday, taking up passengers on the following day at Queenstown. The Tickets are available for any day of departure, and for returning from New York by the same Line only on any Saturday for 6 months after date of departure.

New Line of Guion & Co.

Particulars of this Line will be given in future announcements, as soon as the Boats are named.

The Montreal Ocean Company's Canadian Mail Steamers—Line of Allan Bros. & Company.

The Steamers of this Line, by which the tickets are available, leave Liverpool every Thursday for PORTLAND, from Oct. 25 to April 19, and from April 19 to Oct. 25 for QUEBEC; returning from Portland every Saturday to May 5, and after that date from Quebec.
The Tickets issued for this Line will be available for returning by the Line of the same Company, from Canada to Glasgow, or by the "Anchor Line" of Handyside and Hendersons, from New York to Glasgow, at any time within 6 months from date of departure.

The Montreal Ocean Steamship Company's Glasgow Line of J. & A. Allan.

Until April 19, the Steamers of this Line leave Glasgow for PORTLAND, every other Thursday, returning from Portland every other Saturday to May 5th. After April 19, to QUEBEC, returning from Quebec for Glasgow every other Saturday from May 12 to October.
The Tickets are available for returning by any Steamer of the service for 6 months after date of departure; or they will be available for returning by the same Company's Boats from Portland or Quebec to Liverpool, on payment of 2 guineas extra; or by the "Anchor Line" of Handyside and Hendersons, from New York to Glasgow, free, at any time within 6 months.

The Anchor Line of Transatlantic Steam Packet Ships of Handyside and Hendersons.

Tickets may be had for leaving by this Line from Glasgow for NEW YORK on every alternate Saturday; returning from New York every other Saturday for Glasgow, within 12 months from date of departure.
These Tickets will also be available for returning by the Montreal Lines of Messrs. Allan, from Quebec or Portland to Glasgow, free, or to Liverpool on payment of 2 guineas extra to the Canadian Companies before leaving Quebec or Portland.

98, FLEET-STREET, LONDON.

In reply to numerous enquiries respecting the proposed Tour to America during the ensuing Autumn, I purpose conducting a Tourist party through the same districts detailed in annexed account of a Tour taken by Mr. John M. Cook, subject to slight alterations to meet the wishes of the Tourists; the departures from England and Scotland to be during the second or third week in September. The whole of the Tour as taken by J. M. C. may be made in one month from leaving New York. The travelling expenses in the States and Canada may be estimated at 90 dollars, and the Hotels and incidentals at 4 dollars each per day; so that for 200 dollars over and above the Ocean Return Tickets, the whole Tour may be accomplished.
As I reserve to myself the privilege of not going unless 50 are guarranteed by the second week in August, it is essentially necessary that intending Tourists should send in their names and deposits as early as possible.
Any further information will be gladly forwarded on application.

THOS. COOK.

HASTY NOTES OF THE FIRST EXCURSION TO AMERICA

BY JOHN M. COOK.

To conduct an Excursion Party over nearly 4000 miles of a country never before visited by the "Conductor," is no easy task; but to write an account of such an Excursion, and carry out the instructions of the Editor "to make it short," is a more difficult undertaking for the writer of this article, which must necessarily prove to be only an imperfect sketch. In craving the kind indulgence of critical readers, I think it only necessary to state that this is written the first evening after arrival at home, after a tour of 10,500 miles in nine weeks, which in itself would be a laborious undertaking in our own country, with the assistance of Express Trains at 60 miles an hour. But when we have to contend with 6000 miles of the Atlantic, and a great portion of the remainder by River Steamers and "Lightning Expresses," both running at an average speed of from 15 to 19 miles an hour; to stay in one city 10 days; to correspond and have personal interviews with at least a hundred Railway and Steamboat Officials; to have to cater for everything required by fellow travellers, including attention to all Baggage, and paying Hotel and other expenses, and to arrange the whole so that we only travelled over 90 miles of the same road twice; combined with a detention of three days, through staying to see the Fenian bubble burst.—I flatter myself that even our American friends must admit that a body but a "Britisher" would have been able to successfully cope with such difficulties.

The first arrangement was for me to accompany the Tourists going by the Inman Line from Liverpool; but being anxious, if possible, to be in New York two or three days before the bulk of the passengers, and knowing that I should be quite as likely to require *assistance* during the sea passage as any of our friends, I determined upon leaving by the Caledonia, of the Anchor Line, which left Glasgow on Saturday, April 21st, thus giving me four days' start of those going from Liverpool the following Wednesday, and enabling me to accompany the first detachment of English tourist invaders to America. It proved well for the whole undertaking that I so decided; and so far as comfort, good dietary and a pleasant sea trip were concerned, I may say, without in any way disparaging the facilities afforded to "Cook's Tourists" by other Lines of Steamers, that not one of the passengers who sailed in the Caledonia will ever regret honouring the "Anchor Line" with the conveyance of the first Tourist or Excursion Party from Great Britain to America. I will pass over the voyage out, by saying that we had a most magnificent afternoon for sailing down the Firth of Clyde, affording us an opportunity of appreciating the beauty of the coasts of Argyle, Renfrew, and Ayrshire, Ailsa Craig, the Isles of Arran, Cantire, &c. We were favoured with easterly winds, enabling us to pass the banks of Newfoundland by the eighth day, and giving us hopes of seeing New York on the twelfth; which we certainly should have done, had not the wind turned dead against us for the remainder of the voyage, reducing our speed to 2 or 3 knots per hour for a considerable time, thus making it 3 p.m. on the fourteenth day, when we stopped off Staten Island to be boarded by the Government Medical Inspector and Custom House Officers. We had been favoured with a splendid day, and all were charmed with the scenery on the shores of the finest Bay in the world, which with the exquisite green of the grass and foliage of the trees, combined with the romantic aspect of the "Swiss" cottages, formed one of the most beautiful and placid scenes it has yet been my lot to enjoy.

The first two or three days in New York were spent in visiting the principal features of interest in and around that great city, amongst which may be mentioned, the principal stores and warehouses of the dry goods and other merchants, the magnificent white marble structures in Broadway, &c; the busy throng of Wall street and Washington; the excitement in the Custom House, and "on change;" the interiors of the wonderful Hotels, St. Nicholas, Fifth Avenue, Astor House, Metropolitan, &c., &c.; the taste and splendour of the mansions in Madison and other squares, Fifth Avenue, and neighbouring streets; the extent and beauty of "Central Park;" the wonders of the River Ferry Boat system; and attractions of Brooklyn, New Jersey, Staten Island, &c.

Through the breaking down of the "City of Washington" on her homeward passage, she had not arrived in Liverpool in time to leave with our excursion passengers on April 25th; consequently the Kangaroo had to be substituted, which not proving satisfactory to some of those booked for the "City of Washington," they were allowed the privilege of either going by the Kangaroo or the new and magnificent Steam-ship of the Inman Line, "City of Paris." The majority preferring the latter, compelled me to delay my departure from New York until after the arrival of the last portion: this gave me an opportunity of running over to Boston, to see the Railway and Steamboat Officials of that district. On arrival I was astonished at the great difference between the two cities—Boston and New York—the former having all the stability of our own large commercial towns, combined with the wide streets, fine buildings, and clear atmosphere of the new world; and I consider those who return without seeing Boston will miss one of the finest and most interesting commercial cities of the West. Some of our friends were getting tired of New York, and started off for the South and West before the arrival of the principal portion; others were going through Canada first, thus reversing the Tour I purposed taking, and some were going by the more central districts, so that we became very much divided.

I left New York on Tuesday, May 15th, with a very pleasant party, by the Camden and Amboy route for Philadelphia, passing Newark, Trenton, &c., and skirting the banks of the picturesque Delaware. At Philadelphia we met with the greatest possible kindness from Messrs Killilin, proprietors of the "Merchants' House," who did everything they could to make their hotel a "home from home." All were delighted with their visit to the "home of independence;" but as we had to leave at four o'clock on Wednesday afternoon, we had to make the most of a hurried run through the fine business thoroughfares, and catch hasty glances at the old Hall of Independence, &c., &c. I cannot omit mentioning the beauty and extent of the Market Hall, which is the finest and best adapted building I have ever seen.

From Philadelphia we went to Baltimore, by the Philadelphia, Baltimore, and Wilmington Railway. This short ride was one of great interest, as it brought us in contact with the first views we had of the scenes of the late war. We had to cross the Gunpowder and Bush rivers on temporary bridges, one three-quarters and the other a mile in length, the original ones being destroyed during the engagements; we also had the novelty of having our whole train and engine ferried across the Susquehanna river, on one ferry boat. We arrived at Baltimore at 8.0 p.m., and stayed at the Maltby House, which is situated in one of the streets where an engagement took place. We stayed at Baltimore until 5.0 p.m. on Thursday, when we left by the Steamboat "James T. Brady," of the New Line, for Richmond; our route being one of great interest, through Chesapeake Bay and the James River, passing many ever to be-remembered points of the great struggle, such as Norfolk, Fort Munroe, Harrison's Landing, Malvern Hill, Dutch Gap Canal, "Butler's Look Out," &c., &c. On arriving at Richmond we were first directed to the Libby Prison, now partly used as merchants' stores and partly by the U. S. army. We then visited the ruins of the Treasury House, the Capitol, and the scene of the great conflagration, and were surprised at the great progress being made in the re-building, especially of the public edifices, Post Office, Banks, &c. On Friday we posted to some of the scenes of the war, outside the city, the principal one being Fort Harrison; here all were astonished at the still vivid picture of the effects of the war—the earthworks remaining intact protected by trenches and wooden chevaux-de-frise. The wooden huts that had been head quarters for officers were now used as pig-sties, poultry houses, and goat houses, for the negroes and other workmen and their families, employed in making a cemetery for burying the bones of the killed. Seventy men were employed for that purpose at the time of our visit. We were conducted to a spinney about one mile to the right of the principal earthworks, where the ground was lost and regained several times in a few hours, and in that part we saw skulls, arms, legs, &c., all bleaching in the sun. In some parts we saw large heaps of bones, some of horses, and others the bones of animals slaughtered as food for the armies. I think all of us brought away some mementoes from this point. The panoramic view here of the distant country is wonderfully fine, and close to us the foliage of the trees, especially of the oak, was the finest any of us had ever witnessed; and our ride home, through miles of farms, all desolate and not yet re-cultivated, was productive of sad and strange thoughts on behalf of all the sufferers through the late conflict. We left Richmond at 8·0 p.m. on Saturday, May 19th, by the Richmond, Fredericksburgh and Potomac route, for Washington, arriving there about 4·0 a.m. on Sunday. During our short stay we visited the Capitol, Treasury, War and Navy departments, White House, Patent Museum, Post Office, Smithsonian Institute, &c., &c. One of our rev. friends had the pleasure of opening the Senate with prayer on Monday. All were much pleased with the Capitol, and could not help drawing comparisons between its utility and that of our own House of Parliament. At the same time we were much disappointed with the general appearance of the shops, stores and streets, which fell far short of our expectations of the seat of government.

We left Washington at 6·30 p.m., Monday, May 21st, for Cincinnati, taking the Baltimore and Ohio Railway route, via Harper's Ferry, Grafton, and Parkersburg. This line traverses some of the most interesting districts of American scenery, being romantically diversified with hill, dale, wood, and water; passing also through a portion of the rich mineral and oil regions of Pennsylvania. We arrived at Cincinnati at 6·0 a.m., Wednesday, May 23rd, and after taking a hasty run through the principal streets of this busy city, left at 4·0 p.m. the same day, by the magnificent steamboat "General Lyttle," for Louisville, where we arrived about 1·0 a.m.; sleeping on board until 5·0 a.m., when we left by train for Cave City, from thence taking coach to the Mammoth Cave. By most this was considered the greatest treat we had so far enjoyed; the novelty of staying in an hotel, built of wood, but capable of accommodating about 400 visitors; the peculiarly romantic situation of the hotel, on a clearing from the woods which encircled it; the coolness of the atmosphere as compared with the last few days, combined to make a portion of our party thankful for an opportunity of resting for three days in this most popular resort for honeymoon trips, from all parts of the States. It is impossible to give a description of the Cave—it must be seen to be realised; and even after seeing, you can hardly realise the fact that you have been walking hard for ten hours in a Cave, and have not seen a tenth part of it. To the Geologist this is a wonderful studio, and with the assistance of the highly intelligent guides provided by the proprietors, he cannot fail to be greatly interested in this truly wonderful and romantic spot; the interest of which is to be increased on the first of next month, by the opening of a newly-discovered Cave, nearly as extensive as the "Mammoth." Many ordinary travellers state the expense is too great for this trip, as compared with general sight seeing expenses in America. To obviate this, I completed special arrangements, at greatly reduced rates for our passengers, for the whole of this Tour; and an arrangement for them to extend their trip to Chattanooga for the Look-out Mountains, if they wish, will enable Tourists to traverse a great portion of the district of "Sherman's Great March," which in addition to the magnificence of the mountain scenery, is full of interesting incidents connected with the late war.

From Mammoth Cave we returned to Louisville, staying for a short time at Keane's Louisville Hotel, which is one of the finest and most comfortable establishments in the States, and is the property of a gentleman who takes a warm-hearted interest in the comfort and pleasure of all Europeans, and kindly offers to do everything in his power for Cook's Tourists, and also to reduce his ordinary charges one-third to the holders of our Tickets.

From Louisville we went to St. Louis, by the Ohio and Mississippi Railway route, arriving there at 1·30 a.m., Wednesday, May 30th, making our short stay at the Planter's House. Mr. Fogg, the proprietor, takes an interest in our movement, and has pleasure in affording all information and facilities at his command to our passengers. St. Louis is a wonderfully busy city, and all who can should make a short stay, if it is only to see the immense number of fine River Steamers constantly arriving and departing from the piers.

We left St. Louis the same day, at 5·30 p.m., for Chicago, by the Chicago, Alton, and St. Louis Railway. At the commencement of this journey we met with another novelty in locomotion—we left the hotel in a large omnibus, seating 20 inside, and were drawn by four fine horses to the river, and on to a ferry boat, which conveyed fifteen four-horse conveyances across to the railway depôt at one trip. The Chicago, Alton, and St. Louis Railway runs through the finest agricultural district we had yet seen, the grazing fields being well-stocked with the finest cattle; and the nearer we approached to Chicago, the less did we wonder at the statements of the immense amount of agricultural produce of every description, said to pass through that wonderful "City of the West." We arrived at Chicago about 6·0 a.m., Thursday, May 31st, and stayed at the Brigg's House, where we again had the pleasure of meeting with proprietors anxious to do all in their power for the comfort of English visitors, especially those forming part of our numerous family. We are all apt to think the Americans boasters, but it is impossible for them to say too much in the boasting line respecting this wonderful city. The immense amount of grain passing through and being stored every day; the wonderful system of "elevating" the grain from ship or car, to immense blocks of buildings, ten stories in height, some of which will hold one million bushels; the rapidity with which they can load and unload a dozen vessels at one and the same time; the immense slaughter of pigs and beasts, and rapid curing and packing of the meat; and last, but not least, the (to us) wonderful mode of raising a block of buildings and putting a floor underneath, whilst all the business is going on above—or of removing a building from one side of the street to the other, or setting it back or bringing forward a few feet—all things many of us look upon as Yankee crams; but seeing is believing. The Brigg's House, which is capable of accommodating some hundreds of travellers, was being raised 4 feet 4 inches, whilst we were in the house; and although it was full of visitors, all the business went on without the slightest inconvenience. I here had very reluctantly to leave those of our travellers who so far had kept pace with me, to hurry on through Canada, to enable me to keep appointments advertised for New York and Old England; but as we had now got nearly through the States, and knowing (without in any way reflecting on American Railway Companies) that our system of Tickets would be better understood at the commencement by the Railway Officials of the Canadian Railways, I left in confidence of every one being to manage for themselves, after the training they had received during the previous 3000 miles. I therefore left Chicago at 10·0 p.m. on the same day, by the Michigan Central Railway, for Detroit, which is a very interesting and improving town, and a nice place to rest for a few hours, en route to Canada. After enjoying the company, for a short time, of old friends who had left Leicester years ago, for the New World, I proceeded by Great Western of Canada Railway to Hamilton, arriving there about 2·0 a.m., on Saturday, June 2nd. I left again at 10·0 a.m. the same day for Niagara, and about noon had the pleasure of crossing the suspension Bridge and obtaining my first glimpse of the Falls. This was to me the realization of a day and night dream from childhood; and as I left my baggage at Hamilton, I took the opportunity of walking by the River side from the Suspension Bridge to the Falls, a distance of about two miles, the foot path skirting the top of the cliffs, the Niagara river rolling swiftly below, and the Falls in full view before me. I shall not attempt to describe the feelings created in a walk alone under such circumstances; nor shall I attempt a description of the Falls, as it is an impossibility, at any rate, for my unpoetical pen, to trace the outline of the solemn grandeur of the scene; all I can say is that I had pictured to myself for years the scene in the highest possible colours, and the reality far exceeded even my most sanguine ideas. It takes some little time to be able to realise the awful grandeur and sublimity of the whole scene, and the longer you stay in the neighbourhood, the more difficult it becomes to tear yourself away; and if I am not mistaken, the rushing of the Cataract, the roar of the Falls, the clouds of spray, and the dazzling brilliancy of the numerous rainbows, will be present to my imagination through all the varied scenes of my future life. On Sunday, I visited the Indian Village, a few miles out of Niagara, and went to their church, where I heard a sermon given by an Indian, in their native language; and what appeared most singular, the hymns were sung in English, the choir consisting

entirely of Indians. I should advise all who can, to stay at least three or four days at Niagara, as they will find plenty of change of scenery on Goat Island, and in crossing to and fro between the American and Canadian side, examining the beauties of the Museums and Bazaars, to relieve them from the fascination of the Falls. I must not omit to advise all who go to Niagara, to call first at the Bazaar of our friend Mr. Tugby, standing on the very brink of the Cataract, and close to the entrance to Goat Island. Mr. Tugby is from the old country, and both he and his wife take the greatest possible interest in affording information and assistance to English Tourists. The Hotels are very fine, and a few of them most delightfully situated. I hardly know how to admire or recommend one in preference to another. I made my short stay at the International, and found the present proprietor anxious to do all that he could to add to the comfort of his guests. I had to hurry away on Monday morning back to Hamilton, to keep business appointments, and then proceed to Toronto, leaving there the same evening, by Grand Trunk Line for Kingston, where I arrived at 2 a.m. on Tuesday, intending to take the Mail Steamboat from thence to Montreal by the St. Lawrence and the Thousand Islands; but on arrival at that early hour, found the streets occupied with soldiers and volunteers of every description, and after getting on board the boat, had to leave it again, through the Commander of the Forces claiming it to convey troops and guns, if necessary, so that I had to make my way back to the station and proceed by a mixed train to Montreal. I would caution all future Tourists against attempting a journey by a mixed train, which is really a mixture of passenger and freight cars, and on the occasion in question, took 14 hours to travel 172 miles.

Montreal is a city full of interest to Tourists, and one from which many interesting excursions may be made. In the event of any future Tourists not being able to take the down the St. Lawrence from Kingston, I would advise them by all means to take the 7·0 a.m. train on a fine morning to Lachine, and there get on board the small steamer that plies to Montreal, shooting one portion of the Rapids, sailing under the Victoria Bridge, and arriving at Montreal by 9·30 a.m., with a fine appetite for a hearty breakfast. For a description of Montreal, Quebec, and all the Canadian scenery, I refer our readers to a new book, just published by — Taylor, Esq., of Montreal, a work most carefully compiled, full of very useful and interesting information, and embellished with about a dozen most beautiful photographic views of different portions of Canadian scenery. (I have brought a few copies of this work with me, and shall be glad to send one in return for 5/6 in stamps.) At Montreal I stopped at the Ottawa House, the proprietor of which volunteered to afford every possible facility at his command to our passengers. From Montreal I returned by St. John's, St. Albans, Lake Champlain, Burlington, Rutland, Troy, Albany, and the Hudson River Railway to New York. This was by far the most interesting railway ride I had enjoyed during my whole Tour; the State of Vermont being, in my opinion, the most pastoral and beautiful I had seen, and the Hudson River Railroad being one of great interest, skirting closely the banks of that gloriously picturesque river, all the way to New York. I arrived in New York at 11·30 a.m., on Saturday, June 9; and left at 4 p.m., by the extra steamer of the Anchor Line. We enjoyed a very smooth passage across the Atlantic, but were unfortunate in falling in with a very dense fog, which lasted for about ten days with such density, that we were obliged to steam very slowly for several nights and days, and the atmosphere was so peculiar that we only saw the sun for an hour or two one day from leaving the Bay of New York to coming in sight of the coast of Antrim. But we completed our voyage on one of the most charming days, passing between Torry Island and Greenock; every one on board being in raptures at the lovely scenery of the Irish and Scotch Coasts, seen under such favourable circumstances.

The reader will perceive that I have purposely omitted expressing myself in either approbation or dissatisfaction on the various points of public interest, on some of which I may have been expected to give opinions. I even refrain from giving the last new from the Fenian battle-field, although I was in the immediate neighbourhood of the skirmishing, saw a great portion of what really took place, and spent some portion of my time in the company of the Fenians, as well as British troops and volunteers. I need only say that my views have been altered very much, both as regards America and the Americans. I am convinced there are not any two nations entertaining more erroneous opinions of each other, and with less real cause for it, than do we and our Yankee cousins: and the only way to form true and correct views of the feelings and sentiments of the two nations is to travel amongst each other, with an unprejudiced mind, and a determination to arrive at the true state of all things before forming opinions. This is one of the great objects we had in view in labouring most ardently during the last ten months, to organise a system of Tours; and I am glad to say that, so far as the Railway and Steamboat Officials in America are concerned, they express themselves both anxious and willing to afford us all practicable facilities for the carrying out of this gigantic scheme.

Although on first landing I had some little difficulties to surmount, through not clearly understanding the railway business system of the New World, I am happy to say, that before I left, I not only had ascertained that the 41 Series of Tickets that I had arranged were all recognised and in working order, but also had the pleasure of adding 10 other important arrangements, and receiving offers for more; and we hope in the ensuing Fall to perfect the system in such a way as must ensure to us a good portion of the travellers from the American to the European Continent during 1867. I cannot close without expressing my entire satisfaction with the arrangements for the working of the "Anchor Line;" and in further testimony I may say, that with a full complement of passengers by the outward passage, and a fair average number by the homeward voyage, there was but one opinion, and that was of entire satisfaction. I must also warmly express my thanks to every Officer of the two boats I crossed in, and also to Mr. MacDonald, the agent in New York, for their great personal kindness and attention; and I am convinced, if they continue in the same cordial spirit towards the passengers entrusted to their care, that with the addition of the first-class boats preparing, they will eventually make the "Anchor Line" one of the most favourite for Tourist passengers crossing the Atlantic.

J. M. C.

whole of the a/c's are at once adjusted . . . I shall be reluctantly compelled to place our own cashier and receiver in your office to wind up the business'. The following year he complained to his father about a trip for a Baptist party to the Holy Land which Thomas had arranged with the New York office without telling John Mason, and on which he had agreed not to make a profit.

By 1878 the partnership had reached such a strained state that Jenkins was asking to resign from it and John Mason was prepared to see him go, as long as he put the accounts in order. Thomas, on the other hand, wanted the arrangement to continue. In the midst of the discussion, Jenkins left for Europe with £3000 of the firm's money. John Mason took immediate action. He wrote to every hotelier with whom he did business and every office in Europe:

'Dear Sirs,

I am sorry to think it advisable to inform you that our American partner, Mr Jenkins has acted so dishonestly that I have been compelled to enter an action against him and he has left New York after taking over three thousand pounds sterling, the monies of the firm. I understand that he (accompanied by Mrs Jenkins) has passed through France for Italy. I think it necessary to inform you that they are not travelling in connection with our business; that if you receive them and entertain them free, it will be in direct opposition to my wishes, and you must please understand that if they present hotel coupons to you as payment of their account, you are not to accept them; if you do we shall not pay the same.

Yours truly,
J M Cook'

Jenkins then sued Cook for $50,000 damages, claiming that John Mason's letter had ruined his European trip and that his entry in hotels had been 'cool and unpleasant'. Moreover, he claimed that the money he had drawn from the company funds had been due to him.

In the midst of this lawsuit Jenkins fell ill. A cable was sent to John Mason from his New York office announcing '*Jenkins' life despaired of doctors say end litigation only hope of recovery Ridgeway intimates amicable settlement can be made if you will entertain idea, shall we negotiate?*' John Mason's reply was, '*Yes, with judgment in our favour*'. The upshot of the affair was that Jenkins did die, but it would be wrong to assume, as some have done, that Jenkins' death was caused by his anxiety over the lawsuit as he was already a sick man before it began. Jenkins did win his case, but the judge's award of 6 cents was a judgment which needs no further comment.

It was also an unfortunate beginning to Cook's American venture, a venture which an unknown writer, probably Jenkins himself, had written about in the first issue of the American edition of *The Excursionist*. 'Mr Cook, as I understand the story, went forth under the inspiration of a dream; there was a song in his heart which was not set to the accompaniment of rattling dollars and sovereigns only but rather to the rhythm of those words, "Peace – goodwill towards man"'.

It was not the end of the dream, however, for in the years to come Cook's American business increased enormously, and included in 1896 the offer of travelling arrangements to the gold fields of the Klondyke where that gold for which so many people travelled to America was to be had for the taking for the last time.

Travel helped women to put the feet on the road to emancipation. A symbolic event on cruise ships wa the ladies and gentlemen's tug-of-war.

11 ... and son

When Thomas Cook opened his first London office at 98 Fleet Street in 1865 he had already been in London for two years, operating from his British Museum boarding house. This was run by his wife, Marianne, a capable and strong-minded woman who had managed Cook's Leicester Temperance Hotel. In the boarding house he ran a discreet office in the conservatory, since Bloomsbury was a residential area where businesses were barely tolerated. It was in the conservatory that one of Charles Dickens' reporters caught up with Cook and wrote a sympathetic piece about 'My Excursion Agent' in a Dickens publication called 'All the World Over'. It was in the conservatory, too, that Miss Jemima's trip to Switzerland was planned. It seems evident that, although becoming increasingly well known, Cook was by no means financially secure. The move to Fleet Street was fraught with peril and Cook realised that he must make an enormous effort to achieve success. He also needed the help of a reliable lieutenant; the best he knew was his son John Mason, who had helped Cook to organise and accompany excursions throughout Britain since his early teens.

But John Mason was not eager. He was running a printing business in Leicester and he strongly objected to working as partner with his father, to whom he now wrote expressing his fears that their differences of temperament would make it difficult for them to work well together. In the clash of wills of these two strong-minded men it was John Mason, who rarely gave way to anyone but his father, who finally acquiesced and took over the Fleet Street office with one assistant to help him. To get the maximum value out of it, they set up a Tourist and General boarding house there, and the hotel was run by Marianne and her daughter Anne who also helped in the ground floor office with the sale of the accessories to travel, including baggage, guide books, hat cases and telescopes with which John Mason had stocked it. The Cooks also implemented their income by acting as agents for advertisements in provincial newspapers.

John Mason had married Emma Hodge the year he joined his father and he had therefore an extra reason for wishing to make the new venture a success. Besides, he had to pay debts which had accrued to his business in Leicester and to keep up payments for the mortgage on the hotel. Thomas in the meantime set off to make more contracts with European hotels, and railway companies, and to reconnoitre the Middle East and America.

The Cook's Circular Ticket system, by which people could book a single ticket covering a journey over several different railway companies, was a boon to travellers and attracted hundreds of them into the Fleet Street premises. Cook added his Hotel Coupon system to that of the Circular Tickets in 1867 and was thus able to offer his clients an inclusive tour. The coupons were made up of several sections comprising breakfast, main meals and accommodation, and could be used at any of the hotels with which Cook had an arrangement. Very soon the hoteliers, realising that the acceptance of Hotel Coupons would bring them more tourists, started to queue up for the privilege of being on Cook's list. In all these schemes, John Mason played a leading role, his inexhaustible energy and business flair, so in tune with the spirit of the age, helping him expand and extend the Cook Empire.

Thomas Cook was the pioneer of tourism, but his son, John Mason, was the empire builder. In this picture John Mason is seen with his wife, Emma, and his son Frank, who later joined him in the busine

It was John Mason, as far as can be judged from such fragments of correspondence as remain, who was the most zealous in fighting for the firm's business interests. Having started working for his father at the age of fifteen, and having been inculcated with severe principles by both his parents, his character had a relentless puritanism which he applied to business. In this he was not unlike many late Victorian businessmen who, while they prided themselves on their integrity and their charity, earned for the British that bulldog image which symbolised their inflexible determination. Though he might provide free transport for soldiers going to convalescent camps down the Nile, or sponsor a hospital at Luxor, or give free passes to the widows of former employees, such acts of generosity were carefully weighed against their value or the worthiness of the cause. It was this attitude which created and widened an abyss between John Mason and his father's more impulsive and emotional nature.

In a letter dated 1877 there was already a disagreement between the two men over a property in Jerusalem in which Thomas Cook had become involved. Little imagination is needed to understand why Thomas Cook, the one-time Baptist preacher, should feel drawn to opening some kind of establishment in Jerusalem but, to the pragmatic John Mason, weighing the profit and loss of every venture, his father's impulsive nature was an irritation. 'I was an arrant fool for ever agreeing to it', he wrote, 'but having agreed to it I want to make the best I possibly can of a bad bargain'.

Disagreement between father and son became understandably worse as the son developed the business more and more, sailing ahead on the changing social tide into wider and wider oceans. Inevitably, the founder of the business, the father of the family, felt himself threatened, like any tribal head at the onslaught of a youthful challenger. It appeared that Thomas Cook was spreading the idea that his son was

Ludgate Circus was now the centre of the world of travel and here the Cooks sold tickets, tours, suitcases, guidebooks and ran a temperance hotel on the upper floors.

trying to push him out of the business. 'It is painful to me', wrote John Mason, 'to have to write to you as I have had to do during the past two or three years especially at a time when you ought to keep yourself quite free from all trouble and impiety of this world, but I cannot allow myself to be belied in the manner I have been by my own parents. You know well that I have written letter after letter calling upon you to have a meeting of all concerned to clear up the points at issue; and all the reply you have given me is in one letter in which you say, "we have many more important matters to settle than the personal ones . . . "'.

The breach was difficult to heal, for both the Cooks were obstinate men convinced of the rightness of their opinions, and perhaps lacking in that self-analysis and perception which might have made them understand each others' motives better. They both suffered but refused to give way. John Mason's distress is on record and we can only guess at what his father felt about the breakdown in his relationship with his only son and business partner. Thomas did not make matters easy. He travelled and did not let John Mason know where he was; he made arrangements for parties but did not communicate them to the London office. In spite of this seething personal cauldron the outward face of the business remained calm, confident and increasingly respected.

Perhaps as a means to clear his own mind, or to justify himself John Mason wrote out a list of the accusations that his family were whispering against him, and his answers to them:

One: He was accused of having made his father lose money in taking over his Leicester business. But in fact he had made so much money in the first year or two in London that he had paid off the mortgage of the hotel (£1,100).
'My father', he wrote, 'said he would not believe it possible but flew into a passion and declared I had either robbed him or somebody else to enable the money to be paid'.
Two: John Mason was accused of not helping his mother and sister. But he had paid for the hotel so they lived rent and food free. They had also kept all the money from the sale of books, and the profits made from running the hotel in Paris for the 1867 Exhibition.
Three: He did not understand what it was to be a partner. But he had made a profit for the firm, and he had offered his father an income of £1,000 a year to retire on.
Four: He had borrowed company money to build a new office at Ludgate Circus. But this had been a good investment.
Five: He was killing his father by the horrible things he said. John Mason admitted to having the habit of speaking and writing in plain English, but thought this more honourable than insinuating calumnies. (He could not have guessed then that he would outlive his father by only six years).
Six: That he treated his family as he had treated 'poor dear grandfather who is gone'.

This last accusation, and the one before, make it clear that here was a traditional family quarrel with the traditional accusations of ingratitude and selfishness.

Later, John Mason was driven to write to his father again, this time with an ultimatum. 'I will have it cleared up or *you* leave the business. I don't intend to leave it, I have placed it in the high position it is in and if I have health and strength, will keep it there'. Again, in February 1878 he writes: 'I state distinctly that I will not sign nor enter into any new arrangements for partnership with you upon any terms . . . I deny most in-

Shortly after visiting the Middle East to arrange a tour for the German Emperor Kaiser Wilhelm, John Mason Cook (seated) returned to his big house at Walton-on-Thames. He was ill and died soon after. On the left is John Mason's wife Emma.

dignantly your repeated statement that I meant to kick you out of the business or deprive you of your just rights, and refer to you my repeated offers commencing at least three years back when I asked you to relieve me of a partnership which had always been irksome to me and let me take a railway situation . . . .'. Some of the personal hurt at the situation comes out in another letter in which he expresses the bitterness he feels at the separation between his own and his father's family. 'It is your family that persistently turns their backs upon us. What would your religious and teetotal friends say if I were to tell them that your only son knew nothing of your special parties, held with such apparent sanctity, until he was told of them by those who were astonished at not meeting him at those parties'.

These letters were written by a man in his forties, a man who had travelled all over the world, dealt with princes and rulers and commanded a work force of thousands, yet who could not come to terms with a father whom he loved and wanted to please but with whose ideas on business he did not agree. The situation was the human and timeless one of the son brought up to take over a father's role, but being resented for so doing when the time arrived. In another letter John Mason's demand for recognition is revealed clearly. 'In yours of the 16th you say no father and mother or sister were ever more entitled to the gratitude and love of a son and brother . . . , my reply to that is that no son ever worked and acted more upon that principle than I have done, and that father, mother or sister ever had more right to recognise than the son and brother who has placed them in the position they now hold: but instead of that no son or brother can have been more cruelly and wickedly treated . . . .'.

The rivalry between father and son continued to the end, but underneath the bitterness there was always a feeling of their close attachment to each other, of two lives inextricably bound together. On top of the troubles with his father John Mason had worries about his son, Frank, whom the headmaster of Mill Hill School had threatened to expel. The reason for this remained a mystery as John Mason's letter to the headmaster, showed. 'Your remarks of Tuesday evening have naturally troubled me very much and I feel bound to ask you to give the whole matter further consideration when I think you must see that you are bound to give me the particulars of the cause you have for making such severe complaints about Frank . . . I think upon reflection you will see that you have placed us all in a false position by promising Frank not to tell me the facts . . . I am almost worked to death just now and have a frightful amount of responsibility upon my shoulders, but your insinuations against the character of my eldest son have caused me more sleepless hours and pain than any other present trouble'.

In the middle of success and triumph the events of the Cooks' personal lives moved on with the relentless pace of a Greek tragedy. John Mason, bitter at his treatment by his family now discovered that his sister Anne, who sided with her mother and father in the family quarrel, was secretly engaged to one of his clerks, a man called Higgins. The news, presumably of some consequence in the society to which the Cooks belonged, made John Mason angry. Writing later to his friend Barattoni in New York he said, 'With respect to Higgins, it is quite true that I allowed him to send in his resignation instead of my giving him his discharge and that the circumstance arose thro' it being reported to me that Higgins had for some time been engaged to my sister. I told them both at once that I could not have a brother-in-law a member of my staff and that if they were married he would have to leave our service. He appealed to me in various ways but I declined to be moved from my decision. He has left the service and I know no more than you do when the marriage is to take place'. But the marriage never did take place

Thomas Cook
Annie

Mrs Thomas Cook
John Mason Cook

The Cook business was essentially a family concern and everyone played a part in it. John Mason Cook began in the business in his teens helping his father at the time of the Great Exhibition. Mrs Thomas Cook (Marianne) ran her husband's hotels, first in Leicester then in London. Annie, Thomas Cook's daughter, helped in the London office and in the hotels. Frank, John Mason's son, became the Middle East expert. Ernest developed the banking side of the company which began in 1874 with the introduction of the travel cheque. Thomas travelled over India and Australia with his father and ran the Egyptian office for some years.

Thomas

for Anne Cook was found dead in her bath on Sunday, 8th November, 1880.

Giving his evidence at the inquest her father said, 'I reside at Stoneygate in the township of Knighton. The deceased was my daughter. She was a single lady, 35 years of age. I saw her alive on Saturday evening last about a quarter past eleven, in the bathroom. She occasionally took a bath before going to bed. I had previously been in the bathroom and noticed a strong and very offensive smell. I don't know what to compare it to. It was not merely the gas, though the gas caused it to develop itself – it seemed to come from the interior of the heating apparatus . . . My daughter usually brought me a cup of tea about a quarter past seven in the morning, but yesterday morning she failed to do this and Mrs Cook went to see why it was. She came back and reported that my daughter had not been to her bedroom, and I went to see what was the matter. I burst the bathroom door open and found her in the bath dead, with her face under the water and her legs drawn up'.

The Cook's family doctor then declared, 'Her body was in a rigid condition, the hands tightly clenched, the feet and hands drawn up and the face excessively livid. On raising the body some blood escaped from the left ear . . . The atmosphere of the room was not at all disagreeable. There was no evidence of gaseous or other smells, but the walls were bedewed with moisture which was streaming down and pools of water lay round the skirting of the room'. Summing up, the doctor gave his opinion that Anne had fainted in the bath and drowned and this was accepted by the foreman of the inquest. The death was reported in *The Times*, which said 'The mournful occurrence was attributed to a fit'.

There is no evidence of further family quarrels after this tragedy. Instead the Cooks seem to have gone their still apparently affectionate but separate ways. Thomas Cook began to lose his sight in 1888. Four years before his death he felt a desire to revisit Egypt and the Nile. He wrote to John Mason from Thorncroft, near Leicester, the large mansion where he lived and where he described himself as sitting with blinds drawn and going blind, to ask for berths for himself and some friends. He also referred to a request, presumably from friends in Palestine, to send portraits of himself and his family to Jaffa for an exhibition. John Mason had refused to sit for one. 'I fear', wrote Thomas Cook, 'my picture must stand alone at Jaffa, another addition to my personal isolation'.

At the same time he had written an essay on his life and work for the exhibition, which he described as 'drawn up with great care, and the result of a vivid and true memory of events the history of which form a good part of my present enjoyment and especially those incidents which constitute the luxury of doing good, which is now my highest earthly life'. Having written it, Cook had qualms about its reception at the hands of John Mason, for he added ' . . . in sending you the circular I do not wish to expose myself to severe criticism. I have stated everything as honestly and as honourably to yourself as I could possibly present them'. A nice human touch came at the end of his letter when he asked John Mason to reply to Mr Glasgow who was on the Nile party with him as Cook's blindness made him unable to read and write his own letters ' . . . as I do not want to have such affairs submitted to the reading of gossiping women, mind this remark does not apply to the ladies in your circle to all of whom I send my heartiest love'. He signs himself, 'Your truly affectionate father'.

By now the Cook Empire was growing apace and John Mason, who was determined to keep in touch with every aspect of the business personally, must have had little enough time for any kind of private life. His sons Frank, Ernest and Thomas were now in the

With John Mason's successful leadership the company prospered and so did the family who were able to fill their leisure time with such pursuits as shooting and fishing. The three Cook brothers are seen here after a shooting party with their mother, a friend and their stalkers.

business with him. With Frank in particular there was a friendly correspondence over the business affairs of the Middle East which was his special interest. Ernest accompanied Frank on many of the Middle East ventures and also looked after the business interests in Australasia, later becoming responsible for the banking side of the Company, while young Thomas accompanied his father and Frank on their trips and did his stint at the Cairo office. By 1891 John Mason could look back on fifty years of work in the business, twenty-six of which had been in full employment during the years of the company's great expansion. It is not surprising that he felt a pride of personal achievement in the position that the company had attained.

At the jubilee banquet given that year to commemorate the fiftieth anniversary of the founding of the business, the growth of the firm of Thomas Cook and Son and the various ways in which it had contributed to the expansion of national life, received their due acclaim. Among the 300 guests were the Duke of Cambridge, Prince Henry of Battenberg, Prince Edward of Saxe Weimar and many other notabilities. Three other guests, who were unable to attend through illness or other engagements were W E Gladstone, Lord Wolseley and the Duke of Rutland. It was a great occasion, reported in the newspapers which now unanimously acclaimed the Cooks as benefactors of mankind. John Mason received the acclaim on behalf of his father who lay in his house at Leicester blind and infirm after a wound in his leg, suffered in his youth, had turned gangrenous.

The guests at the party represented the higher strata of society that the Cooks had now gathered into their fold. Over 300 of these distinguished people were listed in Cook's book on the Nile, as having travelled with Thos. Cook and Son. They included Their Royal Highnesses the Duke and Duchess of Saxe Coburg & Gotha, His Royal Highness the Duke of Connaught, Her Royal Highness the Princess Christian of Schleswig-Holstein, Her Royal Highness The Princess Louise, Their Royal Highnesses Prince and Princess Henry of Battenburg, His Royal Highness the Duke of Clarence, His Royal Highness the Duke of York, His Royal Highness the Duke of Cambridge, Her Royal Highness the Princess Mary and Duchess of Teck, His Highness the Duke of Teck, His Highness Prince Edward of Saxe Weimar, His Serene Highness Prince Victor of Hohenlohe, Their Imperial Majesties the Czar and Czarina of Russia, Their Majesties the Emperor and Empress of Germany, The Empress Eugenie, and the Shah of Persia. There were archdukes, maharajahs, sultans, nawabs, lords, earls, bishops, admirals and generals among the Cooks' clients, and many other celebrities of the time, among whom there stand out Sir Arthur Sullivan, Baron Rothschild, Cecil Rhodes, Herr Krupp, General Kitchener, Rider Haggard, Rudyard Kipling, W E Gladstone and Mr Vanderbilt.

There was no doubt that all of society travelled with Cooks. Songs and poems were written about them, and even a musical comedy, written by Seymour Hicks, featured 'The Man from Cooks' and included a popular song about him.

In charge of the whole brilliant assembly was the figure of John Mason, a man less easy to know than his father and who has received less sympathetic treatment from his chroniclers. A contemporary description by G W Steevens in his book 'Egypt 1898' gives what is perhaps the truest picture of the architect of the Cook Empire.

'Some years ago Mr J M Cook was in a hotel opposite two ladies who assured him of their personal knowledge that there was no longer any member of the firm called Cook, but that the business had come entirely into American hands. "I was very interested to hear it", says Mr Cook with that genial grimness which is all his own, "but before I'd done I managed to convince 'em that I was myself" '.

'That is just what he does: he manages to convince everybody that he is himself. He has been doing it in Egypt especially for some thirty years up and down the Nile; and in Egypt, consequently, they know that Mr Cook is himself perhaps better than we do generally at home. One of the first persons to realise the interesting fact was the dragoman of the very first tourist steamer which young Mr Cook – he was the "and son" – took up the Nile. For since he was insubordinate and impertinent, Mr Cook threw him into the Nile at Luxor to think it over there, and dragonmanned the party up to Assouan himself.

A man like this was just the man for Egypt. He knew what he wanted, and he meant to get it: he did get it, and what was as much to the point, it was the right thing to want'.

Steevens gave another example of John Mason's determination and resolution at the launching of the first of the flat-bottomed high deck boats which John Mason built at Boulac and which most people expected to keel over in the first gale.

'The launching of the first boat, the *Prince Abbas* was delayed for no visible reason, thus giving rise to the gossip that "that madman Cook had over-reached himself and was being punished for his rashness". Eventually the launching took place on a day when the falling barometer announced a strong gale, and the boat sailed steady as a rock. It had been what John Mason had been waiting for and it proved his point'.

Ending his reference to John Mason, Steevens gives us this vivid thumbnail sketch.

'Cook is tall, strongly built, he stands erect and firm on his legs. His beard is snow white and his round forehead is bare. His white eyebrows bristle resolutely over the eyes that such a man ought to have, eyes that look out of their sockets like a gun out of a port, blue eyes that seem to have a backward surface looking at the brain, eyes that think as well as see . . . A man of force! a man also of humour, of much kindness, but primarily a man of force. I would sooner have him for my friend than for my enemy. Yet I would sooner have him for my enemy than most men: for he would hit straight and expect to be hit back straight'.

12 Empire building

Britain's good fortune in the nineteenth century was to be spared the internal up-heavals experienced by Germany, France and Italy. She was thus able to devote herself peacefully to the development of her industry and the extension of her influence abroad. The sources of her raw materials and the markets for her exports were enlarged as a result of Empire building, and trade treaties were made in India, the Far East, and, in particular, Africa. To the public these wars, sometimes more skirmishes than wars, were objects of increasing interest and were the basis of a concept of Britain's role as the bearer of enlightenment and progress that lasted for over half a century. This idea permeated the whole of British society, became a regulator of almost every aspect of national life, and conditioned the behaviour of everyone, in particular those who travelled abroad in full awareness of the superiority of their own country over those which they visited.

The extension of British interest abroad provided the Cooks with more fields to conquer. Soon they were busy opening offices in all the new territories often, as in Cape Town (1900), Bombay and Calcutta (1883) to help the troops through their banking as well as their travel services. At other times, the reason for opening was the one which had prompted Thomas Cook many times from the 1850s, the opening of an exhibition. The Melbourne office, from where Cook organised travel throughout Australia and to New Zealand, opened in 1880 for the Melbourne Exhibition.

Where the Government were concerned in the opening of a new territory, Cook made sure of engaging the support of leading personalities. Gladstone approved of Cook's plans for India, and the Admiralty recommended his services for the movement of troops in Egypt during the Gordon crisis. The situation in the Sudan had arisen through Gordon's determination to stay in Khartoum, where he had been sent to maintain order during the rebellion of the Mahdi, a religious leader, coupled with the Government's indecision as to the importance of the Sudan to British interests. John Mason Cook was called in first in an advisory capacity but, because of his unrivalled knowledge of the Nile, he soon found himself in charge of movement of the expedition, under the command of Lord Wolseley sent to relieve Gordon who was besieged in Khartoum. The vacillating and muddled manner in which the Government handled the Gordon crisis is referred to in a journal, now in the possession of Thomas Cook & Co Ltd, which was kept by Colonel G A Furse, CB, who was present in Egypt.

'After the British Government had by clever manoeuvre put a stop to the popular outcry for the relief of General Gordon by sending out five miles of railway plant to Suakim, as if fully prepared to adopt the suggestion of opening communication with him via Berber by means of a light railway, the approaching end of the parliamentary session and the collapse of the conference revived the pressure put on them to fulfil the promise of taking measures for his effectual relief'.

According to Colonel Furse, the Government's idea was that Gordon should retreat to Dongola where he could then make his escape, since the Government was not inclined to get mixed up with the affairs of the Sudan. Gordon however, thought differently, as Colonel Furse suspected. 'No doubt the little that is known of Gordon's telegrams do not go to show that he concurs with the Government in the decision to abandon the country but shows he set himself into opposition to the Cabinet . . . Public opinion would not support him and would be obliged to accept the fact that an expedition is not necessary to further the intentions of a disobedient chief'. At any rate, the Government were committed to some kind of action, and John Mason was called in to carry out a plan suggested by a group of officers who had been involved in the Red River expedition (in America).

The plan was to go up the Nile to Dongola, from where a link with Gordon could be established. Cook's orders from the Admiralty and War office were to arrange for the transport of stores and troops to Wadi Halfa on the second cataract. This meant taking 6,000 men, 10,000 tons of stores, 12,000 tons of coal, and 400 whaleboats by rail to Assiout and shipping them by steamer to Wadi Halfa. The initial talks with the Government took place in April 1884, but John Mason did not receive confirmation of the contract until September and the £600,000 allowed him for this enterprise was not forthcoming. In the meantime, the Mahdi was moving his forces into a position from which he could attack Khartoum. John Mason, who was fully aware of the urgency of the situation, began to arrange for shipment of coal long before the contract was formally signed, and twenty-eight steamers were chartered to carry coal from the Tyne to Alexandria.

In the meantime, the Government had had second thoughts. Instead of 6,000 men there would be 18,000 and the total stores would increase to 130,000 tons. John Mason was also asked to collect 50,000 tons of cereal which were paid in lieu of tax by the fellaheen up river, and transport them down to Cairo. To carry out the enlarged plan, 6,000 railway trucks were put into service between Alexandria and Assiout, and 5,000 men and boys were employed to handle and load the 650 boats used to transport the stores. In spite of all the difficulties, John Mason kept to the date agreed in the contract and delivered the stores and men to Wadi Halfa.

The expedition arrived too late to save Gordon and in the wordy investigations which followed, a report emanated from Whitehall which seemed to suggest that the disaster had been caused by the delay in delivering supplies. John Mason, who was always very vulnerable to any criticism of his work, defended himself, giving a detailed account of his actions in a lecture to the Royal Geographical Society. He need not have bothered, for he had plenty of friends who had been at the scene of the action and knew the efficiency and speed with which he had carried out his task.

One of these was Colonel Furse, who wrote in his journal that John Mason 'was the real Quarter Master General of the expedition. To those who came privately into contact with him he endeared himself by his amiable manners and readiness to answer every question put to him, which coming from a lot of griffs must at times have taxed his patience and equanimity. Here was the man who, in anticipation of work to be done on the Nile, had on his own hook sent out to Egypt some thousand tons of coal, was asked by the War Office when in the midst of his work for some guarantee for fulfilment of his contract: this was really sweet, quite in keeping with the traditions of the Supply and Transport Dept. What a laugh we had about it when Cook told us'.

From the Director of Army Contracts at the War Office came a qualified but nevertheless positive admission of the value of the Cooks' help with the transport of the army:

'Gentlemen,

I am directed by the Secretary of State for War to acknowledge receipt of your letter of the 13th instant, requesting an expression of opinion as to the manner in which the contract for Transport of the Troops on the Nile during the expedition of 1844 was performed by you. In reply, Mr Campbell-Bannerman directs me to inform you that considering the amount of organisation required in arranging for the service the difficulties of the Nile navigation, and the great strain on local resources, he is of the opinion that great credit is due to you for the satisfactory way in which your contract was performed.

I am, gentlemen, your obedient servant,
Evan Colville Nepean'

Having completed his assignment, John Mason and his son Thomas were tempted to go further up the Nile over the rapids and shallows which had to be negotiated on the whale boats which had been brought to Wadi Halfa. Whether or not John Mason would have given way to the temptation had not his son been with him is debatable, but young Thomas, or Bert as he was known in the family, was determined to get to Khartoum with the troops. John Mason did have a reason for wanting to go up river, however. He wished to meet the ruler of Dongola, the Mudir, who controlled this territory and on whom John Mason would need to depend if and when he decided to extend his excursion arrangements to the Sudan.

So the Cooks set off with the army, observing the appalling difficulties with which the men had to contend as they manhandled the boats over the rapids, and against the current. In his report to the Royal Geographical Society John Mason described the arduous journey as he travelled up river with the men of the Staffordshire regiment. He explained how his boat, although only twenty-four feet long, six feet six inches in the beam, and drawing only twenty inches of water, needed 170 men and his own crew to pull it through the cataracts. For soldiers unaccustomed to heat which blistered their feet and exhausted their strength, the task was herculean. The greatest danger came in passing through the cataract, when the boats were in danger of breaking away from the ropes that held them, to hurtle down river in the tumultuous water, smashing themselves on the rocks and dragging the men who held them into the dangerous waters.

Most of the boats got through, although over a hundred of them were damaged, often several times over, as they crashed against the rocks. When this happened they had to be dragged to dry land and repaired. One boat had twenty holes knocked into its inch-and-a-half thick timbers and took two days to repair. In these conditions it is not surprising that there was loss of life. Seven Canadians who had been engaged to help in the expedition, and five soldiers were among those killed. To John Mason, it seemed that the loss of life was surprisingly small considering the conditions.

This part of the journey was not John Mason's responsibility. When he arrived at Dongola he hastened to request an audience with the Mudir, who received him in his

In 1884 General Gordon was besieged in Khartoum. The government decided to send help to him and asked Cook to arrange transport for the whole expedition including weapons and stores at Dongola on the Upper Nile. John Mason arranged for whaleboats to carry troops and set up a hospital ferry service for the wounded.

tent, squatting on a chair and with his holy spear near him. 'He is as thin as a lath', John Mason wrote later, 'his sinews are attenuated, and looking at him you would think he was just going into his grave; but after you have spoken with him for a few minutes and he begins to feel at ease, you would conceive him to be, as I did, one of the most powerful men, from a brain point of view, that I have ever been in the presence of'.

From someone of John Mason's intense power of concentration and single-mindedness, this was respect indeed. Possibly the Mudir felt a similar admiration for his visitor for, after telling him that Mohammet Achmet the rebellious Mahdi was no true Mahdi, and if such a messiah existed it would be himself, he invited John Mason to stay for a fortnight and offered to send him to Khartoum under safe custody. John Mason was amazed. 'Here was England', he wrote, 'spending a few millions to rescue Gordon from Khartoum, and here was a gentleman who offered to send me there in a fortnight'. When John Mason recovered from his surprise he asked the obvious question: 'Why then, couldn't Gordon come away from Khartoum?'

The Mudir pushed back his turban before replying. 'Ask Mr Cook', he said to the interpreter, 'if Gordon leaves Khartoum who will rule there?' The question was soon answered. In January, a few days before the expeditionary force arrived at Khartoum, Gordon was killed and the Sudan fell into the hands of the Mahdi. It was ten years before General Kitchener arrived to revenge Gordon's death, and to mete out punishment for the Mahdi's defiance of British authority, at the battle of Omdurman.

In India, John Mason became involved with yet another Government problem. On his first visit there in 1880 he had asked for and received the recommendation of W E

Gladstone who had personal experience of Cook's services and valued them. This had led to co-operation from Government offices in the sub-continent. The recommendation had been no less warmly confirmed by the Marquess of Salisbury, the leader of the Opposition:

'Mr Cook, I do not hesitate to say that the Government ought to render you every possible assistance to enable you to carry out your ideas, as it is impossible to calculate what benefit you will ultimately be to the nation. If you can only induce a number of wealthy Englishmen to visit India, and to see for themselves the value of that country to England, and also induce even a small number of wealthy Indians to visit England, and enable them to realise who and what the people are at home who govern them in India, you will certainly be of great service from a social and international point of view, and, it may be, politically'.

John Mason's visit to India was to result in far more than either Gladstone or the Marquess of Salisbury could foresee. In 1885, when he was on his way to India to arrange the conveyance of visitors to the Indian and Colonial Exhibition held in London during the Queen's Jubilee, he was approached by Sir Henry Drummond Wolff with a

The average tourist had more than his money's worth from simply observing the strange customs and rituals of the natives, but trophy hunters wanted to hunt the wild animals that abounded in Africa and India.

The British Government were eager that Cook
should encourage Indian princes to travel to
Britain in order to arouse in them a sense of
loyalty to the Empire. Many of the princes travelled
with their entire court and their favourite animals.

request from the Governor General, Lord Dufferin, to interest himself in the transport of pilgrims to Mecca. This was a difficult and challenging job and John Mason realised it. 'I know that this business is surrounded with more difficulties and prejudices than anything I have hitherto undertaken', he said. The difficulties were not only those of providing transport for thousands of pilgrims from all over India, the North West provinces and even farther afield, but also those of avoiding the enmity of the agents who had had the business in their hands until now.

The pilgrims were Mohammedans and came from thousands of miles away to take part in the holy Haj. Some came from Kabul, others from Bokhara, and a few from as far away as Java. Most of them were poor and could not afford to pay for transport to Bombay, the port of embarkation, so they walked. Many of them died on the way and thousands of those who did arrive were in poor condition. At Bombay they had to wait for ships. This was where the troubles really began.

A situation where thousands of people were gathered together with money in their pockets and a demand to be met, would always provide an opportunity for exploiters and crooks. In Bombay, John Mason labelled them 'Liverpool Crimps'. He described how the pilgrims were offered accommodation in houses and stripped of their money for the room, board and steamer passage. After being kept waiting for weeks, the pilgrims would be given a passage on a ship and on embarkation day would have to pay once again for getting from land to ship. No doubt for many of them the pilgrimage ended at Bombay. But those who had managed to get a passage now fought for places on the boats. The weak were elbowed aside or trampled under foot and even crushed to death. Those who managed to find a place were crowded together below decks in conditions hardly better than those on slave ships.

If the sea was rough between Bombay and Jeddah the conditions became appalling, as an article in *The Times of India* described. 'Before we finally get the hatches on, we have a hard time to get the pilgrims below, and in some cases we are obliged to be rough. But still many prefer to stay on deck and be washed about or cling to something in a corner or hold on like grim death and allow water to wash over them. During the whole time the hatches are battened down the shouting, screaming and groaning are sickening'. Even more sickening was the stench, caused by the packed bodies and the fragments of food, including the entrails of the fish sold to the pilgrims by fishermen who came alongside the ship at Aden.

After passing Kamaran, the pilgrims shaved all the hair off their bodies, clothed themselves in calico and prepared for the landing at Jeddah. Inevitably, there was illness aboard, with which the doctors were quite incapable of dealing. 'When I arrived at Aden,' reported the writer of *The Times of India* article, 'I had six cases. My noble doctor would insist upon telling me it was not smallpox, but the post doctor at Aden soon decided the matter, and would have had my doctor's diploma taken from him, only he had none. He was at one time an apothecary and was a good Mussulman: but he got helplessly drunk at every opportunity. The noble doctors we carry are generally as much use as the fifth wheel of a coach'.

John Mason set to, with his son Thomas, to put some order into this state of affairs. He travelled thousands of miles, arranging with railways and steamship lines for the conveyance of pilgrims, and laying down the standards of accommodation he thought necessary. In return for his efforts he received the gratitude of the Governor General, of the Khedive of Egypt and of Mohammedan rulers, but his interference in what had been a thriving business for the exploiters made him enemies, including members of

135

the Governor General's council. In 1893 an abrupt letter from an Under Secretary terminated the arrangement by which John Mason received a subsidy from the Government of India. This prompted him to write a long report on his work; like his father he was touchy about any kind of criticism or implied lack of confidence. In reality, he was pleased to give up this task which had brought him little, if any, profit. In any case, his main work of establishing the standard by which the transportation of pilgrims would be judged in the future, was done. He had plenty of other ventures to occupy him. Since the success of the Colonial and Indian Exhibition, he had been busy looking after the Indian princes who were encouraged to travel in Europe but insisted on doing so with huge entourages, including wives, concubines, cattle, pet tigers, elephants and even cannons.

He had also taken on the Army and Civil Service agency (hence the Cook telegraphic address 'Armagence' used to the present day) and his offices in Calcutta and Bombay were kept busy arranging passages home for soldiers and civil servants and providing banking services. In other parts of the Empire, the Cooks also served the Imperial cause. In South Africa they were entrusted with the job of repatriating undesirables and rebels who were sent to England and then deported to their countries of origin. They arranged trips to Bulawayo, and a personally-conducted tour on the New Congo railway from Metedi to Leopoldville.

By the end of the century Cook offices were serving travellers in India at Bombay and Calcutta; in Burma at Rangoon; in Australia at Sydney, Adelaide and Brisbane; in New Zealand at Auckland; in America at New York, Boston, Chicago, Philadelphia, Jacksonville and San Francisco and through nineteen other agencies; and in Canada, Toronto, Quebec, Montreal, Hamilton, Kingston, St John and Ottawa were part of the Cooks' far flung Empire. John Mason and his sons had worked indefatigably exploring new territories and setting up their ticket and hotel coupon systems, but that was not all, often they had to accompany their more distinguished clients in person. Frank, who ran the Middle East business from the Cairo office, escorted the Duke of Clarence and Avondale and Prince George of Wales round Palestine; Thomas Albert was personal conductor to the Grand Duchess Sergius and the Grand Duke Paul through the Holy Cities and John Mason himself personally looked after Gladstone, Balfour and, his most famous customer of all, the Kaiser of Germany.

The Kaiser met John Mason while on a visit to Vesuvius, and the example of Cook's organising ability he was shown then persuaded him to put his projected tour in Cook's hands. The Imperial party was made up of 105 people. In addition, there were 108 Pashas and their servants representing the Sultan of Turkey. Here again was a major problem of organisation and, although his son Frank was in charge of the operation, John Mason felt it essential that he should keep his word to the Emperor and make a personal appearance, despite his failing health.

To carry out the job of looking after the Kaiser's party, the Cooks gathered 1,430 horses and mules, 116 landaus, baggage carts, 800 muleteers and 290 waiters and servants. Three special trains were hired for the journey from Jerusalem to Jaffa, and three more from Beyrout to Damascus. There was a mixed reaction to the Imperial trip, but the Cooks were proud of their arrangements for this powerful ruler from a country which was regarded as closely associated with Britain. To some of the British Press the Kaiser's visit to Palestine seemed ostentatious and overbearing, but perhaps this was the natural reaction to the new boy in the Imperial Club. On the other hand, German tourists in Jerusalem felt indignant that their Kaiser's procession should be led by a young Englishman, for it was Frank Cook who rode at the head of the party.

The reaction of the French, who were also wrapped in their own Imperial dreams, was more sardonic, and *Le Rire*, a French humorous newspaper, asked whether perhaps the Kaiser and Cook were in league and planning to share the profit of the future tours that the Imperial visit would stimulate. Neither the observers nor the participants in the Imperial visit, which John Mason regarded as the high point of his career, could have guessed that the Imperial rivalries would set up a trend which would destroy the old system of European power politics, and that the age for grandiose visions was already on its way out.

Only the most sceptical regarded the Kaiser's visit to the Holy Land as a means of extending German influence. John Mason Cook was decorated for looking after the arrangements.

13 The naughty nineties

The year 1890, *in spite of some serious financial surprises, was, on the whole, a happy and prosperous period. No grave difficulties occurred between any of the great nations of Europe, and, as we ventured to hope at the beginning of the year, peace was maintained. Trade, especially in the early part of the year, was sound and large . . . The labour market experienced serious strikes, and unskilled labour suffered, but the demand for skilled labour continued, and, although the questions of wages and of how many hours should constitute a working day are sources of anxiety, there seems no immediate prospect of out-breaks incapable of settlement. The general passenger and tourist traffic by rail and by sea at home and abroad, was by far the largest on record, a fair criterion of the progress and prosperity of the world'.*

The editorial in *The Excursionist* for January 1891, reviewing the beginning of the last decade of the century, had an optimistic tone. Here was the voice of the affluent middle classes, full of self assurance and false assumptions, the people for whom *The Times* kept such unpleasant items of news as the prosecution of disorderly houses, white slavery, murder, death owing to malnutrition, factory accidents and workers' unrest, in unobtrusive type at the bottom of columns. To these people the idea of the British as a chosen race, as the bravest of the brave, the justest of the just, and most honourable of the honourable did not seem at all absurd, and they had no doubt at all that if God had to choose a nationality he would not hesitate to be British.

Under the circumstances it is not surprising that British tourists went abroad with the air of landlords inspecting their property, and they went in ever increasing numbers. Half a million at the beginning of the 1890s had turned to a million by the turn of the century. These tourists were no longer driven by a thirst for knowledge, nor were they prepared to put up with inconveniences. They wanted and expected to find themselves treated in the manner suitable to an Englishman's station in the world, to be provided with decent, comfortable food and board, deferential service, and the English newspapers at breakfast.

The Cooks were just the people to see that they got what they wanted. With their vast knowledge of foreign lands and people, and their experience of British travellers, they set about creating a tourist world which could appear to be part of the real world while being isolated from it. They encouraged the building of Grand hotels, promising to send clients with their Hotel coupons to Cannes, Monte Carlo, Baden Baden, Carlsbad, and the great capital cities of Europe. They extended their Circular ticket system throughout the world, they chartered steamers to provide a self-contained world for their 'distinguished travellers'. Foreign travel was the perfect setting for people who liked to deceive themselves about the true condition of their society: foreign countries, particularly the poorer ones, confirmed their belief that everything was all right at home, and the servility which they commanded from the poor who fought for their patronage was interpreted as a natural respect for superior people.

In the sheltered splendour of the hotels, with their palatial decor and their armies of servants, the middle-class tourist who prided himself on his refinement and taste could

Towards the end of the nineteenth century, foreign travel began to acquire a glossy image and many ot those who took part in it became unbearably smug, including the *literati* who wrote about it. These people flocked to the fashionable places at fashionable times. Longchamps in Paris was a favourite Easter rendezvous.

The internal combustion engine brought about
another change in tourist travel but, as with
the train, the new method of locomotion came
in slowly and the traditional systems of transport continued to be used.

Arrivée du train à la Station du Gornergrat-Kulm

388   EDITION PHOTOGLOB CO ZÜRICH

Arrivée d'un Train de Lugeurs à Crêt-d'y-Bau

754   CHARNAUX FRÈRES & Cⁱᵉ. GENÈVE

Ampezzotal - Dolomitenstrasse mit Croda Rossa (3148 m)

Hôtel et Col de la Faucille (alt. 1323 m) et le Mont-Blanc

5. 3 CHARNAUX FRÈRES & C°., GENÈVE

141

live out his dream life to perfection. In the morning there would be a leisurely breakfast on the terrace with an inspiring view over mountains or sea. An English breakfast accompanied by the English papers would be served by a dress-suited waiter wearing white gloves. Then would come the morning constitutional, a stroll round the village where the time of day would be passed with locals who spoke English. In mid-morning there would be a boat trip; the boatman, having been chosen from among the multitude who had offered their services on the first day, was retained throughout the stay. Often the destination of the boat ride would be a small local village where some healthy beverage could be imbibed: on the Italian and Swiss Lakes this was often milk straight from the cow. By the seaside, the snack might include shellfish and a glass of wine. Then came lunch and after lunch the siesta, followed by another expedition to some beauty spot, church or art gallery. All these visits were made with guide book in hand; either Murray, Baedeker or Cook's, the latter being preferable, according to the publisher, for it was less conspicuous than the others and did not attract those undesirable natives who were on the look out for people who looked like tourists.

Tea time would be in the best palm court tradition, and in the evenings the hotel would become the centre of social life, a self contained world in which everyone belonged to the same society, or at least pretended they did, and vied with one another for social ascendancy. While the majority of Cooks' tourists abroad projected an atmosphere of stability and authority, and held the highly moral attitudes usually cultivated in a rigid society which is unsure of itself, others were breaking down the solid walls of what was considered socially acceptable. Both parties to the moral struggle shared one characteristic: snobbery, the snobbery of those who were able to go abroad, or of those who went to the fashionable places, or those who went to places that had just finished being fashionable.

Queen magazine published one of the first regular series of travel articles to reflect this clearly. At Monte Carlo the season was at its best during February and March when there was a constant round of amusements, the magazine told its readers. At San Sebastian life was fashionable and gay, Wiesbaden kept up its reputation for sociability, Trouville was the gayest of North French Coast watering places. 'The cheap Brighton tripper is not felt. The cheap tripper in France again does not proclaim his caste loudly from the third class window of the train, or in his straggling gait, as up the Queens Road, Brighton, penniless on his return'. The 'smart set' went to Monte Carlo and aroused the indignation of the moralists. 'Last of its kind to be tolerated in the neighbourhood of the respectable communities of Europe, the public gambling institutions of Monte Carlo, in the petty principality of Monaco, has been arraigned and found guilty at the bar of public opinion . . . ' said a letter to *The Times*. Another correspondent, admitting that he has only seen the place from the railway, exclaims, 'I know that I am not exaggerating when I say that at Monte Carlo is to be found the very scum of all Europe'.

A more realistic note was struck by *The Pall Mall Gazette*. 'Half the people one meets', said an editorial, 'are going to or have been to Monte Carlo. If friends are invited the probable answer is, "I am going to Monaco, to the classical concert, to the band, or to an operatic performance," but few dare confess that they are going to play, and yet many do'. Hypocrisy was another of the characteristics of the late Victorian. He has been thrashed for it often enough, but in changing times it was a necessary protection. It would be inconceivable that Cook's customers, taking advantage of their 7 guinea 10-day cheap trips to Mentone, Nice and Cannes, should not have made excursions to Monte Carlo to try their luck, but none of them would have liked their neighbours to know.

Perhaps half a century earlier Thomas Cook might have crusaded against the breaking down of taboos and moral stringencies but times had changed and the Cooks had changed with them. In the 1860s Cook had written of Paris, 'the cafés thronged with smoking men and tippling women consuming all sorts of liquor from eau de vie to sugar water, whilst the low wine shops are reeking with the fumes and excitement of ouvriers and men in blouses . . . night afforded ample evidence of the untruthful representation of many that drunkenness is a rare sin in Paris'.

Now, in the nineties, when Paris had its Folies Bergères, Olympia and other music halls, its brothels and strolling prostitutes, its street cafés and night clubs, Cook's customers were assured that 'Paris cafés are a feature of the daily life of the city. The cafés of Paris are so numerous that it is unnecessary to specify any particular establishments . . . Ladies, may, without any impropriety, visit the best cafés, or sit at the tables outside'. But there is a warning given. 'Ladies should, however, on no account enter the cafés on the north side of the boulevard, between the Grand Opera and St Denis'. And Cook still cannot accept the Can-Can establishments which, 'though presenting some attraction to the visitor on account of the "fast" reputation which they formerly had, are now of the most dreary description. The Can-Can is danced by paid performers and is altogether of an unnatural and forced abandon'.

The forces which had emancipated the middle classes were now liberating those lower down the scale, working class movements were gathering strength and shaking the social structure, Karl Marx had drawn up his blue-print for another kind of future and Darwin had started a worm of doubt which would gnaw its way through the divine furniture. This doubt and uncertainty underlay the last decade of the Victorian age and came out more openly in that of the Edwardians; most were unaware of it but reacted to it instinctively, fighting to preserve the *status quo* of the society they had, and increasingly looking to pleasure to drive away the dark thoughts.

John Mason, above all else a good businessman, recognised the new trends in society and, with his sons Frank, Thomas and Ernest working with him, continued to supply his customers with what they desired, whatever their station in life. For those who could afford the Nile he offered private dahabeahs, a vessel he had previously criticised when it had been to his interest to guide the public onto his steamers. Now John Mason, with an ingenuous frankness which would be alien to a modern businessman, admitted that 'although we have merited to a certain extent the accusation that we have ridiculed the expensive luxury of the dahabeah, still we have at the request of private families arranged for their voyage to the 1st or 2nd cataract'.

For others he built ever more luxurious steamers at Boulac, whose shipyards are still owned by Cooks. The *Ramses the Great*, the proudest possession of the Cooks' Nile fleet, was 221 feet long, with a beam of 30 feet, and a draught of only 2 feet 6 inches to enable it to navigate the shallow waters of the river. It had a 400 horse power engine. On these steamers, distinguished tourists would sail up the Nile served by unobtrusive but numerous white-robed Arabs, with red tarbooshes and cummerbunds, protected from the inconveniences of the land they had come to visit. But wherever they went, Cook's tourists could depend on the long arm of the Cook Organisation to be ever ready to help and succour them and to reassure them of the protection of British Authority. In Paris, Marseilles, Nice, Geneva, Turin, Milan, Florence, Genoa, Venice, Vienna, Rome, Brindisi, Naples, Algiers, Athens, Constantinople, Alexandria, Jaffa or Beyrout

There was no more luxurious way of travelling than in a sleeping car of the Wagons Lits Company. Cossetted by a polite attendant, fed in a first class restaurant, the rich and beautiful people of the 'belle epoque' travelled the length and breadth of Europe.

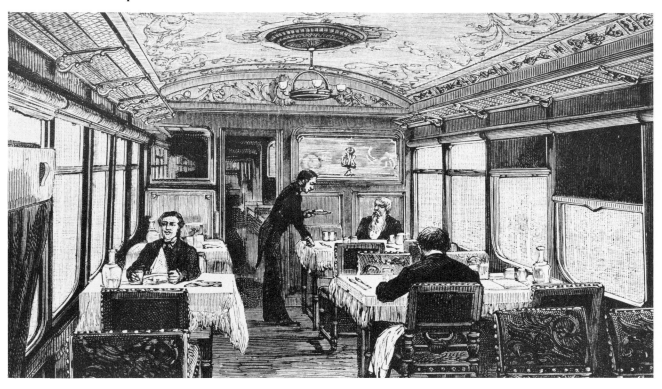

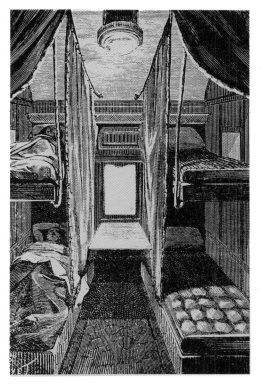

the Cook's man in his resplendent blue uniform with gold buttons would be waiting to attend to the customers' needs: a symbol of the Britain who was mistress of the world.

John Mason also offered his customers the comforts of a system of travel introduced by George Nagelmackers, a Belgian, in 1872. This was the sleeping car of the Cie. Internationale des Wagons Lits. After a slow start during which Nagelmackers had had some difficulty in persuading railway companies to include one of his cars on their trains, the sleeping car idea had taken on. The restaurant car was added to it in 1882. Railway travel, which until then had been regarded as comfortable enough, but which had such inconveniences as passengers having to sit up all night and having either to carry food or fight for attention at railway buffets, was now transformed. Passengers could sit calmly in their sleeping compartment or their first class carriage and wait until they were invited to attend the first or second sitting for lunch or dinner. The restaurant, with its gleaming white tablecloths, its leather padded chairs and walls, and its stuccoed ceiling from which hung miniature chandeliers, echoed the atmosphere of Europe's best hotels. The cuisine was of an equally high standard; although how this was achieved in the constrained quarters allotted to the chef was something of a miracle, and still is on those trains which still carry a top class restaurant service. In the evening, the sleeping compartment would be transformed from its daytime appearance to that of a small bedroom, usually while its occupants were at the evening meal. The attendant would be ever ready to provide drinks and other services for those who wanted to entertain friends. It was a civilised way of travelling and attracted all those who could afford it, including crowned heads, industrial magnates and the better-off Cook's tourists. The most glamorous of these trains was the Orient Express which first left the Gare de L'Est in Paris in 1883 after a send off which the fashionable world of Paris attended, as well as the curiosity-driven public.

In their eagerness to provide for the ever-increasing number of their passengers and their needs, the Cooks became involved in more and more enterprises, extending their organisation 'wider still and wider' both geographically and in the range of its services. Printing had always been an activity that interested the Cooks, and it now grew into publishing. Guide books poured out, on Italy, Florence, Rome, Venice, Holland, Switzerland, France, the French Riviera, Paris, Scandinavia, Sydney, India, Palestine, Algeria, Tunisia, Burma, New Zealand, and even Iceland. Although preferring to remain an agent for other companies, the Cooks were sometimes obliged to take on the role of principal, as they did in Egypt where they actually owned the Nile fleet. One of their most unexpected acquisitions was that of the Vesuvius Railway, which took tourists up the volcano. There was great difficulties in operating this line, arising mainly out of the opposition of the men who had earned a living by carrying people to the top in sedan chairs and who saw the railway as a threat to their livelihood. The men had demanded that every passenger carried on the railway should pay a tax in compensation, and the original owners of the railway had agreed to this. John Mason Cook was made of sterner stuff and refused to give way to what he considered extortionate blackmail. War was declared, with the Vesuvius men damaging the railway, throwing the carriages down the volcano and setting fire to the station. Cook's answer was to keep his tourists away from Vesuvius until he succeeded in convincing the local 'brigands' that by allowing the railway to operate peacefully they could profit in other ways from the tourists who travelled on it.

Despite their interest in distinguished customers, the Cooks did not neglect less favoured tourists. Indeed, in the 1890s cheap tours were intensified; there were Circular tickets to Spain and Portugal from 10 guineas, a 15 guinea voyage on the Currie Line to the Canary Islands and Madeira, and the now long-established excursions to British

While the Empire called its sons to its distant outposts, others only dipped their toes into the waves which were ruled by Britannia.

watering places and seaside resorts.

In the nineties, the bicycle – which had been considered improper for ladies to ride – became the vehicle on which they began their determined but unsteady charge towards emancipation. Thousands of them took to the wheel and, accompanied by male companions, began to tour Britain and then the Continent on cycling parties. For the sake of propriety a cycling dress was designed which comprised a coat which 'gracefully defined the figure' and knickerbockers which discreetly concealed their legs. Others wore a divided skirt, 'the skirt having a very wide side wrap so that no possible peep at the knickerbockers can be obtained'. Another solution to the modesty problem was to weigh the skirt down. The Cooks lent their support to the new craze; they had always championed the rights of women to travel, encouraging single ladies to join their parties, and now here was another opportunity to support their female customers and incidentally increase their business.

The first cycling parties took place in Normandy and Brittany and 'ladies accompanied by a relative or friend' were invited to join the parties which would cycle 20 to 50 miles a day, still finding time to eat three meals a day. Cycling tours were carried on in a dignified and gracious way, for the Cooks offered to arrange for heavy luggage to be forwarded to each of the daily destinations. After Brittany the cycling tours became more ambitious. Italy, Switzerland, Belgium, Holland and France soon became accustomed to the sight of the English tourist pedalling up hill and down dale, through towns and villages, adding to the legends of the British abroad.

COOK'S
VESUVIUS
RAILWAY

During this very active decade the company lost both its leaders. Thomas Cook died on 9th July, 1892. *The Times* wrote of him:

'The late Mr Thomas Cook who died on Monday night at Leicester in his 84th year was a typical middle class nineteenth-century Englishman. Starting from small beginnings, he had the good luck and the insight to discover a want, and to provide for it'.

Referring to John Mason's part in building up the company, the editorial said,

'They have organised travel as it was never organised before, they have their reward in the enormous increase in the number of travellers, of whom so many come to them for help. Much credit is due to the late Mr Thomas Cook, the founder, and to his son, the consolidator of the business – the Julius and the Augustus of modern travel. They have applied the resources of civilisation to a very general modern need, and for this they deserve and obtain full recognition'.

The praise was grudging however, for *The Times* represented a class who had been obliged to accept the self-made people like the Cooks, but who did not welcome them. The editorial continues:

'The world is not altogether reformed by cheap tours, nor is the inherent vulgarity of the British Philistine going to be eradicated by sending him with a through ticket and a bundle of hotel coupons to Egypt and the Holy Land. Sometimes, indeed, the only effect of such a tour is to noise that vulgarity abroad, and to make the average Englishman even less beloved than he is at present by foreign nations. If only Messrs Cook could guarantee a benefit to mind and manners as easily as they can guarantee a comfortable journey! But this unfortunately, is beyond their skill'.

After his father's death, John Mason carried on with redoubled energy as if he too could feel 'time's winged chariot hurrying near'. The existing correspondence of the period shows him answering scores of charitable appeals. The British and Foreign Sailors' Society, a home for blind people at Leicester, the Hackney and East Middlesex Band of Hope Union, the Dave Row Sunday and Ragged School Junior Band of Hope, the Academy of Music for the Blind, the Anglo Indian Temperance Society, Jaffa schools, and a number of charitable institutions for railway workers all received his help. At the same time he examined a variety of business ventures, from the import of ostrich feathers from the Sudan to the buying of Brighton's Marine and Palace Piers. He also found time to persuade the Thames Conservancy to install lavatories at some of the locks.

After his trip to the Middle East in 1898 to superintend the arrangements for the Kaiser's tour he fell ill and retired to his recently-acquired home, Mount Felix, at Walton-on-Thames. In this magnificent house, in the coach house of which were the new brougham, landau and Victoria coaches for which he had paid over £400, John Mason wrote:

'Thus ended my public career as a Personal Conductor, which commenced in 1844, as a small boy with a long wand assisting the guidance of 500 other small children

One of the strangest acquisitions of John Mason Cook was the Vesuvius Railway. He had to e firm with sabo- eurs when he took ver its operation, ut he made it safe nough for even Edward VII (seen at he lower station in his picture).

149

from Leicester to Syston by special train five miles; then two miles across the fields to the Mount Sorrel Hills for an afternoon picnic, and back the same route to Leicester. Since then I have taken part in conducting almost all classes and conditions of people to all the chief parts of the globe, and I think I may fairly claim to be satisfied with concluding such a career with the German Emperor in Palestine'.

John Mason died in 1899 at the age of 64, and was buried in Leicester next to the father whom he had loved and struggled with throughout his life. Together these two men had helped change the face of British Society, not by their acts of charity, but by the introduction of a new concept of freedom in leisure. Their work received little real acclaim, and still does not. Few people even considered the difficulties of their vocation; only Jerome K Jerome, describing a meeting with a nameless tourist agent in the 'Diary of a Pilgrimage' takes time to consider the arduous nature of his work.

'We travelled from Oberammergau with a tourist agent, and he told us all his troubles. It seems that a tourist agent is an ordinary human man, and has feelings just like we have. This has never occurred to me before. I told him so. "No," he replied "It never does occur to you tourists. You treat us as if we were mere Providence, or even the Government itself. If all goes well, you say, what is the good of us, contemptuously; and if things go wrong, you say what is the good of us, indignantly. I work sixteen hours a day to fix things comfortably for you and you cannot even look satisfied: while if a train is late, or a hotel proprietor overcharges, you come and bully me about it. If I see after you, you mutter that I am officious; and if I leave you alone, you grumble that I am neglectful. You swoop down in your hundreds upon a tiny village like Oberammergau without ever letting us know you are coming, and then threaten to write to *The Times* because there is not a suite of apartments and a hot dinner ready for each of you. You want the best lodgings in the place, and then, when at tremendous cost of trouble, they have been obtained for you, you object to the price asked for them. You all try to palm youselves off for dukes and duchesses travelling in disguise" '.

Since it was the Cooks who had the sole agency for the Oberammergau Passion play, it is possible that the unknown excursion agent was one of them, or at least one of their couriers. At any rate, the discretion usual to the Cooks and their care not to upset their customers would accord with the anonymity of Jerome's tourist agent. As the century came to a close the burdens of the excursion agents, laid on them by a new class of travellers on the fringes of the middle class, became more acute.

'I must candidly confess' [says Jerome] 'that the English-speaking people one meets with on the Continent are, taken as a whole, a most disagreeable contingent. One hardly ever hears the English Language spoken on the Continent without hearing grumbling and sneering. The women are the most objectionable. Foreigners undoubtedly see the very poorest specimens of the female kind we Anglo-Saxons have to show. The average female English or American Tourist is rude and self-assertive, while at the same time, ridiculously helpless and awkward. She is intensely selfish, utterly inconsiderate of others; everlastingly complaining, and, in herself, drearily uninteresting'.

The tourist of the 1890s was, it seems, no different from the tourist who had so offended the susceptibilities of O'Dowd forty years earlier. Perhaps it was not so much the quality of the tourist which remained constant as the relationship between the established traveller and the tenderfoot who was venturing abroad for the first time and whose numbers, ever increasing, were threatening all those places which had become popular with those at one remove on the ladder of society.

All Europe was open to tourists who travelled by coach, car or ferry on Thomas Cook's tours.

151

14 The new century

In the period that lies between the death of Queen Victoria and the Great War, society, which had been in the process of evolution since the beginning of the Industrial Revolution had in some sections, the middle classes, become hierarchic with divisions and sub-divisions jealously guarded by those who belonged to them against trespass by those lower down. Snobbery was rampant among the upper levels while the lower middle strata kept a watchful and critical eye on each other and on everyone else. Everyone except the working class who didn't care and the upper class who were above that kind of thing, was hanging perilously to their rung of the social ladder and waiting for an opportunity to place their feet on the one above. The reason for this kind of behaviour, was that society was again undergoing a profound change, and those who had achieved middle class status feared that the change would sweep away all the privileges which they enjoyed.

For the upper middle classes who controlled Parliament, commerce and law and who were accustomed to standards of life made possible only by the vast numbers of under-paid workers and servants, the new socialist ideas and the growth of trade unionism were as disturbing as the agitation for female suffrage. For the lower middles the increasing militancy of the working class and its threat to the established order seemed like the hot breath of competition panting at the area gates of the houses which stretched in unending terraces in the suburbs of all the great cities.

The anxiety, expressed by a growing intolerance and chauvinism was added to by the new and outrageous ideas aired by writers and artists. Fortunately, for the peace of mind of most of people, the theories of Einstein who had just begun his work on rela-tivity, or Freud who had just written The Psychopathology of Everyday Life were little known at the time. In normal human fashion most people pretended that nothing was happening and that life would go on forever in the way that they imagined it to be. And none more so than the Cooks' tourists. The Cooks had by now perfected the illusory world of travel in which everything was exactly, or as near as possible, what it should be, and for their travellers there was unending deference and attention to every detail concerned with a customer's comfort. The words of their advertisements sum it all up. 'The main object of a Conducted Tour, apart from the advantage of being able to calculate the exact cost before starting, is to enhance the enjoyment by relieving the travellers of all the petty troubles and annoyances inseparable from a journey one of which may be said to be never absent in the quasi-conducted tours so frequently advertised in these days, viz. the incessant call for the payment of extras . . . '. Clearly, although the Cooks' customers expected every service due to ladies and gentlemen they were also concerned about getting it at the lowest possible price, and the Cooks saw that they did.

On the Nile steamers, of which there were seven, cabins had electric light and electric bells for calling the servants, windows with sliding glass, venetian blinds and wire gauze to discourage such petty annoyances as mosquitoes and insects, and the linen was changed daily. The bathroom had hot and cold water, there was a deck lounge and a dining room at which the best table was kept by a first class chef who drew the raw

The Alps were tunnelled through to make a
passage for the trains, roads encouraged the more
intrepid motorists and motor charabancs took
tourists on excursions round the cities.

materials for his dishes from a refrigerated room and, most important of all, there was a 'liberally maintained cellar of wines' for the passengers' comfort. On cruise ships there were Cooks' representatives in attendance; at ports and railway stations the ubiquitous man from Cooks stood ready to help. Aware that travellers could also be found among members of the middle classes who, while not able to afford what their betters enjoyed nevertheless wanted to copy their habits, the Cooks instituted a series of Popular tours. In Egypt these took the form of Express tours from Cairo to Assouan which took one week instead of the three normally allotted, and cost only £22.

On the Continent of Europe the tours to Switzerland cost from 5 guineas for one week at Lucerne or Geneva; to Rome for 10 guineas and to the Italian Lakes for 29 guineas for two weeks. The new centre of fashion with its 'fast' reputation, the Côte d'Azur and Monte Carlo, was not forgotten either and, in the season which stretched through winter and spring, unlike today when summer is the most popular time, there were tours to Nice, Mentone and Monte Carlo. At the former all the festivities of the season

were listed in order to encourage travellers. In the January *Travellers' Gazette* of 1905 we read that events began on February 5 with the Automobile week and parades along the Promenade des Anglais, then came the Annual Lawn tennis tournament. King Carnival arrived on February 23, and on the 26th there was the procession of Masks, followed on the 28th by the first of three Battles of Flowers. More tennis, International Regattas, Flower fetes, Childrens' fetes chased each other through the season providing visitors with a new, but inadmissisble, motive for holidays which was simply pleasure.

At the same time as they were promoting the established resorts the Cooks were searching for new places to develop, and it is interesting to note that in 1905 there appears the first mention of the Balearic Islands which, they note with regret, 'have certainly not received that attention from the winter and spring traveller which their scenic and climatic attraction would seem to entitle them to. Palma, the capital of the group, is easily reached from Marseilles and, now that it possesses a first class hotel, the

"Grand" opened a year or two ago, we have decided to tempt the tourist to try this comparatively unknown field . . . '.

Other spheres of fresh activity were provided by the new means of transport, and chief among these was the motor car which aroused the deepest feelings of partisanship. As eighty years before with the railways, the motor car divided the country into two camps, those who saw in it a symbol of progress and freedom and those who identified it as a destroyer of the *status quo*. Among the former were the Cooks who first announced in 1903 that they could arrange motoring tours at home or abroad. They described the pleasures of this new method of transport enthusiastically. 'There can be no doubt about the growing popularity of motoring,' remarked *The Excursionist*, which now suddenly changed its name to *The Travellers' Gazette* in deference to the higher social status of its readers. 'It is unquestionably a pleasurable mode of locomotion, and, when rationally indulged in, is an excellent method of travel for making the acquaintance of these islands'.

The Cooks were simply identifying themselves with a new development which they realised could become commercially viable for them. Among pioneers in the new activity of motoring were women, who seized on the car, as they had on the bicycle, as a symbol of their emancipation. A magazine called *The New Travellers*, on the board of which was the Countess of Drogheda, expressed the new devil-may-care spirit which women were defiantly adopting. 'There are actually people living today who are so benighted as to call motoring "a nasty, smelly, dangerous pastime". Isn't it quaint, and so old fashioned?' *The New Travellers'* woman writer asked. Such a favourable view of the motor car, apart from the fact that she had expressed any views about it at all, must have shocked her contemporaries. But the lady was not content to leave things at that. She declared that motoring was like that other pastime which so many people regard as reprehensible: gambling at Monte Carlo and, to make matters worse, she encouraged all her readers to join her in a smart woman's favourite sport of 'bobby baiting'.

The little war against the police resulted from the incompatibility of the laws regarding road traffic and the growing speed of the motor car, and it certainly added to the thrill of driving. Police traps, with bobbies lurking in ditches and hedges, pursuit and capture, even prison, were among the hazards of the new sport. The motorists' bid to outwit the police led to the formation of a protective society, the Automobile Association, whose patrol men warned member motorists of police activity by the simple expedient of not saluting them.

Motoring was only one of the many sporting activities which women were taking up with such energy and, to some, such lack of decorum. Another which women took to in order to show they were no longer on the pedestal on which the Victorian male preferred to preserve them was winter sports. The numbers who engaged in this form of sport in the early years of the twentieth century was small however, for the pioneer work in developing skiing techniques done by Richardson, Caulfield and Arnold Lunn had not yet popularised the sport. In the 1880s, Switzerland in winter had been considered a place where only invalids or devoted mountain lovers were to be encountered and its adoption by the tourist did not begin until the 1890s, when a boom in the building of mountain railways and the accessibility of the mountains led to the building of winter resorts where visitors could be provided with those amenities they considered essential.

By the turn of the century this development had grown to a considerable extent, turning into a reality the fears expressed by such devotees of the silence and emptiness of the mountains as Leslie Stephen who had rejoiced twenty years earlier that some

THE NILE IS EGYPT

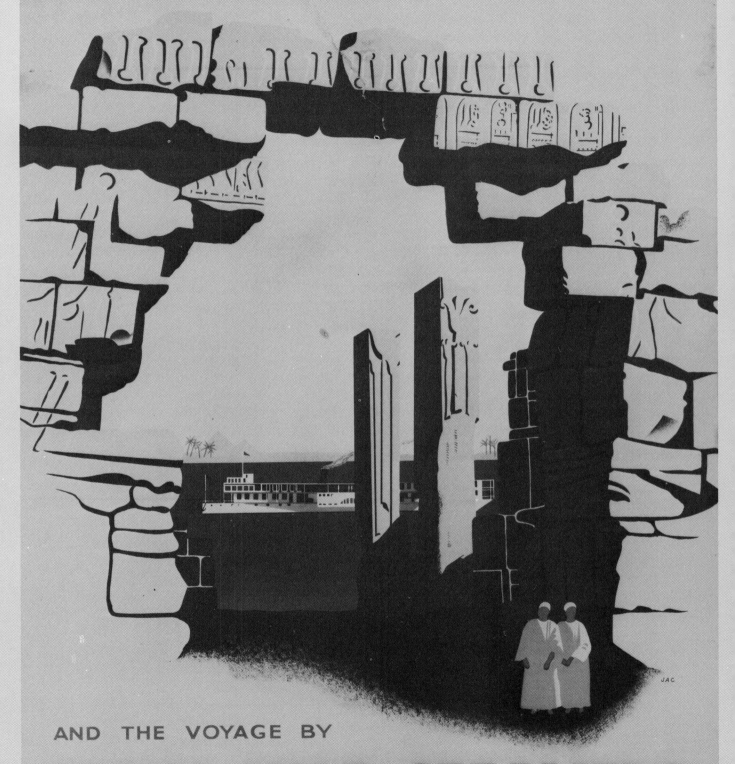

AND THE VOYAGE BY

COOKS NILE STEAMERS

Emancipated women grasped at the freedom
from social pressure offered by holidays abroad.
They defied much censure and took up skiing and
sledding and revealed more than their ankles as
they stumbled up glaciers.

161 - Course de Skis pour dames - L'Arri ee

Swiss valleys had still not 'bowed the knee to Baal' in the shape of Cooks customers. Not unnaturally the Swiss resorts now had to follow the pattern set by Monte Carlo and Nice, and luxury and entertainment became the aim of all those which wanted to achieve popularity. Despite the older type of Alpine visitors' regret at the passing of simplicity and absence of affectation the Swiss resorts began to fill with visitors bent on pleasure.

St Moritz became the centre of the social life of the winter tourists; hotels sprang up and provided the standards of accommodation food and service which the visitor now demanded and the evenings were filled with dances, galas and concerts. During the day tobogganing, skating and sleigh rides occupied those with sporting inclinations while others merely strolled about, sat on terraces admiring the views or watched their more active companions. While some, very few, and, among them, women as well as men, climbed laboriously up snow covered slopes in order to enjoy the thrills and spills of the new sport of skiing. The Cook's customers who represented the more conservative sections of the middle class were more inclined however to visit the less fashionable, and cheaper, resorts.

In *The Travellers' Gazette* of 1905 we find a description of a holiday at the Bear Hotel Grindelwald. 'We were all very glad to receive a warm welcome from our host, and a cup of tea, as English as possible, was a boon to the tired and weary traveller'. After lunch the visitors devoted themselves to the toboggan runs where things were especially lively on a Sunday afternoon with 'everybody on toboggans – old men and maidens, young men and babies'.

In the hotel there were log fires blazing and everything was 'so arranged that English people are enabled to obtain every home comfort'. The pleasures of St Moritz were not required by the visitors to Grindelwald according to the writer of this report who goes out of his way to point out the defects of the Engadine. 'In the Engadine the pleasure is marred to some extent by the host of invalids one meets at every turn whose daring feats in skating and tobogganing have been too much for their frail bodies . . . ' With that irresistible urge to decry the resorts which he cannot afford to visit, a tendency still in evidence today among some tourists, the writer continues. 'The halls here do not resound with the coughs of the consumptive'.

With the founding of the Davos English Ski Club and the Ski Club of Great Britain at the beginning of the decade the sport of skiing began to get under way and provided excitement to those Edwardians who sought a means of expressing feelings which the formal society of the day preferred not to see openly displayed. Even the Cooks were carried away by the physical joys of winter sports when they wrote. 'Winter sport exhilarates and rejuvenates; it generates a glow of pleasure in the mind which acts powerfully upon the whole physical organisation, while all the time the nerves and muscles are directly braced up by the keen dry air, tempered by bright general sunshine. The exercises are extremely elating, whether gracefully gliding over level surfaces of ice, or rushing down the snow slopes at express speed with just the qualifying spice of uncertainty to add piquancy to the sensation'.

This open appeal to the delights of the senses although related in the first place to the 'pleasures of the mind' reveals a change occurring in social attitudes. The physical side of life, for so long banished from the idealised life of respectable people, was beginning to force its way through the weaknesses in the solid layer of social form that covered it. This applied in particular to women who, ceasing to be housebound angels, were demonstrating their capacity and desire for enjoyment of activities for which, it had hitherto been assumed, they had neither the interest nor the inclination. They went on Cook's tours unaccompanied, they climbed the Swiss mountains, they rode on bicycles, they played tennis and they even spoke to strange men without a formal introduction.

There were, of course, plenty of people who were aghast at what was going on, one of these was Mrs Humphrey one of those ladies who take it upon themselves to lay down the rules of etiquette. Finding perhaps that her advice is falling on deaf ears where the women are concerned she addresses the men in a book of manners published in 1898, and warns them of girls who will talk to men of whom they know nothing, pointing out that these chance acquaintances are most likely to occur at the seaside or on a bicycling tour. Although Mrs Humphrey blamed the lower middle classes for the loose behaviour that she described, in fact, a more familiar attitude between the sexes was also prevalent in the upper middle class, who however were more constrained by their social attitudes, and who more than anyone else found in foreign travel the opportunity to escape the inhibitions of life at home.

Much of the more relaxed attitude came perhaps from America, imported by the tourists who brought their mid-western accents, their dollars and their sons and daughters on European visits. Despised by the upper middle class for their so-called vulgarity, but really envied for their wealth and, perhaps, their supreme self confidence, the American tourist became the butt of cartoonists' jokes but also a power in the resorts where holidaymakers congregated. Certainly they were essential to the growth of the transatlantic tourist business and to the transatlantic steamship lines which competed for their patronage with luxurious ships like the *Mauretania*, the *Lusitania* and the *Titanic*.

Life on board ship with its self-contained world where status was quickly established and acquaintanceship made without formality lent itself admirably to a more relaxed relationship between the sexes, as long as they belonged to the same class. Cruises therefore flourished and these were offered in a variety of forms: there were the ships chartered by the Cooks such as the P & O *Vestris* a steam yacht which visited Sicily, Greece, Syria, the Holy Land and Naples on a 28 day cruise costing 25 guineas; and there were trips on the regular runs of such lines as the Orient, Moss, Papayanni, John Hall and Messageries Maritimes which operated in the Mediterranean.

Other aspects of behaviour also became more open during this period and became the subject of more serious concern than that of Mrs Humphrey. The brothels and cabarets of big cities and their concomitant the white slave trade aroused a fierce denunciation by reformers, but received little notice from the middle class press other than an occasional law report on the apprehension of men who kept disorderly houses. Egypt was renowned, and continued to be renowned until its independence, for its erotic entertainments and some evidence of what took place remains in a book dramatically entitled 'Anti-Christ in Egypt' by W N Willis:

'Tourists young and old go to Egypt to "do" the Pyramids, Tombs, the wells . . . But they scarcely ever leave the land of the Pharoahs without seeing the abomination of all humanity, Ibrim Gharhi . . . a painted, perfumed, bejewelled pervert surrounded by his court of prostitutes and fanned by two handsome youths from the Upper Soudan dressed in gawdy raiment like women'.

Ibrim Gharhi was, it seems, the 'godfather' of the Wazzak Bazaar, and the entertainment that this quarter offered was under his care. Visiting Ibrim's tourist entertainments seems to have been as much a 'must' for visiting male tourists as the night club

Suez was the door to the Empire of the East and Egypt the springboard to the dream of a Cairo to the Cape Imperial corridor. Besides, the climate was perfect in winter, so the tourists arrived in ever growing numbers.

tour was in Paris. In Egypt, however, there were two tours, one during the afternoon which the more daring ladies could attend, and another in the evening which was touted for by the charming guides who flattered the ladies and also knew the requirements of the gentlemen. 'Nice girl tonight. Very good show: quite de prize. Nothing wrong, only de sights of the East. All are fine ladies, oh very good', went the patter, an assignment was made for an hour when the ladies of the party would be preparing to retire to bed.

Visits to hashish dens were also a tourist attraction, as were the *café dansants* where everyone went, much as they might have done to the night clubs of Paris, and where officers and officials could be seen tangoing until the early hours. A more respectable gaiety was available for men with their wives and daughters at Shepheard's Hotel where 'society' met and danced and flirted. Those who patronised the places of entertainment were, however, a small number of the minority who took tours abroad. Nevertheless, it was the influx of visitors seeking amusement and freed from the moral codes of their home environment which encouraged the creation of the centres of vice. As today the motivation behind them was a commercial one, and they were probably patronised in most cases simply because they were there.

For the majority of tourists abroad in the years before the Great War, travel was still more concerned with notions of social status and intellectual improvement than with the attractions of exotic forms of vice, while for those who stayed at home the seaside resort was a place where relaxation, amusement and sea air could be enjoyed by one and all. For both these types of tourists the Cooks and their competitors had plenty to offer, and their efforts to provide for everyone encouraged more people to take a holiday away from home and helped to establish the holiday habit on a national scale.

At the famous Shepheards Hotel in Cairo every whim of the tourist was satisfied and the company was congenial. Like Cook's Nile steamers the hotel provided a refuge from the realities of local life.

15 The Cooks' last trip

The social changes accelerated by the Great War were not very apparent in the society which took Cooks tours abroad. On the contrary it seemed as if the victory over Germany had confirmed their way of life. The pride in Empire became ever stronger, the belief in the unchangeability of the British class system more entrenched, and the affirmation of middle class ascendancy expressed ever more strongly by the tightening of the social rules by which they played their game.

Nowhere was this more evident than abroad. On the Nile steamers, on the shores of the Italian lakes, on the snowy slopes of Switzerland the middle class gathered, the men in their sweaters and blazers in public school or regimental colours, the women with the shingled hair and short skirts which symbolised their emancipation. Outwardly a new generation, in fact these people clung to the forms of a past in which the manners and habits of their class were the norm and the status of their kind of people assured.

So, while society trundled towards the General Strike of 1926 and the Depression of 1929, they isolated themselves in a world where gentility was waited upon by the increasingly unwilling service of others. These tourists were not the jazz age escapists of the Fitzgerald novels, ever seeking new sensations to blot out their sense of insecurity but people whose attitudes were firmly entrenched in a past glory. It was a confused age, however; a world in which Sanders of the River, Bulldog Drummond, and the Forsyte family rubbed shoulders with Bertie Wooster and Christopher Robin and were faintly but disagreeably aware of Lady Chatterley and Sweeney.

In this uncertainty, which grew into a positive lack of confidence and led to the neurotic anxiety of our own day, preservation of the past struggled against the demands of a new society. Among the tourists who travelled with the Cooks, there was a reverence for old stones, irrespective of their merit and an adherence to old attitudes and outworn forms of social behaviour whether or not they were relevant to contemporary society. The Cooks' tours, with their hotels conditioned for generations to provide the needs of English tourists and their steamers and cruise ships reserved for a particular class of passengers, offered the illusion of a stability which was all too evidently disappearing from the real world, and the business flourished.

The surplus of ships after the War provided opportunities for the expansion of sea-going holiday traffic. The Cooks chartered ocean liners for their cruises, the *Homeric* made a Mediterranean cruise, and the *Franconia* began a series of annual world cruises in 1921. Ships other than those specially chartered also carried a large number of the Cooks' customers, and at least half the ships cruising in the Mediterranean had a man from Cooks aboard to provide service and arrange shore excursions.

The Round the World Cruise was followed by another ambitious project in 1922 when the Cooks arranged a Cairo-to-the-Cape tour under the leadership of Sir Alfred Sharpe, the explorer. The Cape-to-Cairo Railway, the dream of Cecil Rhodes, was still incomplete but the journey was accomplished by a combination of rail, river steamer and motor transport. The journey to Egypt was by P & O then the party went by rail to Assouan, steamer to Halfa, and on to Khartoum, safari to Nimule, by motor car to Butiaba and Masindi, steamer to Mamasagali, rail to Jinga and Entebbe, steamer to

11 Décembre 1922

SUNSHINE IS LIFE

Albertville on Lake Tanganyka, rail to Kabalo, steamer to Bukama and then on by rail to the Cape. The trip took seven weeks and cost £1,500. Hunting was included *en route*, but the difficulties that might arise from too much accurate shooting had been foreseen by the Cooks who warned their customers. 'As it will be impossible to carry large quantities of shooting trophies throughout the tour, it will be necessary for members to despatch them direct to England from time to time as opportunity offers'.

Other members of the Cooks' select and distinguished clientele who received special attention were the Indian princes who had a special department set up to serve them. The lengths to which Cooks went to provide for the needs of customers, who were not only enormously wealthy but were politically important personages who helped to maintain British rule in India at a time when a nationalist movement was under way, was prodigious. Entire hotels were hired for them, special trains chartered for their trips around Europe, audiences arranged with important people including the Pope. The amount of money spent was enormous and those among the Cooks' staff who attended to their needs were presented with gold cigarette lighters, watches and other gifts.

The authority of the name of Cooks wherever British people travelled was such that it was not unusual for the firm to become involved in the affairs of the highest people in the land. All these arrangements however were carried out under the greatest secrecy and known only to the Cooks themselves or perhaps to their top managers. All the evidence that remains of what must have been to some extent a cloak and dagger activity of Cooks' managers in the Middle East and East are faint echoes of rumours about secret midnight departures of members of royal families and of governments in danger from the *coups* of their enemies, of mysterious meetings arranged in European capitals, and of unscheduled stops of trains to allow anonymous passengers to board or leave their Pullman sleepers at unusual hours.

One mystery which has been documented by an ex-Cooks man Mr A E Moore, refers to a large crated chest which arrived in London from Constantinople after the Great War. This had been in the possession of the Dutch Legation which, as a neutral in Turkey, had looked after British business interests during 1914-18. The case, formerly believed to have been a safe from the Cooks' Constantinople office, was opened in the presence of Frank Cook and was found to contain, not office files, but jewellery, bank notes, gold coins and some gold and silver ingots.

Since this was not the property of the Cooks and no details about its true owners could be discovered, Frank Cook deposited the box with a firm of Dutch bankers in the City of London. The receipt for this was kept by Cooks in a safe, but during World War II the receipt disappeared. It is possible that the original owners of the property, who perhaps had given their case to the Cooks' Constantinople office for safe keeping before 1914, may have been killed during the war. No-one knows, and the present whereabouts of the case is also a mystery.

Although engaged in providing every kind of travel facility for the upper rungs of the social ladder the Cooks' business still rested on a foundation which included every section of society that travelled. After World War I the trips to France, Switzerland, and Italy recommenced although, unlike their new competitors, who offered cycling tours, camping tours and parties in chalets, the Cooks kept rigidly to the principle of hotel accommodation and first or second class rail travel. Particularly popular were the trips to visit the battlefields where millions of men had died, but which now had a ghoulish fascination for some and the attractions of a pilgrimage to hallowed ground for others. There were a number of trips offered, among them a week at Ostend with excursions to Ypres, Zeebrugge, Bruges, Knocke where the Wilhelm II battery could be examined and to Couckelaere to see the gun known as 'Long Max'. The cost of this tour was £9 10s 6d.

On a tour to Amiens a coach tour was included in order to visit the famous 'Big Bertha' which had shelled Paris. The trip to Arras and the Somme was described in some detail. 'The route traversed (from Amiens to Arras) is most interesting the ground having been continuously fought over throughout the war and for some time it formed practically the front line. Albert, the jumping-off point of two great offensives, the battle of the Somme in 1916 and 1918, and now a mere rubbish heap – the famous Ancre Railway with Aveluy Wood, Thiepval, Harnel, Beaucourt and Miraumont is a devastated region of shellholes and dismantled trees'.

One of the characteristics of the 1920s was the accelerated pace in living, epitomised by the new dances imported from America and known by such exciting and, to British society at any rate, such outlandish names as the Shimmy, the Bunny hug, the Black Bottom and the Charleston. Speed was the new god, exciting, adventurous, the ultimate in escapism, or progress, depending on the point of view, and those who dealt in speed were the heroes and heroines of the age. It was in the 1920s that the motor car reached the incredible speed of 200 miles an hour (in 1927, a Sunbeam driven by H Segrave). It was also in the 1920s that a Supermarine S.5 piloted by Flight Lieutenant Webster reached an airspeed of 281.68 mph. Railways were travelling at over 100 mph and ocean liners ploughed their way across the Atlantic in just over four days.

It was flight that captured the public's imagination more than anything else and stories of the achievements of Alcock and Brown, of James Mollison, Amy Johnson, Charles Kingsford Smith and the greatest hero of them all, Charles Lindbergh, filled the daily papers during this and the following decade. For the public, flight was something dangerous as well as exciting and it was essential for those involved in the business of travel to woo them gently into this new method of transport. The Cooks, quick off the mark after the war, published their first flying brochure in 1919 and the editorial both excited and reassured the prospective customer.

'The Handley Page is the largest aeroplane in existence and probably the most widely known of machines. Built as a night bomber to fly long distances it was designed mainly with a view to safety and reliability . . . It is not a high speed aeroplane, its maximum being about 100 miles an hour and its average speed between sixty-five and seventy miles. Neither is it a "stunt" machine. The ailerons and rudders not being dimensioned for trick flying it is impossible for the pilot to loop or perform any other spectacular but useless and dangerous stunts'.

In 1924 the Imperial Airways Co was formed and operated out of Croydon to Europe and later to India but there was plenty of competition and the Cooks offered all the air companies to their customers: London to Paris for £10 return was available through Imperial Airways, Air Union, or the Cie. Messageries Aeriennes, which also offered aerial trips over the battlefields. Even London to Moscow was possible by a combination of air services provided by Imperial Airways, Deutscher Aero Lloyd and Deutsche Russische Luftvekhers Gesellschaft. Running an airline became as widespread as running a railway had been in the nineteenth century. There was the Cie Franco Roumaine de Navigation Aerienne with services to Warsaw, the Cie. Generale des Entreprises Aeronautiques to Casablanca and companies such as the Handley Page Transport Ltd.,

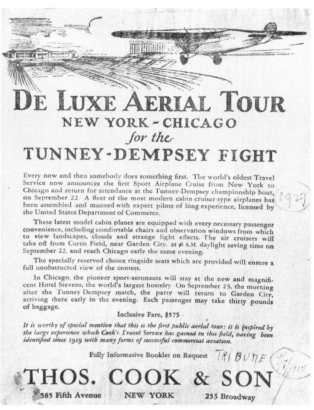

World War I dealt a damaging blow to the society which had made tourism its recreation, but it brought in a new form of transport which would later introduce a different section of society to the delights of tourism.

Aircraft Transport and Travel Co., Grahame White Aviation Co. Ltd. and North Sea Aerial Navigation Co. which hired out their aircraft to parties of four, ten or more individuals.

To encourage air travellers special tea flights were operated from Croydon airport and nervous passengers would be regaled with India or China tea and cucumber sandwiches as they floated over the Tower and the Houses of Parliament. Heavier-than-air craft were not the only new means of aerial travel, for Count Zeppelin had launched his great airship and regular trips across the Atlantic were started providing comfort impossible in an aeroplane. The Cooks supported the Graf Zeppelin service advertising a trip to Brazil with connecting service to Buenos Aires and announcing a service to North America in $2\frac{1}{2}$ days. Later disasters and the improvement in long distance aircraft were to put a stop to this line of experimentation, and the flying boat concept was also to become obsolete as airfields were built all over the world, to accommodate new long distance aircraft.

Throughout the decade the Cooks' Empire continued to expand with offices in America, the East and Far East, Africa and the hotels that accepted Cooks' coupons ran into thousands. Over all this reigned the two remaining Cook brothers Frank, who like his father devoted himself to the meticulous care of the tour business, and Ernest, who looked after the banking side, (Tom had earlier left the business after his father's

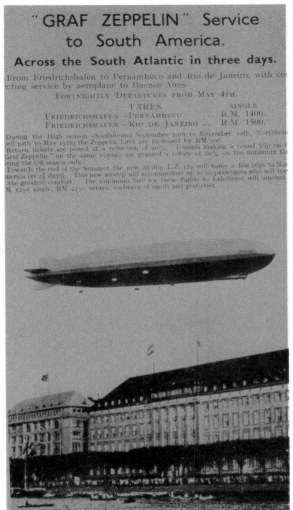

death). The staff saw them but little, and the stairs to the floor from where they ruled their kingdom was guarded by one or sometimes two men in Cook's uniform. To the people who worked for Cooks and to its customers the world-wide organisation was as permanent and immutable as the British Empire itself. The structure and the operations of the company were along the more or less military lines which prevailed in all the national institutions whether they represented education, religion, charity, business and even in the home.

A retired member of the staff who joined in 1904 remembers that every member was obliged to furnish a guarantee of integrity in the form of a bond for £100 for the lowest grade and more if the new employee was applying for a higher rank. Marriage without permission of the management was not allowed under the age of 27. Everyone was obliged to learn to type and take shorthand, (female typists did not become acceptable in business until just before the Great War), dress was strictly controlled, and the juniors had the job of fetching the bucket of coal for the fire and buying the buns for afternoon tea.

The main business of the Cooks was the issue of rail tickets, a complicated business as each of the hundreds of railway companies throughout Europe and the rest of the world continued to issue separate tickets. Cooks' ability to issue a through ticket or a book of tickets was, therefore, a boon to travellers. Similarly with hotels; since Cooks

171

were the only agents for thousands of hotels overseas, the public turned to them when they needed accommodation. For this work the Cooks collected money in advance from their customers and, since the payment for fares and rooms did not have to be made until the passenger had made use of the facilities, there were always liquid assets which could be invested to increase the profits. The money collected for travel cheques was employed in a similar manner and represents a profitable aspect of this business to this day. The service was highly individual with small groups travelling all over Europe and accompanied by a Cooks travelling representative of whom there were many.

In the twenties however, the pressure of change in British society began to be felt; pensions, paid holidays, women staff, and lower middle and working class demand for foreign travel brought about a revolutionary change in the travel business. But before the changes had really begun to take effect, and before the great Depression and the Second World War, which broke the power of the middle classes on which Cooks had come to depend, Frank and Ernest Cook had come to the end of their journey as the captains of the Cook organisation. The announcement of their retirement was unobtrusive and appeared only once in the editorial columns of the March issue of *The Travellers' Gazette* of 1928.

> 'In view of the many rumours and unofficial paragraphs in the press relating to the fusion of interest that has recently taken place between us and the Compagnie Internationale des Wagons Lits we reprint the following official statement which appeared in *The Times* and other leading newspapers in Great Britain signed by Mr F H Cook and Lord Dalziel. "A fusion of interests has been arranged between Thomas Cook & Son, Thomas Cook & Son Ltd., and its associated companies, including Thomas Cook & Son (Bankers) Ltd., and the Compagnie Internationale des Wagons Lits will join the boards of Thomas Cook & Son Ltd, and Thomas Cook & Son (Bankers) Ltd., as vice chairman, and Mr Frank Henry Cook will continue to be chairman of both the Cook companies" '.

The fusion of interests was merely a fiction in order to get through the business of transferring public loyalty and, in fact, Ernest Cook retired immediately and was followed by Frank Cook who held the chairmanship only a few months. Information about the sum paid for the vast world wide organisation which had started with a shilling excursion for Temperance workers is not available but the new company began with a share capital of £2,000,000.

A few years later on Christmas day 1931 Frank Cook died at his home, Barnet Hill, Wonersh. Only Ernest remained of the travelling Cooks and he retired into a quiet anonymity at Bath. He was a rich man, however, and he now devoted the rest of his life to a collection of works of art and to the preservation of great British estates. His interest in buildings had perhaps been awakened by his contact with the architecture of the Renaissance and there is a story of his enthusiasm for the baroque style leading him to cap one of the Cooks buildings, the one at Pall Mall, with a dome.

His interest in buying paintings began in 1927 when the Holford collection was sold at Christies and he spent £90,000 in acquiring some of the pictures. During the next ten years the Ernest Cook collection was built up with works by Claud Lorain, G B Tiepolo, Stubbs, Guardi, Turner, Raeburn, Reynolds and many others. At the same time Ernest Cook began to acquire properties in order to preserve buildings of historic value. Montacute was bought and presented to the National Trust in 1931, and so were the Bath Assembly Rooms. In 1935 Trent Manor near Sherborne became part of the Ernest Cook Estates, then came Hartwell House, Dalby Hall, and Broughton Place. During the War and after it, more estates were added, most of them intended for the National Trust to the funds of which he donated £100,000.

All his contributions to the preservation of historic monuments and to the various funds to which he provided financial assistance were made unobtrusively; to such an extent that when the Queen Mother wanted to thank the donor of £100,000 to a fund for retired District Nurses in which she was deeply interested, she had some difficulty in discovering that it was Ernest Cook. The grandchild of Thomas Cook, the publisher and publicist of excursions, was a very different man from his grandfather and his father, but perhaps he achieved Thomas Cook's ambition to serve society in an unexpected way.

Thomas had visions of a brave new world which would open up a new and more enlightened life for everyone through the medium of travel. Ernest, by his collection of paintings of British artists and his help in the preservation of historic buildings returned to the nation some of its heritage. Moreover, the Ernest Cook Trust, which owns over 15,000 acres, enables many boys to be educated at schools which they could otherwise not afford and through which they may have access to that Utopian World of which Thomas Cook had dreamt.

Italian Riviera by Flying Boat

DEPARTURES FROM SOUTHAMPTON EVERY SATURDAY AND SUNDAY FROM JUNE 4 TO SEPTEMBER 18

These specimen fares are based on minimum-grade hotel accommodation. Full details regarding accommodation of superior grades will be given on application to any of our offices.

An Aquila Airways Flying Boat

Tour J.226

	8 days' holiday (7 nights at resort) £ s. d.	15 days' holiday (14 nights at resort) £ s. d.
Bordighera	43 6 0	51 15 0
Ospedaletti	44 13 0	54 6 0
San Remo	43 13 6	52 3 0
Nervi	43 7 0	52 7 6
Santa Margherita	46 11 0	59 18 0
Rapallo	43 2 6	53 0 0
Sestri Levante	48 0 0	62 18 0
Viareggio	42 4 0	51 2 0

THE CHARGES INCLUDE: Travel tickets Southampton to Genoa or Santa Margherita and back by flying boat; full board accommodation at hotel including gratuities and taxes; conveyance of passenger and hand-baggage from flying boat to hotel at resort and back (travel tickets 3rd class by rail are provided between Genoa or Santa Margherita and Bordighera, Ospedaletti or San Remo).

Alassio

Alassio Tour J.229

8 days' Holiday £25 15 0

15 days' Holiday £34 17 0

DEPARTURES FROM LONDON:
BY RAIL (via the short sea route and Vintimille)
EVERY SATURDAY FROM MAY 21 TO SEPTEMBER 24 (see page 4)
BY TOURIST NIGHT AIR SERVICE TO NICE—Daily from May 1

With its gently shelving, sandy beach, five miles of plage, modern entertainment and delightful setting by the blue Mediterranean, Alassio is one of the most popular of the smaller resorts of Italy. From a point at the eastern end of the Gulf of Genoa, protected by a circle of olive-covered hills on the north, it commands wide views of the glorious Ligurian coast, and is within reach of the San Remo golf course.

BY RAIL (3rd class)		CHOICE OF HOTELS	BY TOURIST NIGHT AIR SERVICE		Daily high season charges	PERIOD		OPTIONAL SUPPLEMENTS:
8 days' holiday (5 nights at resort) £ s. d.	15 days' holiday (12 nights at resort) £ s. d.		8 days' holiday (7 nights at resort) £ s. d.	15 days' holiday (14 nights at resort) £ s. d.	s. d.	From	To	
25 15 0	34 17 0	PENSION EDEN	42 19 0	52 1 0	14 0	June 20 to September 10		1st class on steamers, 2nd class rail
26 2 0	35 12 0	PENSION SAN ROSSORE	43 8 6	52 18 6	9 0	July 1 to September 13		£6 4 8
27 19 0	37 4 0	VILLA IDEALE	45 19 6	54 14 0	12 6	July 1 to August 31		1st class travel throughout, £11 11 4
29 2 6	43 10 6	BEAU SEJOUR	47 11 6	61 19 6	11 0	June 15 to September 15		By AIR to Nice, by tourist day service direct, £4 9 6
30 10 6	46 16 6	EUROPA AND CONCORDIA	49 10 6	65 16 6	7 0	July 1 to September 13		by tourist day service (via Paris), £2 9 0

Arrangements can also be made to travel by General Steam Navigation Co.'s *Royal Daffodil* from Gravesend or Southend-on-Sea to Boulogne on Saturdays from July 2 to September 10. Full details will be given on application.
For meals en route, itinerary, what the charges include, etc. please see pages 4 and 5.

16 The competitors

The dominance achieved by the Cooks in the business of travel at the end of the nineteenth century was not accidental nor had it been arrived at without competition. Even in the earliest days, when excursions to the seaside resorts and the spas marked the limit of its possibilities, the excursion business had attracted other men with initiative and imagination. All these early ventures were localised however, owing to the limited nature of communications, and competition on a national scale did not arrive until the Cooks moved to London in 1865. Nevertheless, competition, though Cook was perhaps unaware of it, did exist.

One of the more ambitious travel promoters, who was a contemporary of Thomas Cook, was Joseph Crisp of Liverpool. As early as 1844 Crisp made an agreement with the Grand Junction and London and Birmingham railways, probably the first of its kind, by which he was given a 5 per cent commission on traffic introduced by him, and an advertising subsidy of £100. Crisp's business was evidently successful and there is a record of group business, including a party of Orangemen who travelled from Liverpool to a meeting at Manchester on July 12, 1848. Like so many travel entrepreneurs, Crisp became ambitious and started to set up schemes for travel abroad before he had sufficient support. A trip to Paris via London, Southampton and Le Havre on which Crisp was to receive a 50 per cent reduction on the fares and for which he was charging 7 guineas first class, never came off and no more is heard of Crisp after this failure.

A more persistent excursion agent who later became a real rival of the Cooks was Henry Gaze. It wasn't until the 1880s however that the full story of Gaze's business is told, when he published a brochure on the subject. Gaze had started his excursion business in 1844 when he took a tour from the 'Thames' (presumably London) to Boulogne, a journey of twenty-two hours, and then on to Paris by diligence. In 1854 Gaze arranged a trip to Brussels and the battlefields of Waterloo, a year before Thomas Cook's own first excursion down the Rhine. Four years later Gaze's senior partner went to Switzerland and wrote a book entitled 'Switzerland and How to See it for Ten Guineas'. The book was ridiculed in *Punch* in an article entitled 'A week in the Moon for a Pound'.

It was at this time that Cook began to take notice of Gaze and, feeling perhaps that an ally in the trade might be an advantage he praised Gaze's book. 'We recommend Mr Gaze's "Switzerland for Ten Guineas" ', Cook wrote, 'the book is written in good style, and displays the spirit of energy, self denial, and perseverance that should characterise Alpine travellers . . . *Mr Gaze is labouring in the same line as ourselves . . . and regarding him in the light of a co-worker* we shall be glad to promote the circulation of his guides'.

This friendly spirit of co-operation did not survive the years of evolution of the business for, in the fifties, we find Cook and Gaze clashing over the most lucrative travel market yet to appear: The Middle East. Gaze had already arranged travel to the Middle East before Cook took his first tour in 1869 and Gaze does not hesitate to rub this in. ' . . . it was not until the *third* party under the personal escort of the senior member of our firm was in the East', he says, 'that the *first* associated party under any other auspices arrived at Jaffa'. He also claims that Cook employed Gaze's own dragoman, Mr Howard, to conduct his parties. 'If imitation is a crime', says Gaze sombrely, 'then it is clear who is guilty of it'.

The parallel career of Gaze and Cook and the increasing competition was further exacerbated by the proximity of their offices, Cooks at 108 Fleet Street, and that of Gaze at 163 Strand, opened in 1870. Like Cook, Gaze realised that the future of the business lay with the middle classes and he too made a point of the fact that among his customers were what he calls the 'elite' many of whom, he claimed, had come over with his company from France for Napoleon III's funeral at Chislehurst.

The Exhibition at Vienna was another bone of contention between the two firms, and Cook, who had won the agency appointment, and announced the fact in his literature, was criticised by Gaze who considered the term 'useless and unmeaning'. The Paris Exhibitions and most of all, Oberammergau, where Gaze transported furniture over the passes in spring in order to prepare a hotel, were further scenes of rivalry. After the publication of the book in which this information is made public, Gaze continued to operate his tours to the Middle East and the Continent and introduced a parcel and baggage delivery service in competition to the Cooks' own forwarding business.

In the 1900s the Thewfikieh Line of Nile steamers, which Gaze used, began to put its own advertisement in *The Times* and, after 1902, when Gaze & Sons wrote a letter to this newspaper protesting at the rumours of high hotel prices for the Coronation of Edward VII, there is no further trace of them. It is probable that the year 1881 when the booklet with the Gaze history was published, was a crucial one, certainly the introduction betrays anxiety at their chief competitor's success.

'Compelled now and again to assert ourselves and our claims, by reason of the inflated pretensions and grossly exaggerated statements which are continually being urged by some upon public attention' [says Gaze] 'so long (being absorbed in the development of our business) have we quietly allowed these matters to pass unnoticed, that these pretensions, growing bolder because uncontradicted, have now reached the most extravagant proportions, and we feel constrained to interpose a formal protest against such attempts as are being continually made by those referred to, to claims and inventions and to monopolise powers which are the property of all Tourist Agents, and in the development of which we have ourselves borne so important a part'.

Whether or not Gaze was correct in his accusations, the fact is that he did not survive the competition, whereas the Cooks did, and the reason for their triumph was partly that theirs was a family business with five male members to carry it on. Thomas Cook had laid the foundations with the help of John Mason and at the moment when the opportunity to expand arrived, there were three sons who had been schooled in the business from early on to carry out the expansion. Such a team was unbeatable.

John Mason whose formidable character is revealed in the correspondence with his

175

sons whom he keeps constantly on their toes by demands for their attention to the details of the business, whether it relates to the fact that towel hooks in the Nile steamers have been placed at the wrong height, or his correspondence is not sent ahead to him while travelling, had their complete backing. All of them travelled, inspected offices, set up new ticket and hotel coupon arrangements and dealt with the managers of the branch offices with the same firmness as their father. It was only this personal involvement, that made it possible to maintain the control of standards of accommodation, food and service which brought everyone to the Cooks for their travels.

The demands of their public, and the requests for travel arrangements for small groups kept the Cooks too busy to deal with all sections of the public who wanted to travel however, and it was this that left gaps in the field of travel which were filled by other competitors. One of these was Joseph Dean, who had joined John Dawson, an agent of the Manchester, Sheffield and Lincolnshire Railway in Sheffield, and formed the firm of Dean & Dawson. Dean had himself become the Stockport agent of the M S & L and when he was offered another agency in Sheffield, an amalgamation took

Georges Nagelmackers, founder of the Compagnie des Wagons Lits.

WAGON-RESTAURANT

Cie WAGONS-LITS

The **GOLDEN ARROW**
ALL PULLMAN TRAIN
DAILY BETWEEN

NORD Ry. BELGIAN Rys. NETHERLAND Rys. WAGONS-LITS Co.

ÉTOILE DU NORD
(NORTH STAR)

CÔTE D'AZUR
PULLMAN – EXPRESS

Paris Côte Belge
PULLMAN EXPRESS
Ire CLASSE   IIe CLASSE

ZOUTE
KNOCKE
BLANKENBERGHE
HEYST
OSTENDE

LILLE

PARIS

**SUMMER ON THE FRENCH RIVIERA
BY THE BLUE TRAIN**

place. Because of Dean's knowledge of the Continent, the firm began to develop tours abroad through the Great Central Railway as the M S & L came to be called when it established its lines into London.

Dean & Dawson's business expanded during the fruitful decades at the end of the century and by the end of the first decade of the twentieth they had 24 branches and were dealing with group as well as individual traffic. One of the largest groups to go abroad since the start of foreign tourism was arranged by Dean & Dawson when they took 1,500 Lever Brothers' employees to Paris in 1900. In 1904 the business was bought by the Great Central Railway which later merged with the London North Eastern. It was this railway ownership which eventually brought Dean & Dawson into the hands of Cooks when it was taken over by the railways during World War II.

The 1880s with their increasing middle class affluence and opportunities for travel, encouraged others to follow the example of Cook. Many of the newcomers were motivated by similar ideas of reform and improvement that had stimulated the older Cook. Now, however, it was the artisan class and lower paid clerks who were to be provided with recreation and spiritual improvement. John Frame who ran his first tour in 1881 was driven by the same enthusiasm for Temperance as Thomas Cook. The Polytechnic Touring Association which began in 1888 with a tour to Belgium, Germany and Switzerland was the product of Quintin Hogg's enthusiasm for providing opportunities for education and useful recreation to young people.

The development of winter sports as a holiday attraction was largely the work of Henry Lunn, later knighted for his services to the Methodist Church. Lunn first hit on the idea of organising tourist trips at a Reunion meeting at Grindelwald. His first organised party was to Rome and in his autobiography entitled, 'Reaching Harbour', he writes,

'We hoped for a party of fifty or sixty for Easter 1893. The response was surprising, and we took in all four-hundred-and-fifty passengers to Rome that Easter, at twenty guineas each. Thomas Cook & Son's representative, Mr Bredall, warned me that this powerful company has never been able to make a twenty-five guinea tour pay. That was simply because they aimed at small parties'.

This comment casts an interesting light on the Cooks' business at this time, the small parties of select people were made up of the middle class market that the Cooks were now catering to and, in doing so, he was leaving open other sectors of the market to those with the talent and flair for seizing business opportunities.

Henry Lunn's talent for organisation was quickly perceived by the chairman of the London, Chatham and Dover Railway, who had recently had a difference of opinion with the Cooks and was looking around for a new ally in the continental tourism business. He approached Lunn and offered him an agency to carry on the general business along the lines of the Cooks. Lunn accepted, but in his autobiography he admits that it was a mistake.

' . . . this was a disastrous incident in my business life' [he says] 'Messrs Thomas Cook & Son had an immense organisation carried on by a large army of experts, and David was better armed with his smooth stones from the brook against Goliath, than I was armed with the support of one of the three railways to the Continent, which have since been amalgamated with the Southern Railway'.

Lunn's real success and contribution to the history of travel was to begin at Adelboden, a small village in the Bernese Oberland where he took parties of Etonians and Harrovians whose enthusiasm led to the formation of the Public Schools Alpine Sports Club in 1902. Once more it was the middle class clientele that were to help in the creation of a new and successful travel agency. In the meantime, Lunn seems to have formed a business association with Woolrych Perowne, a travel organiser of Co-operative Educational parties one of the features of which, in 1895, was lectures by the Bishop of Peterborough. Together, Lunn and Perowne advertised cruises to Palma, Algiers and Malta for £21, and to the Holy Land and thus launched the cultural Hellenic cruises for which Lunn's became famous.

On an international scale, however, there was only one company that grew in a comparable manner to the Cooks', this was American Express, but its development was in shipping, freight and banking. William F Harnden was the founder of this world-wide company: a young Bostonian who, on finding that office life did not suit either his temperament or his health, gave it up and set up an express letter and parcels service. By 1841 Harnden had extended his business to England, France and Scotland and was also promoting immigration to America.

Working with Harnden was a young man called Henry Wells and it was he who, in 1844, set up a partnership with William Fargo and founded the famous Wells Fargo stage coach and pony express service whose romantic early days have been portrayed in many a western movie. There were other competitors on the scene during these years, men like Butterfield and Wasson, and Livingston, and in 1848 these men and Wells and Fargo decided to merge their companies and thus American Express was born. The Express business was a lucrative one and now the company was carrying not only letters and parcels but gold bullion, jewellery, bank notes, as well as passengers, on its stages. The travel business as such however, did not seem attractive enough and, even in 1902 when American Express were expanding into Europe, President Fargo refused to have anything to do with it. 'I will not,' he said, 'have gangs of trippers starting off in charabancs from in front of our offices the way they do from Cooks'. A more powerful reason for not entering into the travel business was its lack of profitability and President Fargo did not hesitate to say so. 'There is no profit in the tourist business as conducted by Thos Cook & Son, and even if there were, this company would not undertake it'.

Nevertheless American Express did become selling agents for railroads and steamship lines in 1909, offering rates and tickets but no other arrangements. Little by little however, the travel service increased, tickets for the main railway routes of Europe were sold at American Express offices and excursions in Naples, Berlin, Paris and London were arranged. Despite his protests, President Fargo's worst fears were realised and charabancs began to leave American Express offices filled with tourists.

Despite the propitious circumstances for launching into the business of travel none of their competitors of the decades following 1880 could hope to do more than emulate the Cooks. Here and there there were particular opportunities such as those grouped by Wayfarers, Workers Travel Association and others, who came into the business at the beginning of this century, but the bulk of the business was under the Cooks' control. It wasn't until a further major change occurred in society after World War II that challengers arose who were of the stature of the Company which had by then become a property of the state.

17 The Compagnie des Wagons Lits

The company formed by Georges Nagelmackers to construct and develop the use of sleeping cars and restaurant cars on Continental trains grew rapidly and became as important in the evolution of tourism as the organisation founded by Thomas Cook. Like Cook, Nagelmackers realised that the travellers who would make up his clientele were those whose affluent circumstances permitted them to undertake long journeys·and that they would expect to find the comfort habitual to their social class wherever they went.

He therefore set about providing his sleeping cars and, later, his restaurants, with every possible luxury. His enthusiasm for sleeping cars was inspired by his studies of the system evolved by George Mortimer Pullman in the U.S.A., and when another American, Colonel William d'Alton Mann, arrived in Europe to launch the sleeping car idea he became an enthusiastic ally.

Nagelmackers' contribution was an acute business sense and a knowledge of the European scene. He immediately grasped the fact that for the system he envisaged to be effective in a Europe separated by national rivalries, it would have to be neutral. Fortunately, he was a Belgian, and with his neutrality guaranteed he set about persuading nationalistic railway companies of the advantages of through coaches which would provide passengers with luxurious sleeping quarters as they travelled across Europe. By 1876, Nagelmackers was the sole owner of fifty-eight sleeping cars, Colonel Mann having gone back to America. With the patronage of the King of the Belgians, Leopold II, Nagelmackers officially established the Cie. Internationale des Wagons Lits in 1876.

A year later, by persistent persuading and string-pulling, he had signed contracts with twenty European national railway systems. He added restaurant cars to his system in 1883, the year when the Orient Express made its inaugural journey from Paris to Constantinople, as Istanbul was then called. This was not yet a direct route, for passengers had to accomplish the last part of the journey by ship. The through route did not operate till 1889. Of all his luxury trains, it is Nagelmackers' Orient Express that has captured the public imagination: this was the train that pierced the mysterious curtain of the East, taking its passengers into a city of mosques and harems, of veiled women and swarthy men, of crowded bazaars and vast palaces. Here was the ultimate for that late Victorian flowering of the romantic spirit to which Tennyson and Elroy Flecker gave tongue.

Moreover, in a practical sense Constantinople was the threshold to the East; a short boat-ride away was Asia Minor, and services to Palestine and Egypt were frequent. No wonder then that passengers on the Orient Express were a cut above all others and that Nagelmackers made sure that the service was *de luxe* throughout, as advertised.

The story of the first journey of the Orient Express in June 1883 is admirably recounted by George Behrend in his book 'Grand European Expresses', and need not concern us here except to examine the standards of the accommodation. The train, as with all Wagons Lits trains, was short and the carriages were six wheelers; bogies were

The Wagon Lits image expressed through their crest and imaginative advertising

AT YOUR SERVICE

EVERYWHERE

WAGONS LITS COOK

CIE DES WAGONS-LITS

CHEMIN DE FER DU NORD

CHEMINS DE FER BELGES

L'OISEAU BLEU
TRAIN PULLMAN

ANVERS
BRUXELLES
PARIS

181

LE CALORIFÈRE.   LE COULOIR.   LE CABINET DE TOILETTE.

UN COMPARTIMENT: INSTALLATION DE JOUR.   COMPARTIMENT TRANSFORMÉ EN DORTOIR.

182   SECTION BELGE. — LA COMPAGNIE INTERNATIONALE DES WAGONS-LITS   1878

Luxuriously appointed railway compartments became part of the continental travelling scene, after Nagelmackers established the Compagnie Internationale des Wagons Lits in 1876 under the patronage of Leopold II of Belgium, who was a cousin of Queen Victoria.

VOYAGE
D'INAUGURATION
DES NOUVELLES
VOITURES-LITS
DE LA
COMPAGNIE INTERNATIONALE
DES WAGONS-LITS ET DES
GRANDS EXPRESS EUROPÉENS

introduced the same year. There were two sleeping cars, a dining car, a mailvan, and a luggage van in which passengers were permitted to carry 330 lbs of luggage each.

The sleeping cars were designed for day and night travel; the lower berths were made up from the four armchairs with which each compartment was provided, while the upper ones were let down by ropes which held them out of the way during the day. There were two w.c.'s in the carriage and two hand basins, provided with hot water throughout the journey.

The Côte d'Azur was the epitome of the twenties style. Most smart people still went there in winter however.

Each car was looked after by an attendant who could provide drinks for his travellers and who served them faithfully in the hope of receiving something in appreciation of the attention he had given to their comfort.

The dining cars were also six wheelers and seated about a dozen people at a time in individual, padded leather chairs, arranged at tables for two or four. The decor of the restaurant was that of the Grand hotels; there were leather-covered walls, stuccoed ceilings, chandeliers and the table service was of the best. The food claimed to be of an *haute cuisine* standard. The cooking was done by a master chef, and his assistants, over a wood stove provisions often being bought *en route*, so that travellers from northern countries were often surprised and pleased to eat fresh vegetables and fruit that seemed out of season to them. The menus give some idea of the quality of the dishes offered to the diners. The Orient Express dinner menu of December 1884 consisted of soup, olives and butter, fish with Hollandaise sauce, lamb, chicken and desserts and cheese, and one on the Rome Express a few years later offered *hors d'oeuvres*, sole, lamb cutlets, chicken galantine and tongue. Certainly nothing like it had ever been seen before and now, with the advent of mass travel at cheaper rates, will probably never be seen again.

Having succeeded in establishing the Orient Express, Nagelmackers embarked on an even more ambitious project: the Nord-Sud Express which was planned to provide a service from St Petersburg (Leningrad) to Lisbon. However, lack of co-operation from the Prussians made this impossible until 1896 when a through journey from St Petersburg to Paris became feasible. A variation of this service was the St Petersburg-Cannes Express which was much used by the aristocratic Russians who frequented the French Riviera until World War I brought their world to an end.

An even more audacious service was the one that Nagelmackers provided on the Trans Siberian Railway. This in its early stages terminated at Tomsk, the eastern portion to Vladivostok reaching completion in 1902.

Of all the *de luxe* trains that seem to epitomise the luxury and glamour of Wagons Lits travel perhaps none is more evocative than the Blue Train. Inaugurated in 1889, this train became a symbol of all that the Côte de'Azur stood for in the twenties and was the scene of many romantic encounters in contemporary fiction. There was even a ballet called 'Le Train Bleu' which was part of the repertoire of the Diaghilev ballet company. It was the popularity of this service, which ran three times a week after 1897, that led the Wagons Lits company to build the Riviera Palace Hotel at Nice.

The Wagons Lits involvement with hotels had begun in 1890 and was the natural outcome of a desire to provide the patrons of the sleeping cars and restaurant cars with every comfort *en route*. In a publication listing all the Wagons Lits Grand hotels at a later date, the company expounded its policy:

'The Cie. Internationale des Grands Hotels has created first class establishments at all the termini of the luxury trains and at spas and pleasure resorts, in a useful collaboration with Wagons Lits company in order to encourage travelling and to develop international understanding'.

It was essential that the travellers who had come from the centres of civilised life in Europe should not be dissuaded from travelling by having to put up with inferior accommodation on the way and at their destinations. Like John Mason Cook with his Nile steamers, Nagelmackers was concerned to provide his passengers with a cocoon which would protect them from too real a contact with the sordid conditions of the picturesque and poverty-stricken inhabitants of the glamorous places that they visited.

The first hotel built by Nagelmackers was erected with the participation of the P & O Line. This was at Brindisi, the terminus of the Brindisi Peninsular and Orient Express which linked London to the Italian port where passengers embarked for the Middle East. The Hotel International Brindisi gave rest to travellers after their long journey and possessed bathrooms as well as electric light.

In Ostend, the northern end of a number of Wagons Lits services, the Wagons Lits company developed no less than four hotels; the Terminus, de la Plage, the Grand Hotel du Palais and the Royal Palace Hotel.

The latter was a model of what the Palace hotels should be.

'The Royal Palace, [said the brochure of the time] has been built by the Compagnie de Grands Hotels, close by the Chalet of the King of the Belgians, and a stone's throw from the Wellington race course, not far from the clay pigeon shoot and in a part of Ostend which will become the future centre of the town and is already the most aristocratic quarter. This hotel, the most beautiful and most important in Ostend, is a kind of huge modernised chateau in the style of Louis XIV, and its planning is the work of M Georges Chedanne, Prix de Rome'.

The words reflect the character of the residents for whom the hotel was designed. Through the 300-metre long covered gallery strolled the haut bourgeoisie, the successful bankers and merchants, and now and again, those noblemen who were hoping to marry their daughters to money. One of the most important public rooms was the ballroom, decorated in eighteenth century style with chandeliers and rococo plasterwork, a room suitable, as the brochure pointed out, for the balls, concerts and other entertainments at which all the notable people passing through Ostend would gather.

The restaurant was equally astounding with individual tables from which diners could see the sea through the large bay windows. In the evening this splendid room came into its full glory as the men in evening dress and the ladies in their low-necked bodices and trailing skirts displayed their bosoms with averted eyes. The showpiece of the room was the ceiling, which was made of glass decorated with colourful designs and lit by hundreds of fairy lights. While the orchestra played behind its palms and aspidistras the social life of the 'belle epoque' unfolded with a formality which disguised its true intentions, intentions which were perhaps hinted at in the announcement that owing to a most ingenious design, rooms could be turned into apartments at the unlocking of a connecting door.

The most exotic of settings for the Wagons Lits hotels were those in the Eastern Mediterranean. In Constantinople the Therapia Summer Palace became a sort of unofficial residence of ambassadors and titled residents, while in Egypt the Gezire Palace was the centre of life for British officers. Later, the famous Shepheards Hotel also became a part of the Wagons Lits hotel chain. This, too, was the centre of social life for the British in Egypt and its 300 rooms, all illuminated by electric light, and its bathrooms and water closets were the wonders of Cairo.

Like the Gezire Palace, which had once belonged to the Khedive, many of the Wagons Lits hotels had been the houses and palaces of royalty and aristocracy, a fact which provided an additional attraction for their new residents. The Pavillon de Meudon had been the home of Madame de Pompadour, the Grand Hotel Stephanie at Abbazia in

Austria, the palace of the Emperors, the Palace Hotel, Ardennes, a royal palace of Leopold II.

At the beginning of the century Wagons Lits company embarked on even more audacious adventures in hotel building. Having taken over the operation of the Cairo Luxor Express the company now built a hotel in the Upper Nile. With the long-term prospects for the Trans Siberian Express it set up a hotel in Peking. But already the 'belle epoque' was beginning to crumble; the Russo-Japanese war and the beginnings of revolutionary tremors in Russia were discouraging travel Eastwards and the unsettled conditions in the Balkans were leading to a cataclysm which would destroy the peaceful and privileged world of Nagelmakers' clients.

Nagelmackers himself died in 1905 and after his death the decline of the Grand hotels was accelerated until in 1914 they were given a death blow.

After the First World War the Cie. Internationale des Wagons Lits was first taken up with reconstituting its rolling stock and those hotels which remained in its hands continued to decay. By 1930, however, the hotel chain began to be revived, but once again war brought the business to an end.

In the post-war period the activities of the Cie. Internationale des Wagons Lits, et des Grands Express Europeens, a title now changed to Cie. Internationale des Wagons Lits et du Tourisme, have taken a different turn. Its know-how in the field of catering has been profitably employed in the development of a service for airlines and on motorways, and in snack bars, pubs, cafeterias and drugstores, in which it serves some six million meals a year. Three million tray meals are prepared for airlines, and some million and a half meals served in the Restop, motorway restaurants. Its hotel activities have also been revived and the company handles over 700,000 passenger nights accommodation every year.

In diversifying its activities the Wagons Lits company has pioneered the idea of total involvement in the various components of the travel operation. With its more than 60 subsidiaries and holdings in companies which are concerned with catering, hotels, transport and travel agencies throughout the world it indicates the direction in which travel businesses will undoubtedly develop in the years to come.

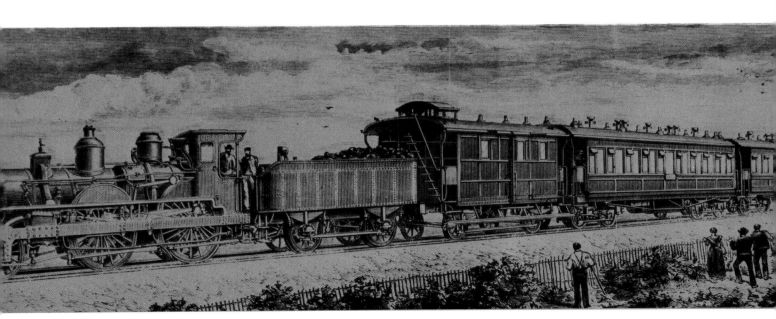

18 ... and after

'Why oh why do the wrong people travel and the right people stay at home?' asked Noel Coward in 1961 surveying the embattled social scene in foreign resorts where once only middle and upper classes had taken their winter leisure in the assurance that everyone else in the place would be their kind of people.

In the 1960s the right people were not, of course, staying at home. They were travelling, too, and what they saw of their fellow countrymen abroad made them shudder with dismay. Foreign travel had at last reached those sections of society for whom Thomas Cook had envisaged the benefits of railway journeys, and those strata of society which had got abroad first were as indignant as the master of the house who finds his butler drinking his best brandy.

The process of social change which had brought about this state of affairs had begun with the reformers of the nineteenth century but had not imposed itself until after World War II. Then, in the idealistic aftermath of war and much talk of the rights of men and the fundamental freedoms, the working class, which had for so many generations carried the burden of Britain's supremacy, broke through into a region of political and social power which left it and most of the rest of society breathless and bewildered.

Among the many rights to which everyone felt entitled was the freedom of movement, and among the working class that freedom extended into those areas where once there had been no opportunity for them to visit, and where in any case they would not hitherto have been welcome. The post war period provided the means to achieve this freedom through a number of factors.

The first and most important, though one not noticed by *The Times* until 1956 when, in slightly amazed tones it noted in a leading article that 'Europe is a workers' playground now that holidays are with pay', was that nearly 30 million people were now a potential market for people in the holiday business.

Next, but equally significant, was the fact of the travel allowance. The limitation of foreign currency imposed by the Treasury in order to control the outflow of money at a time when the country's resources had not yet recovered from the War, was an un-suspected boon to the propagation of the idea of foreign travel. On the one hand it made the travel agents devise a cheap way of providing holidays, and on the other it produced a state of social equality which encouraged the working class to travel without the fear of finding themselves at a disadvantage. These factors were vital in the creation of the idea of mass tourism and are responsible for the evolution of the travel industry in the quarter century since the end of World War II.

The beginnings were, like most beginnings, not immediately apparent. In fact, in the late forties and early fifties many people were under the impression that society would settle down to a pattern not unlike that of pre-war, and there were expensive middle class tours by flying boat to Rome, Cyprus and Egypt, cruises (although ships were scarce), weekends at fashionable Le Touquet, the Riviera during Carnival time, a grand tour of Scandinavia and hundreds of other individual holidays offered in the same terms as those of pre-war.

It soon became evident, however, that the business of travel organising had moved on to a new phase, and that the problem that travel agents had to cope with was how to deal with ever increasing numbers within the scope of the travel allowance. Foreseeing the growth prospects of the industry and realising that its encouragement must depend on providing holidays within the limits set by the Treasury the leading agents, Cooks, Frames, Poly, Workers Travel Association, Sir Henry Lunn, Co-operative Travel, Dean & Dawson and Pickfords, who were loosely associated in a body named the Creative Travel Agents' Conference, set about finding the means of supplying the public's growing demand for cheap holidays abroad.

The principal obstacle to cheap holidays was the fare, since most of the popular holiday centres of pre-war lay in Switzerland and France. The CTAC therefore sought to reduce the cost of the rail journey and did so by the same methods used by Thomas Cook over a hundred years earlier, and by themselves in the period immediately before 1939, that is they chartered trains which they then shared between the members of the Conference. In the decade between 1950 and 1960 there were special trains to the Riviera, to Italy, to Spain, to Switzerland and to Austria. Each of these trains was manned by travelling representatives of the companies involved who as the train sped to Nice, Ventimiglia, Barcelona, Lucerne, and Innsbruck looked after the welfare of the passengers, many of whom were travelling for the first time.

Inevitably in an operation of this magnitude all kinds of things happened and since such a great mass movement of people by train is never likely to take place again anywhere in the world it is worth recording the events of a typical journey.

The weekend special train for Barcelona left Victoria at 10.30 am every Sunday morning and at least half an hour before departure the representatives of each of the travel agencies concerned would be waiting for their passengers, with lists of their names in their hands. Cooks' men usually stood out from the others, their expensive, quasi-military blue and gold uniforms lending them an air of authority which made them a focus point for arriving passengers. For the most part the rest wore armbands, which in many cases revealed the transient seasonal character of their jobs. The travelling representative fraternity were a mixed lot, many of them dedicated to the work, a few making what they could out of a season, one or two, especially those engaged only for the high season period, the kind of men who drift from job to job, often self indulgent and given to drinking too much. At least half the passengers had never been abroad before and they were anxious, edgy, given to asking absurd questions or expecting unreasonable services. Some were the old middle class customers of pre-war years who, unable to go abroad independently with the travel allowance, took advantage of the cheap fares offered by travel agents.

The Channel crossing via Newhaven and Dieppe was usually chaotic during the season, the steamers were overcrowded, the bar a swarming mass of dishevelled passengers demanding duty free drinks and cigarettes. In the mêlée of Dieppe it was the Cooks' man again who distilled calm in the midst of the hurricane. He was the Dieppe port representative and he knew the exact location of each of the carriages in each of the trains standing in the still unrebuilt station. Between Dieppe and Paris it was the representative's duty to check his passenger lists again, in case anyone had fallen by the wayside, and at the same time to help the French Passport officer to perform his duty. That having been done a drink or two was taken with the authorities and preparations were made for the rush across Paris, from St Lazare to Austerlitz by coach.

According to the itinerary worked out by the holiday planners in London there was ample time for the bus journey across Paris to the station from which the Spanish

All the best holidays
are better at
COOKS

bound trains departed. In fact there were often delays, bad Channel crossings, confusion caused by the sheer quantity of the travellers, and on one occasion time lost owing to the fireman getting his head knocked off by a stone bridge, and the journey across Paris was often a frantic race against time. So much so that the resourceful representatives had a permanent arrangement with the station master at Austerlitz that the gates to the goods yard would be left open in an emergency and passengers transhipped directly from coach to train. Even with this arrangement there was often barely enough time to heave hundreds of passengers and their luggage into the last carriage or two of the Port Bou Express before it left for the Spanish frontier.

In the season there were often two or sometimes three trains, carrying thousands of people, which left almost concurrently and the possibility of confusion was a nightmare to the representatives. Despite the numbers, the travel agencies and the railway companies strained every nerve to provide that gracious form of travel of an earlier period. Dinner was served in three sittings in a dining car suitable for sixty people, and only those who were lucky or who were travelling in the care of an experienced, and sometimes ruthless, representative got it.

In the dining car the form of service was in the same traditions as that which had served the upper middle classes and gentry of Nagelmackers' day. It was superb, and the chef, penned in his ten by five cubicle, performed miracles. Meals began with the offer of an assortment of aperitifs and ended with coffee and cigars, all served at top speed and with frequent hammerings at the dining car door as the queue lengthened outside, their wait often prolonged by the confusion which reigned as the time for settling up the extras came round. (Most travel agency customers carried pre-paid meal coupons but these did not include drinks and coffee.)

As the train tore through the night, often making up for time lost in order to keep up the French railway tradition of always arriving on time, passengers settled themselves in their couchettes, ladies often finding to their discomfiture that these were issued with no regard to the sex of the occupants, or in their seats.

The experienced representative who had provided himself with a pass key, since all the communicating doors between carriages were locked at night, would then patrol the train, often looking for an empty compartment which he could lock and keep for himself or, on the rare occasion, share with a female traveller in need of company. Space was always at a premium on night journeys in high season and ruthless passengers sometimes resorted to all kinds of ruses in order to get more elbow room, feigning illness, even madness, or resorting to bribery.

The last critical stage of the journey was at the Spanish frontier where, owing to the different gauge of the railways, all passengers had to transfer to the Spanish train. The transfer of thousands of passengers was achieved via the Customs shed, the exit doors of which were locked until everyone was present. In the heat of summer the temperature inside the corrugated iron shed was such that people often fainted and the Spanish authorities and especially the Civil Guard with their patent leather hats had not yet learned that a hospitable manner can be converted into foreign currency. As the Spanish train moved off, spewing coal dust and smoke which fell over the white table cloths in the restaurant car, the passengers received yet another shock which made more than one of them remark that they wished they had stayed at home: the food was uncompromisingly Spanish, cooked in oil and flavoured with garlic!

The Costa Brava, however, lived up to nearly everybody's expectations. After the
grimy, sunless industrial cities of Britain and the austerity of the war and post war it

was heaven indeed, and even if the incidence of what the British called 'Spanish tummy' and the Spaniards called 'English stomach' was high it did not dim the romantic glory of the holiday.

Although travel agents had solved the problem of cheap travel on railways they had not found the really adequate way of dealing with the problem of finding suitable accommodation for hundreds of thousands of tourists all demanding high standards of hygiene and comfort. Such hotels as existed, in Switzerland, Italy, France and Spain were either the grand hotels of the Edwardian era or small places unable to cope with more than twenty or thirty guests at a time.

In the absence of anything else the travel agents had to make do with these and they tied up as many hotel beds as they could in order to satisfy their customers' demands. The hoteliers were only too glad to co-operate: after all the business of Continental tourism was due to the British and they looked forward to a new and prosperous era of co-operation. When the travel agents demanded extraordinarily low prices in return for promises to keep the hotels filled, even in the off season, the hoteliers reluctantly agreed, they even agreed to allow the travel agent to have the rooms on a sale or return basis. As a result of the negotiations the public were able to spend holidays abroad at incredibly low prices, and a principle was established which was to lead the travel industry into serious problems later on.

The results of the efforts of travel agents to find accommodation for their tourists at a cheap rate had an enormous effect on foreign hoteliers. Those of the small hotel or pension category rapidly learnt to adapt themselves to the new market and soon small hotels were busy building extensions to premises and adapting their menus to English tastes.

For the Grand hotels the new situation presented certain difficulties of organisation and administration. Most of the Grand hotels had been built with a view to serving a comfortably off middle class clientele. Their rooms were large, often arranged in connecting suites with one bathroom per suite; they had large staffs, and they were used to offering large and varied menus. In order to meet the cost requirements of the travel agents they were obliged to divide their suites into separate rooms, often turning particularly big rooms into two by means of a partition, and to reduce their menus to a table d'hôte which would be within the terms offered.

Unfortunately many of the Grand hotels still possessed a clientele which expected former standards, and indeed, the middle class travel agency customers often chose to stay at a Grand hotel in the expectation that it would provide the kind of gracious living which they remembered from pre-war.

A certain dichotomy was inevitable and in many cases the hotels, although a unit, carried on a schizophrenic life. On the one hand they tried to maintain the amenities that their full-rate paying customers expected and on the other they often were obliged to operate a separate dining room service for tourist parties and charge supplements, which the new customers objected to, for entrance to the hotel night club, the hotel tennis courts, and the hotel lido, in order to compensate for the low price which the travel agency customer was paying.

It was not a happy arrangement and the fact that on the whole this makeshift compromise worked without too much friction and irritation is a compliment to the hard work and endeavour of the hotel managers and others who had to make the transition between their past operation and that with which they were now faced.

The most extraordinary effect of the situation was seen in the social life of the hotels.

193

Accustomed in the past to a clientele who sought peace and quiet after a day of enjoying visits to natural beauty spots or historic places, the hotels provided lounges where three piece orchestras played discreetly behind potted palms and rubber plants, billiard rooms, and afternoon teas in the palm court. Now suddenly the tea hour was broken into by what *The Times* described as the new type of British tourist 'seething *en masse* through hotel lounges'. Most of the arrivals from small houses in industrial cities, suddenly arriving in the palatial entrance of a once Grand hotel with its marble columns, its plants and liveried footmen, felt overawed and at the same time edgily on the *qui vive* for any fancied slight or any sign of being put upon. Moreover they were in search of fun rather than gracious life.

In these circumstances the resident representatives of the travel agents who acted as go between for hotel management and the travel agency customers had to stretch their tact and diplomacy to its utmost.

The representative's role of mediator extended throughout every aspect of hotel life: in the restaurant there was the delicate matter of explaining to customers that it was customary to wear a tie and jacket to dinner, and that the hotel preferred guests not to have breakfast in their vests, or lunch in their bathing suits. The menu had to be tactfully explained and the customers encouraged to eat the pizza that the chef had specially prepared, or warned that any dish ordered à la carte would be charged extra. There was the continual need to explain that the hotel concierge felt entitled to place a service charge on collecting daily newspapers or that the receptionist was obliged to make a charge for cashing a travel cheque and that tea and coffee were not included on the bill.

Moreover, there was the constant effort to help the hotel management to come to terms with their situation. Many of the hoteliers had served their apprenticeship in the great hotels of Europe and were set in their ways regarding the standards which they offered, as well as those they expected from their guests. Many of them did not take easily to the idea that a night club would be more useful than a billiard room, or that their new customers did not have any desire to participate in formal gala nights but preferred to congregate in the village bar where the drinks were cheap and the proprietor spoke English.

Hotel managers were concerned, too, about their private guests and were anxious that the behaviour of the tourists should not upset them; when the ballroom was filled with bands of British visitors doing the Hokey-cokey, or when they sat about on the hotel lido eating food brought in from a village shop the hotel manager began to wonder whether he was jeopardising the future of the establishment for which he was responsible by allowing such lowering of the hotel's tone.

Concern about the behaviour of tourists and its effect on Britain's name abroad was not restricted to the hotels at which they stayed. As early as 1949 *The Times* reflected the anxiety of its readers about the new tourists and their behaviour, 'It is implied', an editorial said, 'that the Anglo Saxon reputation for refined behaviour is being ruined by high spirits and horseplay, and failure to observe the decencies of dress and deportment.'

The problems that arose from the invasion of the continent by the new tourists had nothing to do with failure to observe decencies, although they may have been guilty of horseplay and high spirits. Such friction as there was arose from the different attitude of the new working class tourist, who was more extroverted and less concerned with the polite decorum of the pre war middle class. Faced with a situation which had moral undertones the foreign resorts tried to find a compromise between the traditional social

194

Not everyone was happy with Cooks service, of course, and *Punch* made a point when they depicted a Cook's courier being set upon by tourists on their return to England.

code of their residents and the more liberal behaviour of their visitors.

On the beaches in Spain policemen were provided with leaflets which explained, in English, the amount of exposure which was permitted. Occasionally couples were arrested for kissing in public and at the same time sometimes advised where this kind of thing, and what it led to, was provided for in private hotels where rooms could be booked by the hour.

The people most affected by the tourist wave were the young, and the freedom which British society embodied, the evident fact of the economic gains of the working classes through their political emancipation, the liberty of the young with regard to the opinions of their elders became potent factors in breaking down age old systems, particularly in the Mediterranean countries. Meanwhile foreign travel was also helping to accelerate the progress towards freer attitudes in Britain. The privilege myth regarding foreign travel was being destroyed, sexual freedom was more easily practised abroad than at home and, despite a tendency to seek the familiar, some of the Continental ways of life were being unconsciously absorbed and Continental foods, fashions and life styles gradually began to take root at home.

The great era of the Special train continued until the 1960s, but at its height its end was already in sight when in 1950 Vladimir Raitz advertised a holiday by air charter. The holiday he offered was completely different in concept to any that were on the market, it was an air holiday, but instead of hotel accommodation it offered a tent and the price was £35.10s. Raitz was banking on the new type of holiday-maker being more concerned with getting to his resort quickly than on gracious living when he got there. During the first few years it looked as if Raitz had guessed wrong but by 1954 his business venture was a success. That year he added Sardinia to his programme, two

years later the Costa Brava and Costa del Sol and Portugal, then Minorca and Tangier. Now, however, the holidays included a hotel room. The years 1955 to 1960 were crucial for the holiday business and many including Bill Cormack, Cooks' Publicity Manager could see the writing on the wall.

'In the late twenties and early thirties', he wrote in *Travel Topics*, a trade publication, 'Social classes were almost identical with economic classes . . . today how different is the scene. No longer can the anxious booking clerk anticipate his clients' requirements by accent alone, nor indeed by appearance. Correlation between the social and economic classes has largely disappeared'.

It had indeed, but class had not and a new classless class was arising which wanted to cut itself off entirely from the past and anything associated with it. It heralded a society where merit was measured by ability, where nothing was accepted as proved until it was experienced, and which embraced everything that was new with an almost religious fervour. These were the people who wanted a holiday without frills, but demanded the maximum value for their money.

One of the means of giving it to them was already at hand and the way to use it had already been indicated by Raitz. At this point material progress and the demands of society coincided as much as they had at the moment when Thomas Cook was inspired to run his first excursion.

The jet engine was the cause of the new opportunity which presented itself to travel agents. Although flying holidays had already been pioneered by Raitz, the public in general, and in particular the public of the leading travel agents, regarded a holiday by air as too expensive, if by regular air, or too unreliable and possibly unsafe on the only aircraft available for charter. The arrival of the Comet changed all that for, suddenly,

the airlines were obliged to change their fleets to jets and in doing so found themselves with a number of almost new aircraft, that the public trusted, available for charter.

The opportunity which now presented itself for cheap air holidays on new aircraft brought a number of new business men into the travel industry. One of these was Harold Bamberg, owner of Eagle Aviation who now bought an interest in Sir Henry Lunn and began an ambitious series of holidays using his own airline and the resources of his travel agency; in doing so Bamberg introduced the idea of vertical integration, or the business association of the various ingredients of an inclusive holiday. Another new-comer to the scene in 1954 was Sky Tourist services which operated their air holidays through the Sky Tours agency (later absorbed by Thomson Holidays).

The Travel Trade Gazette, a trade paper which was launched in 1953 and represented the travel trade's expansion and its growing need to keep in touch with the various aspects of its operation, remarked on the new developments in its lead editorial headed 'New travel pattern for 1955. Bid for new classes of travellers'. The report continued, 'New organisations coming into the inclusive tour field for the first time are particularly active in plans for this traffic, and keen competition to capture new classes of travellers – those in the lower income groups and those who have never been abroad before – is likely to produce a number of original experiments in low price holidays'.

In the same year (1954) the travel allowance was raised to £100 and the race was on.

All the established travel agents, members of CTAC, joined, though in most cases their clientele were reluctant to take to the air. BEA, becoming aware of the threat posed by charter flights, began to accept block bookings, the Skyways company which sought to keep prices down by combining a coach air operation joined the ranks of carriers. Seventy three applications for air charters were make to the Air Transport Commission.

In this competitive atmosphere, with airlines vying with each other for a lead in regular traffic and trying to stave off the effects of charter operations on their holiday traffic, and travel agents seeking ways of making holidays by air as cheap as those by rail, the tourist business moved into the sixties. The pressure on the air travel industry was becoming a source of anxiety to some: the International Air Transport Association which had been founded in 1956 in order to safeguard standards and prevent price cutting warned that with a margin of only 1.1 per cent on all operations, all international operators must run at a loss. Sir William Hildred, Director General of IATA declared in Edinburgh however that, 'Airlines must find out how to go all out for the mass market, and recommended to Governments a fare pared down to the lowest level consistent with sound operation'.

The problem was one that affected travel agents, who were now being defined as tour operators if they were organisers of the holidays and agents if they were merely the retailers, and the former had to concern themselves more and more with the exact costing of their programmes. More than ever tour operators had to look at the cost of producing and selling holidays and try to estimate at what point an increase in price would lose them customers, and how many customers they could afford to lose without returning to a low profit position.

To meet this perilous tight-rope situation the travel industry introduced all sorts of ingenious and daring innovations: the charter of aircraft was made a more economical operation by the adoption of the concept, introduced by Freddy Laker, of 'Time' chartering by which an operator hires an aircraft for a number of years and obtains a specially good price for his long term plans: the cost of hotel rooms had been lowered by

199

investment in the hotels or advance payments for long contracts on hotel rooms. In either case the tour operator had to bear the brunt of finding the customers and if he didn't he went broke.

To survive in this situation required careful calculation and a lot of capital. Small companies were obliged to merge, the large companies became fewer and fewer. Cooks, partly because they had been nationalised in 1946, and would hardly risk public money on experiments, and partly because they felt they did not need to take risks any longer, but could wait and see which way the trend was going, kept out of the conflict; but others like Clarksons and Thomson Holidays jumped into the arena eager to face risks for the big prize of a virtual monopoly on package holidays.

Whether or not there is a big prize to win remains to be seen. At present everyone is getting into the business, air companies anxious to use their aircraft fully have become tour operators, so have motoring organisations foreseeing a growth in motorised holiday-makers. Banks and stationers are being tempted with the idea of swamping the retail business, others are foreseeing the day when all holidays will be sold in supermarkets or through a mail order catalogue.

The necessary rationalisation of the holiday product has made it as easy to sell as detergents, and those who prophesy the disappearance of the retail travel agent with his much vaunted but often non existent expertise may be right. Whatever the future holds the chances are that the tourist will do well out of it; he has achieved the desirable status of an essential consumer for an industry in which large financial interests are now involved.

But what kind of holiday will the holiday consumer want? According to Knebler a German sociologist, who made a study of the subject in 1900, the holiday trends showed a tendency towards larger and larger holiday cities in which all the desires of the holiday customer would be satisfied. Already the growth of such resorts as Torremolinos and Palma seem to indicate that the tourist seeks not isolation but gregariousness and non stop entertainment. Crowded cafes, shops, hotel swimming pools, beaches, provide an endless spectacle of the human comedy and they are the real attraction of the big resorts which, because they are collecting adequate revenue from their thousands of visitors, can also provide free side shows for public amusement.

In such places as these, as in any big city, the individual can express himself in any way he likes, conforming to the pattern of the traditional middle class holidaymaker or wearing carpet slippers and hair curlers to lunch if that is what is natural to him or her. For those to whom such conduct is anathema or who simply find a more selective community more congenial there will be the resorts reserved for those on a higher plateau of the social Himalayas. Here, in places like the Aga Khans' Costa Esmeralda, and surrounded, not by walls but a price barrier, the meritocrats will enjoy the company of their equals, much as the Cooks' Nile steamer customers did a century earlier, insulated from the realities of local life.

Reality, in any case, has very little to do with tourism or any kind of journey for that matter. All forms of travel are a kind of romantic dreaming, a form of that essential human activity we call play.

All the great explorers were driven on by their dreams rather than by hope of material gain. Thomas Cook was impelled by a zeal for reform, his son by a Kiplingesque vision of the role of the British businessman. The early tourists shared many of the feelings of the pioneers and of their Cook leaders. They too when they stood on the summit of the Rigi felt a supreme confidence in the destiny of their nation and its alliance with the

Natural and Divine order. When they rode uncomfortably across the deserts of the Middle East they were the lost tribe coming back to affirm their identity. The Nile steamer passengers were a closed group, like the officer class at Simla. They knew they belonged to a higher order of the greatest nation on earth. When this dream was shattered by two World wars the tourist turned introspectively in upon himself.

In the Grand hotels the plump ladies from Wigan felt themselves young and vulnerable under the burning glances of the sergeants of the local police force, the young girls dreamt of undying passion – for many of them their first trip abroad had the breathless excitement and terror of a Victorian wedding night; the old men gave the foreigners avuncular advice on how they should have conducted the war or their way of life. Solitary people threw off their inhibitions and appeared in hardly recognisable guises, others sat quietly reviving old memories.

In recent times the great holiday wonderlands are also reflecting a more universal dream. The tall white blocks with their identical cells, the practised gaiety of the decor by swimming pool and bar, the provision of all essential amenities, the solicitude of the tour operators' representatives are an echo of that rationalised society from which, hopefully, all ills will be removed and everyone will be equal.

If things haven't quite worked out at home, people seem to say, here at least its a perfect world or, if it isn't, we shall want to know why.

PHOTOGRAPHED ON 76TH BIRTHDAY
NOVEMBER 22, 1884.

Index

INT. WAGONS-LITS CO.
**SUMMER
ON THE FRENCH RIVIERA**
BY THE
BLUE TRAIN

OSTENDE — CONSTANTZA EXPRESS
CONSTANTINOPLE

Londres-Constantinople: 71 heures.

Bruxelles-Constantinople: 63 heures.

Londres-Vienne: 29 heures.

Cⁱᵉ INTERNᵗˡᵉ DES WAGONS-LITS

**GRANDS EXPRESS
EUROPÉENS**

In searching for material an author must read far more books than those which provide him with quotes about, or background to, the subject which he is writing about. I have limited this bibliographical list to those books from which quotes have been taken or which will provide the reader with interesting territory for further exploration of the subject.

Adams, W H   *Celebrated women travellers*, W Swan Sonnenschein & Co, London.
Bridges, Mrs F D   *Journal of a lady's travels round the world*, John Murray, London, 1883.
Burton, Isobel   *Syria, Palestine and the Holy Land*, H E King & Co, London, 1875.
Cobbett, William   *Rural rides*, J M Dent & Sons, London, 1912.
Croall, Thomas   *A book about travelling*, William P Nimmo, London and Edinburgh, 1877.
Dowd, O (Charles Lever).   *Upon men and women*, Chapman & Hall, London, 1874.
Eldon, Dr Abraham   *The Continental oracle*, London, 1828.
    Excursionist, The, Archives of Thos. Cook & Son Ltd.
Fraser, Rae   *The business of travel*, Private printing.
Furse, Col   Hand-written diary in possession of Thos. Cook & Son Ltd.
Gaze, Henry   Booklet on his company in possession of Thos. Cook & Son Ltd.
Granville, A B   *The spas of England*, London, 1841.
Hatch, Alden   *American Express*, Doubleday, New York, 1950.
    Illustrated London News.
Jerome, K Jerome   *Diary of a pilgrimage.*
Kemble, Fanny   *Records of a girlhood*, Beckes, London, 1878;
    Further records, R. Bentley & Son, London, 1890;
    Records of a later life, R. Bentley & Son, London, 1882;
    A year of consolation, R. Bentley & Son, London, 1847.
Lunn, Arnold   *The story of skiing*, 1952.
Lunn, Sir Henry   *Nearing harbour*, 1934.
Montgomery, A N   *Hints about Egypt*, Houghton & Co, London, 1882.
Morrell, Jemima   *Miss Jemima's Swiss journal*, Putnam, London, 1963.
    Orient Line guide, 1890.
P & O   *Travellers' pocket book*, 1888.
Packard, J H   *Sea air and sea bathing*, Presley Blakiston, Philadelphia, 1880.
    Pall Mall Gazette.
Pimlott, A R   *The Englishman's holiday.*
Pudney, John   *The Thomas Cook story*, Michael Joseph, London, 1952.
    Queen magazine, Book of travel, 1904.
    Miss Riggs diary, In possession of Thos. Cook & Son Ltd.
Roget   *Travel in the last two centuries*, 1921.
Russell, Richard   *A dissertation on the use of sea water*, London, 1752.
Russell, William Howard   Cook T excursion and tourist manager, 1870; Monte Carlo and public opinion, 1884.
Sketchley, Arthur   *Mrs Brown on the Grand Tour*, Routledge, London, 1871;
    Mrs Brown up the Nile, Routledge, London, 1871;
    Out for a holiday with Cooks, Routledge, London, 1870.
Smith, William   *A Yorkshireman's trip*, 1892.
Steevens, G W   *Egypt*, William Blackwood, London and Edinburgh, 1898.
Stephen, Leslie   *The playground of Europe*, Longmans, London, 1871.
    Travel Trade Gazette, Archives of *Travel Trade Gazette*; *Travellers Gazette, The.*
Twain, Mark   *Innocents abroad.*
Viator, Verax   *Cautions for the first tour*, London, 1863.
Willis, W N   *Anti-Christ in Egypt*, Anglo Eastern Publishing Co, London, 1915.